T0330037

Economics of Transition

The intention of The Vienna Institute for Comparative Economic Studies series is to encourage discussion on the economic theory and policy of transition and European economic integration. For more than 20 years, the Wiener Institut für Internationale Wirtschaftsvergleiche (WIIW) has facilitated academic dialogue on economic theory and policy in Eastern Europe and the former Soviet Union. WIIW also assembles comparable statistics for the transition economies and monitors their economic performance. Information on publications and services is available on the Internet by opening the URL: http://www.wsr.ac.at/wiiw-html/, or by writing the institute at wiiw@wsr.ac.at. The series editor is Mark Knell (knell@wsr.ac.at).

Economics of Transition

Structural Adjustments and Growth Prospects in Eastern Europe

Edited by
Mark Knell

Department of Economics
De Montfort University, Leicester, UK

THE VIENNA INSTITUTE FOR COMPARATIVE ECONOMIC STUDIES SERIES

Edward Elgar
Cheltenham, UK • Brookfield, Vermont, US

Published by
Edward Elgar Publishing Limited
8 Lansdown Place
Cheltenham
Glos GL50 2HU
UK

Edward Elgar Publishing Company
Old Post Road
Brookfield
Vermont 05036
US

A catalogue record for this book
is available from the British Library

Library of Congress Cataloguing in Publication Data
Economics of transition : structural adjustments and growth prospects
    in Eastern Europe / edited by Mark Knell.
        (Vienna Institute for Comparative Economic Studies)
        Includes bibliographical references and index.
        1. Structural adjustment (Economic policy)—Europe, Eastern.
    2. Europe, Eastern—Economic policy—1989–   I. Knell, Mark, 1956–
    . II. Series.
    HC244.E2449   1996
    339.5'0947—dc20   96–15346
                                                                              CIP
ISBN 1 85898 312 6

Printed and bound in Great Britain by Antony Rowe Ltd, Chippenham, Wiltshire

Contents

vi   *Contents*

Tables

Editor's Introduction

The first volume of The Vienna Institute for Comparative Economic Studies series brings together a variety of different perspectives on structural adjustments and the prospect for sustainable economic growth in Eastern Europe. In the 1995 World Bank conference on development economics, Michael Bruno and Stanley Fischer pointed to the range of divergence across transition countries and the need to shift emphasis from the issues of stabilization and liberalization to longer-term issues of growth and structural change. Now that the behaviours of producers are more market oriented in the advanced Central and East European countries, the longer-term aspects of economic transformation have become increasingly relevant. How to bring about structural change and competitive advantage is perhaps the most important policy question faced by the transition economies in the second half of the 1990s. And it will surely excite lively debates over economic theory and policy over the next few years.

This volume brings together diverse streams of analysis on structural adjustments and growth prospects in Eastern Europe. These chapters go beyond the standard neoclassical assumptions by including different analytical traditions that recognize effective demand, institutional change, and technological learning as important issues in the economics of transition. If catching up is desirable, then it is necessary to ascertain how effective demand induces growth; how diffusion takes place; how economic policy influences incentives, motivations, and behaviours; how institutions influence organizational and technological capability building; and how institutions both constrain and guide economic policy.

The first paper introduces some of the important themes developed in the volume by asking whether Eastern Europe is catching up. Making extensive use of the WIIW statistical database (as of March 1996), Peter Havlik makes a general inquiry into the impact of stabilization on economic growth and future growth prospects. Alec Nove provides a strong case against using standard neoclassical assumptions to analyse the transition process by emphasizing the need to recognize investment not as a function, but as a path-dependent process. Basing their argument on chaos theory, J. Barkley Rosser, Jr. and Marina Vcherashnaya Rosser show how the rapid stabilization and liberalization strategy caused a complete institutional breakdown in Eastern Europe. Kazimierz Laski argues that conventional stabilization theory exaggerates the need for demand-side restraints because it assumes output is independent of the level of effective demand. Amit Bhaduri develops a two-sector model to show that sustainable growth depends on the pattern and extent of economic interaction between the public and private sectors. Michael Landesmann and Josef Pöschl extend the balance-of-payments growth model developed by A.P. Thirlwall to show, through scenarios, how export growth, the real exchange rate, capital imports, and the income and price elasticities affect the longer-term growth rate. Developing the idea of creative destruction from the neo-Schumpeterian perspective, Vladimir Gligorov and Niclas Sundström point out some of the difficulties faced by the transition economies. Slavo Radošević discusses how technology policy and institution-building facilitate technological and organizational learning by combining market and non-market incentives. Developing the need for an evolutionary approach to institutional change, Richard Kožul-Wright and Paul Rayment discuss why economic interaction between institutions, the state, and public and private firms is necessary for building entrepreneurial and technological capabilities. Aggregations often used in the chapters cover the CEEC-5 (the Czech Republic, Hungary, Poland, the Slovak Republic, and Slovenia), the CEEC-7 (the previous group plus Bulgaria and Romania), and Eastern Europe (all the European economies in transition).

The Vienna Institute for Comparative Economic Studies (WIIW) dedicates this yearbook to the memory of Alec Nove. Alec Nove was a friend of WIIW, having visited the institute several times, and contributed to an institute workshop in Moscow shortly before his death. It was during his visit to the institute in late 1993 that Alec circulated and discussed the paper included in this volume. Then I proposed that we jointly edit a volume questioning the use of standard neoclassical assumptions in economics of transition; he accepted knowing that we would not pursue it until autumn 1994, when I planned to begin a new teaching post at De Montfort University. To our great loss Alec Nove died on 15 May 1994. This volume is what we had envisaged, so it is fitting to dedicate it in his memory.

At the same time we thank Westview Press for allowing us to include Alec Nove's chapter. This chapter is an edited version of a conference paper published in the book *Markets, States and Democracy*, edited by Beverly Crawford. Many thanks also go to Ian Thatcher for assisting me in editing the chapter by Alec Nove and to June Corbett for typing it.

Particular thanks go to Eva Strobl who painstakingly read everything, putting every word and figure in their proper place, and to Alfonso De Caro for compiling the index. I am also thankful for all the support received from my friends and colleagues at the Vienna Institute and to editorial staff at Edward Elgar. Finally I would like to thank my father, whose passing this summer unexpectedly interrupted the flow of the first chapter, but not the inquisitiveness he inculcated in me as a child.

Mark Knell
Vienna, Austria

Contributors

Amit Bhaduri is professor of economics at Jawaharlal Nehru University, New Delhi, India and research associate at WIIW

Vladimir Gligorov is professor of economics at the Institute of Economic Sciences, Belgrade, Yugoslavia and research economist at WIIW

Peter Havlik is senior research economist and deputy director of WIIW

Mark Knell is senior lecturer in economics at De Monfort University at Leicester and Milton Keynes, UK and research associate at WIIW

Richard Kožul-Wright is associate economic affairs officer, Global Interdependence Division, UNCTAD, Geneva

Michael Landesmann is professor of economics at the Johannes Kepler University, Linz, Austria and research associate at WIIW

Kazimierz Laski is emeritus professor of economics at the Johannes Kepler University, Linz, Austria and research director at WIIW

Alec Nove was professor emeritus and senior research fellow in the Institute of Soviet and East European Affairs, University of Glasgow, UK

Josef Pöschl is lecturer in economics at the Johannes Kepler University, Linz, Austria and research economist at WIIW

Slavo Radošević is a research fellow in the Science Policy Research Unit (SPRU) at the University of Sussex, Falmer, UK

Paul Rayment is senior economic affairs officer, Economic Commission for Europe, United Nations, Geneva

J. Barkley Rosser, Jr. is professor of economics at James Madison University, Harrisonburg, Virginia, USA

Marina Vcherashnaya Rosser is associate professor of economics at James Madison University, Harrisonburg, Virginia, USA

Niclas Sundström is researcher in the Department of East European Studies, Uppsala University, Sweden

1 Structural Adjustments and Growth: Is Eastern Europe Catching Up?

Mark Knell

1 Introduction

This volume brings together a variety of different perspectives on structural adjustments and prospects for sustainable economic growth in Eastern Europe. With an average growth rate exceeding the European Union (EU) average in 1994 and 1995, the Czech Republic, Hungary, Poland, the Slovak Republic and Slovenia all appear to be moving on to a new growth path. All of these countries have undergone some structural adjustments, but it is still not clear whether a convergence in per capita incomes across Europe is possible and, if so, whether it is sustainable. The sustainability of economic growth depends on the accumulation and utilization of production capacity and the creation of new technological and organizational capabilities. The prospect for economic growth and real convergence in economic performance to the EU hence depends on the ability of Eastern Europe to generate and manage technical change and technological learning.

To ask whether there is enough technical change and technological learning in Eastern Europe for catching up and whether it is sustainable may be premature. Nevertheless one should begin contemplating some of the longer-term aspects of economic transformation. Now that the behaviours of producers are more market oriented in the five most advanced Central and East European countries (CEECs), the ability to create an economic environment conducive to growth and innovation is of central importance. Crucial to this economic environment is an institutional infrastructure that induces technological and organizational learning and reinforces the effects of economic policy. Once technological accumulation begins, it becomes possible to observe structural change and changing competitive advantage in the CEECs. Structural change and changing competitive advantage reflect then the changing behaviours of managers and firms and the creation of new technological and organizational capabilities.

How to bring about structural change and competitive advantage is perhaps the most important policy question faced by the transition economies in the second half of the 1990s. The ability of Eastern Europe to restructure their economies depends to a large extent on the speed and effectiveness of the restructuring process. The creation of competitive advantage requires investment in new production capacity and a lengthy and arduous process of building technological and organizational capabilities. Most of the chapters in this volume consider, either directly or indirectly, the conditions necessary for sustained economic growth and convergence of per capita income across Europe.

Despite the variety of perspectives contained in the volume, a common theme is the view that standard neoclassical assumptions do not provide a basis for a satisfactory economics of transition (see also Murrell, 1991; Stiglitz, 1994). At the centre of this discussion is Nove's claim in chapter 3 that the investment function is not applicable for an economics of transition because the investment process is path dependent and occurs under the conditions of disequilibrium and institutional diversity. Laski also questions the policy implications of the investment function in chapter 5 by examining the role stabilization programmes played in reducing effective demand and potential output in the early 1990s. In like manner, innovation and diffusion models based on the investment function imply policies that more often hinder, rather than accelerate industrial restructuring and the catching-up process. Several chapters provide alternative explanations of how structural change and economic growth take place and suggest policies for generating and managing investment and technological and organizational learning. Radošević stresses in chapter 9 the importance of combining market and non-market incentives for technological and organizational learning. Kožul-Wright and Rayment propose in chapter 10 that organizational learning also involves building an entrepreneurial state that can facilitate growth by providing a strategy or vision for structural change.

The economic performance of a nation depends to a large extent on the institutional context and the corresponding incentives and policies for building technological and organizational capabilities. The following sections of this chapter elaborate on this topic by bringing together some common themes developed in the volume.

2 Convergence and divergence in Eastern Europe

The objective of catching up was important for the Soviet strategy of economic growth and it is important for the transition strategies of Eastern Europe. The continued existence and divergence of gaps in technology between Eastern and Western Europe before 1990 questions the viability of the institutional arrangements of central planning and the application of the standard assumptions of neoclassical economic theory. By transforming the institutional arrangements of central planning into market-based ones, the expectation is that structural adjustment policies will facilitate the diffusion of technology, just as the diffusion of technology will facilitate structural adjustment and improve the competitiveness of industry.

Systemic differences in the way institutions affect incentives, and in consequence, the diffusion of new technologies, products and processes, explain international differences in growth rates. The diversity of innovation systems arises from differences in the way the economic and social organization of a nation influences technological and organizational learning. Hanson and Pavitt (1987), Brus and Laski (1989) and Freeman (1995) argue that the institutions embedded in the Soviet system of innovation impeded the economy from catching up with the West. To close the technology gap the Soviets pursued a strategy that gave priority to certain sectors and activities, namely the production of certain basic goods (heavy machinery and strategic materials) and full utilization of capital and labour. The experience of real socialism proved to be a disappointment, however. While estimates of Soviet economic growth suggest that the technology gap narrowed from 1929 to 1940, Brus and Laski (1989) suggest that it may have widened from 1951 to 1985.[1] Instead of catching up, the centrally planned economy fell further behind as there was little incentive to introduce new products, new processes and organizational innovation. The reason, Freeman (1995) points out, is that the Soviet innovation system committed a large share of R&D funds to the military and space without many technological spillovers to other industries. Although research and development (R&D) was 4 per cent of GNP in the 1970s, very high compared with the industrialized countries, enterprise R&D accounted for less that 10 per cent of the total. By contrast, in Japan R&D was 2.5 per cent of GNP with industry financing about two thirds of the total amount and in Western Europe the civil R&D to GNP ratio was more than double the Soviet ratio.

The inability to create a dynamic relationship between productivity and output growth is perhaps the most important economic reason for the collapse of the centrally planned economy.[2] The institutionalization of sellers' markets and dependence of enterprises on the planning authority created little incentive to innovate (Kornai, 1992).[3] Despite the allocation of substantial resources to R&D activities, the economic environment created little incentive to improve products and the lack of the profit motive and financial responsibility created little incentive for process innovation. The result was an almost complete separation of the R&D process from the enterprise and the consumer. This, combined with decentralized managerial decision making, led to the 'soft' negotiability of credit between the enterprise and planning authority, with the semi-autonomous enterprise attempting to obtain as much credit as possible. Because there was little or no incentive to gain profit, innovation activities involved high risk with little reward. Nevertheless, some innovation took place in industries tied closely to the planning authority such as military and space. Even in these cases, enterprises were more often followers than leaders in the development of technology. Trade barriers also limited technological diffusion from the West. The accumulation of technical knowledge was costly and often done by reverse engineering. Ultimately, the centrally planned economies followed an extensive growth path with declining productivity, making it increasingly difficult for them to catch up with the advanced market economies and even provide essential goods and services.

After the collapse of the centrally planned economy, the CEECs moved rather quickly toward a capitalist market economy partly because of the belief that this would speed up technological progress. Although the capitalist innovation system appears to be superior to the Soviet system, it is not clear whether the particular innovation system adopted in each of the CEECs will generate rapid technological progress and catching up. The European Union also faces the dilemma of continuing uneven and divergent patterns of technological accumulation even after trade liberalization (Patel and Pavitt, 1994). Convergence in per capita incomes across Europe is a fundamental objective of the EU,[4] yet there are as many different innovation systems within the EU as there are members. The diversity of institutional and industrial structures within Europe may be the most difficult obstacle to overcome in creating a single European market, integrating the more advanced CEECs into this market and fulfilling the EU objective. For this reason it may be too early to tell whether any or all the innovation systems of Eastern Europe will improve the prospect of convergence.[5]

The level of development of the CEECs suggests that the East Asian development strategy could provide some valuable lessons for Eastern Europe. Table 1.1 shows the 1993 gross national product (GNP) per capita for selected countries and the change in GNP from 1987 to 1993 compared to the United States. Eastern Europe fell significantly behind the United States after the deep recession in the early 1990s, while there was considerable catching up in East Asia. Radošević (chapter 9) and Kožul-Wright and Rayment (chapter 10) point to the importance of institution-building and technological learning in the East Asian development strategy. East Asia strongly supported infrastructural investment in education, research and development, telecommunications, and scientific and technical activities and sometimes used interest rate subsidies to support firms in building certain technological capabilities (Dosi et al., 1994). By contrast, much of Latin America fell behind the United States from 1987 to 1993, partly because of an innovation system that retarded the development of a national infrastructure but also because of mismanaged economic policy. In reality, East Asia attempted catching up by developing a highly integrated system of innovation that is conducive to technological and organizational learning.

Table 1.1   PPP estimates of GNP per capita for selected countries

	PPP estimates of GNP per capita (USA = 100)		Current intl. dollars
	1987	1993	1993
Bulgaria	28.5	16.6	4,100
Czech Republic	39.2	30.5	7,550
Hungary	28.5	24.5	6,050
Poland	23.0	20.2	5,000
Romania	18.4	11.3	2,800
Slovak Republic	35.0	25.4	6,290
Latvia	35.7	20.3	5,010
Lithuania	27.9	12.6	3,110
Russian Federation	35.8	20.4	5,050
Georgia	28.5	7.1	1,750
Kazakhstan	24.6	15.0	3,710
Ukraine	26.6	18.0	4,450
Greece	35.8	36.4	9,000
Ireland	43.2	54.5	13,490
Brazil	24.8	21.7	5,370
Mexico	28.2	27.5	6,810
Korea	27.7	38.9	9,630
Japan	74.6	84.3	20,850
China	6.3	9.4	2,330
USA	100.0	100.0	24,740

Source: World Bank estimates. World Development Report 1995, Oxford University Press, pp. 220–21.

One way neoclassical economics can explain the rapid divergence of per capita incomes of transition countries away from the United States is through the so-called 'J-curve' response to rapid price liberalization. While there is considerable controversy over what causes the 'J-curve' effect, Gylfason (1995) argues that rapid price liberalization induces the rapid exit of uncompetitive capital and the gradual entry of new, more competitive, capital. As the economy moves onto a new growth path, stabilization measures initially cause declining output and employment but then engender a stable economic environment that encourages entry into the market, increasing output and reducing unemployment. Gylfason then uses a neoclassical endogenous growth model to explain how the new economic environment will generate dynamic gains through technical change and technological learning (Gligorov and Sundström also discuss these types of models in chapter 8). But it is not clear that the transformation process will move this smoothly, nor that it will automatically follow a higher growth path without a clear strategy for technological accumulation. Rosser and Rosser suggest in chapter 4 that there could be a complete institutional breakdown causing a pervasive and severe macroeconomic collapse if the transformation process moves too quickly. Laski argues in chapter 5 that active demand management policies would temper the 'J-curve' effect and improve the prospect of moving to a higher growth path. Several of the other chapters suggest that stable prices and exchange rates do not necessarily lead to a higher growth path unless accompanied by additional incentives to facilitate technological and organizational learning.

Table 1.2 Approximate years required after 1994 for convergence to the EU average

	growth differential				
	1%	2%	3%	4%	5%
Bulgaria	170	85	57	43	35
Czech Republic	80	40	27	20	16
Hungary	99	50	33	25	20
Poland	120	60	40	30	24
Romania	183	92	62	46	37
Russia	152	76	51	39	31
Slovenia	80	40	27	20	16
Slovak Republic	110	55	37	28	22

The most difficult problem faced by the transition economies is to close the technology gap. Table 1.2 uses Havlik's statistics in Table 2.11 to show the number of years it would take the CEECs and Russia to catch up with the European Union average given a positive growth differential. In this table, the two leading countries, the Czech Republic and Slovenia, would need a 5 per cent growth differential for convergence to take place by 2010. This requires sufficient technological and organizational learning for catching up to take place. Even if Poland maintains its current growth rate it would take more than 30 years to catch up to the EU average.

3 Strategies of economic growth and transformation

Building an economic environment conducive to growth and innovation is an important component of a successful transition strategy. Even before policy debates started shifting towards long-run problems of transformation, there has been considerable controversy over whether the stabilization and liberalization programmes implemented in Eastern Europe were conducive to economic growth. For many economists there appears to be 'a striking degree of unanimity' in accepting the standard prescription of the rapid liberalization of prices and privatization of state assets, while simultaneously creating the institutions of a market economy (Blanchard et al., 1994; Murrell, 1995).

Debates in the economics of transition during the first half of the 1990s centred primarily on the speed of stabilization and liberalization and not on the sequencing of institutional change. Discussion often focused on the differences between 'shock therapy', the term generally used to describe the strategy adopted by Poland and Russia to liberalize prices by decree, and 'gradualism', the term used to describe the strategy adopted by Hungary to liberalize prices in stages. In adopting this distinction there was a tendency to overlook differences between institutional change and behavioural change. Any change in the formal institutions (e.g. rules, laws, constitutions) and informal institutions (e.g. norms, conventions) of society are a 'shock' to the system in that individuals and organizations must find new ways to handle the new rules, conventions, etc. The behaviour of individuals changed in the CEECs as the rules governing transactions between individuals and organizations changed. Changing the rules that determined prices under the old system was a 'shock' to the system, irrespective of whether price liberalization occurred at once or in stages. Similarly, the introduction of the production responsibility system and limited rights to private property in China were a 'shock' to the system because the rules governing that society had changed. Routines and behaviours of individuals and organizations change gradually because acceptance of the new rules and the capability to respond to them are part of the learning process. In the theoretical argument underlying the strategy of Lipton and Sachs (1990) there is the expectation that routines change quickly, otherwise prices would not send the proper signals. For Nelson and Winter (1982) these routines provide predictability of rule-governed behaviour. Since the appearance of new routines today influences the appearance of other routines in the future, the sequencing of institutional change is important.

Strategies that neglect institutions generally rely on explicit and implicit neoclassical imperatives (see chapters 3 and 10). In the strategy of shock therapy, price liberalization is requisite for economic stabilization, institutional change and privatization. Only correct prices send the proper signals for entrepreneurs and managers to enter and exit the market. Underlying this argument is a functioning market based on an organizing principle that describes economic rationality of individuals and enterprises as maximizing preferences and profits, respectively, provided sufficient information is readily available. In capitalist market economies buyers and sellers receive many different kinds of signals other than prices and routines are important for reducing uncertainty. The reasoning by Lipton and Sachs (1990) suggests that if entrepreneurs have the right of entry and the state maintained prices at artificially low levels, these entrepreneurs would engage in rent-seeking behaviour by buying state goods and selling them at a higher price in private markets, a type of unproductive entrepreneurship defined by Baumol (1993). The Chinese system of innovation shows that non-price and quantity signals encourage productive entrepreneurship and that penalties discourage unproductive entrepreneurship. GNP and industrial output growth averaged 9.4 and 14 per cent respectively from 1979 to 1994 causing the share of state enterprise output to fall below 50 per cent in 1992. While the output of state enterprises increased during this period, production by individual and collective township and village enterprises explains most of the growth. The irony is that there has been significant unproductive entrepreneurship in Eastern Europe after price liberalization because of the inability to enforce laws, especially new rules of taxation and other regulations. This entrepreneurship can become destructive when it impedes financing of public investment and the balance of payments.

The establishment of clear property rights in China before liberalizing prices is also an illustration of the importance of maintaining effective demand during the transition process. By combining excess effective demand with the right of entry and exit, there is an incentive to enter the market or expand production because of the expectation of making above average profits (or quasi-rents). This incentive, combined with large productivity gains in agriculture resulting in surplus savings and labour, led to the *creation* of new township, village and private enterprises that were often in direct competition with state-owned enterprises. To ensure that entrepreneurial activity is predominately productive, the Chinese encouraged private initiative and used quotas when necessary. The result was that the ratio of free market prices to state prices narrowed from 270 to 112 between 1962 and 1989, while the percentage of market-determined agricultural prices and consumer prices rose to 65 and 55 per cent respectively by 1991. This was a very different strategy from the one followed by Eastern Europe.

Although politics may have forced much of Eastern Europe to liberalize prices before establishing clear property rights, there are two important implications of the Chinese strategy for the economics of transition.[6] The first concerns whether scarcity prices provide the sufficient information for a transition strategy. Nove points out in chapter 3 that (perfectly) competitive scarcity prices do not contain the kind of information (profit-seeking) entrepreneurs want and real world scarcity prices do not contain the kind of information necessary to arrive at a (Pareto-optimal) competitive equilibrium. Laski suggests in chapter 5 that the excessive declines in output observed in Eastern Europe were partly due to the dependence of conventional structural adjustment programmes on (neoclassical) scarcity prices. A second implication concerns whether certain institutions should be in place before liberalization and privatization. Rosser and Rosser argue in chapter 4 that China avoided total institutional breakdown and a collapse in output by gradually changing the institutional arrangements and subsequent behaviours and building entrepreneurial capabilities, while retaining a strong presence of the public sector. This leads to a further concern over whether the privatization of state assets is necessary to improve competitive advantage or the private sector is the main source of growth and structural change. Bhaduri suggests in chapter 6 that neither may be true because investment, and hence growth, depend on the pattern and extent of economic interaction between the public and private sectors, given the institutional framework. Kožul-Wright and Rayment argue in chapter 10 that economic interaction between institutions, the state, and public and private firms is necessary for building entrepreneurial and technological capabilities.

4 From structural adjustment to growth in Eastern Europe?

Perhaps the single most important influence on the transition process is the International Monetary Fund (see Bhaduri, 1992; Knell, 1993). Although there are many different personalities influencing policy in Eastern Europe, such as J. Sachs, L. Balcerowicz and V. Klaus, it is the analytical framework and the policy instruments used by the IMF that defines the essence of the various strategies followed in Eastern Europe. The IMF is market-oriented, so to improve efficiency and the prospect of economic growth it advocates rapid price liberalization, eliminating subsidies, lessening trade barriers and privatizing state assets. Because rapid liberalization might lead to high inflation when there is excess demand, the IMF imposes excessively austere measures. After stabilization, the expectation is that new behaviours and motivations will put these economies on a stable, full employment growth path with more rapid technological accumulation.

The main objective of an IMF-supported structural adjustment programme 'is to provide for an orderly adjustment of both macroeconomic and structural imbalances so as to foster economic growth while bringing about a balance-of-payments position that is sustainable in the medium term' (IMF, 1987). Virtually all the IMF stabilization and adjustment programmes in Eastern Europe call for various forms of liberalization, fiscal austerity, monetary tightness, currency devaluation and wage restraints. Although the IMF claims not to endorse 'a particular view of the economy or on the convictions of a single school of economic thought', it essentially applies the balance-of-payments approach to the 'quantity theory of money' (see Mills and Nallari, 1992; Tarp, 1993). The three main targets in this approach are: (1) international reserves; (2) the domestic price level; and (3) domestic credit. The theoretical foundation of this approach is not strictly monetarist, though the IMF uses a neoclassical version of the 'quantity theory of money'. To obtain the 'quantity equation' (monetary equilibrium), the IMF defines the money supply as the sum of foreign reserves R and domestic credit DC and assumes a money demand function M^d that is positively related to real income Y, the domestic price level P_d and other unspecified variables. Leaving out the unspecified variables, the demand for money may be written as $M^d/P_d = (1/v)Y$, where v is the velocity of circulation and is constant by assumption. Given output Y is independent of the level of demand and determined through an aggregate neoclassical production function, it follows that the price level is a function of the monetary authorities' ability to control the money supply. The IMF uses essentially three policy instruments to control the money supply: (1) a domestic credit ceiling; (2) net government borrowing; and (3) the exchange rate. The assumption of scarce resources implies complete crowding out of private investment when public spending (consumption or investment) increases. Accordingly, the IMF advocates reducing the fiscal deficit, but may also reduce the domestic credit ceiling and increase the interest rate. Since the quantity equation also implies that $R = (1/v)YP_d - DC$, that is domestic credit expansion leads directly to foreign reserve contraction, *ceteris paribus*, the Fund proposes an exchange-rate devaluation along with domestic credit controls to improve the balance-of-payments position. Imperfectly competitive markets, originating mainly from the continued presence of public enterprises, strong trade unions, and missing or underdeveloped institutions of the labour market, etc., may induce the IMF to use wage anchors or any other policy instrument when necessary.

Whether IMF-supported adjustment programmes are conducive to growth and innovation is unclear. From 1990 and 1991 GDP and industrial production fell by more than 16 per cent and 32 per cent respectively in the five most advanced CEECs (see chapter 2 by Havlik). In almost all the individual countries, actual declines were much greater than those expected (see ECE, 1992 and chapter 5 by Laski).[7] While the extent to which the austere fiscal and monetary policies caused the collapse in output is debatable, they did create an economic environment that made it difficult for new entrepreneurs to enter the market and for consumers to spend. Because the IMF approach does not have adequate microfoundations, it is not possible to investigate supply-side problems or the impact of institutions on maintaining a stable economic environment and building technological capabilities. Instead the IMF approach focuses on demand-side restraints and the assumed stability of the demand for money function.

The IMF was unable to anticipate the large decline in output because it considers the level of output as exogenous in the theoretical analysis, causing it to exaggerate the need for demand-side restraints. Because tight credit and austere fiscal policies may affect output through demand, the IMF tends to underestimate inflation and declines in output, suggesting policies that are prone to the possibility of 'overkill'. As Laski points out in chapter 5, these 'overkill' policies caused a contraction in effective demand and investment, leading to a contraction in GDP and industrial output through the multiplier process. The collapse in CMEA (Council for Mutual Economic Assistance) trade was not an important factor because exports to the West rose immediately and by almost as much. Paradoxically, the most neglected features of conventional stabilization theory, namely effective demand (especially investment demand) and missing institutions, explain most of the decline in industrial output observed early in the transformation process.

Effective demand is perhaps the most important of many variables that determine the level and composition of output. Laski argues in chapter 5 that output is not independent of the level of demand and employment dependent on marginal revenue products, but instead is dependent on the level of effective demand (and the investment multiplier) and wage–cost mark-up pricing behaviour. In a credit money economy, monetary growth may not be a cause of inflation as the 'quantity theory' claims, as administered pricing behaviour, distributional conflict and full employment policies may also cause inflation.[8] If money is endogenous, as suggested by Kaldor, the supply of money does not cause inflation because it can only respond to the demand for money. And if money is an asset (credit) in the central bank, then institutional factors play an important role in monetary policy. Even if the monetary authorities can control the money supply, it is not clear whether changes in the money supply affect the level of output permanently (Keynesian), temporarily (monetarist), or never (rational expectations). In truth, distributional conflict and the inability to control the money supply may explain why Fund-supported programmes use nominal wage and exchange rate anchors so extensively in the CEECs.

What type of economic environment is conducive to growth and innovation is highly controversial. The IMF attempts to reduce inflation because it believes that high inflation is the primary cause of economic disturbances, including falling output and rising unemployment. Given the scarcity of resources and a belief in the self-organizing market, they discourage the use of fiscal and industrial policies to stimulate the economy and encourage the use of monetary policy to create a stable entrepreneurial economic environment. Keynesians also believe that high inflation is detrimental to economic growth, often suggesting incomes policies to reduce it, but try to stimulate growth and innovation with fiscal, monetary and industrial policies, while recognizing the limits (and possible misuse) of these policies. Even in the more basic financial markets of the CEECs, government deficits can generate additional income (and profits) through the deposit creation process. Financing government debt without crowding out private investment depends on whether the financial intermediaries can turn 'high-powered' money into 'low-powered' through deposit creation and banks and individuals want to hold this debt in their asset portfolio. The creation and acceptance of indirect taxes is another way to manage the debt over the cycle. Industrial and technology policies complement fiscal policies by directing expenditures toward infrastructural investment, education and training, support for R&D activity, etc. and by facilitating the development of financial intermediaries, industrial restructuring, export promotion, etc.

The lack of finance is probably the most important factor hindering growth and innovation during the first years of the transformation process. Innovation surveys taken in Czechoslovakia, Eastern Germany, Hungary, Poland and Russia all point to the problem of obtaining finance for innovation activities.[9] In Poland, almost 80 per cent of those who responded said that lack of accumulated retained earnings and the ability to issue shares hindered innovation activity and 75 per cent said that high interest rates was another constraint. Although these obstacles may appear as resource constraints in neoclassical theory, they are demand-constraints in that the excessively austere economic policies implemented in Eastern Europe created them. The collapse of effective demand contributed to the decline in profits, just as the lack of finance contributed to the fall in demand. As the austerity measures eased in the mid-1990s, effective demand and profits increased, and domestic credit became more readily available to finance investment. Evidence from Poland suggests that profits (retained earnings) were the primary source of investment in 1994 and that rising capacity utilization is the primary source of growth, though competitiveness may have improved in some industries such as automotive, televisions, etc.

Balance-of-payments difficulties may become an increasingly important factor hindering growth and innovation in Eastern Europe in the second half of the 1990s. Serious balance-of-payments problems could constrain growth in almost all of the CEECs if the competitiveness of these countries does not improve (see chapter 2 by Havlik). A typical IMF adjustment programme tries to reduce the current-account deficit by controlling domestic credit to reduce imports and, if the sum of the price elasticities of demand exceeds unity, by devaluing the exchange rate to improve competitiveness. Although devaluation is only an expenditure-reducing policy on the demand side in the simple framework, they also regard it as an expenditure-switching policy on the supply side, influencing the terms of trade through price incentives. Initially expansionary, output and the current account balance return to their original levels as the money supply and the domestic prices of labour and capital gradually increase if individuals hold the same money balances.

The role devaluation plays in improving the current-account balance is controversial. If output is dependent on the level of effective demand, the investment multiplier and wage–cost mark-up pricing behaviour, two opposing outcomes are possible. First, if the sum of the price elasticities of demand exceeds unity (the Marshall-Lerner condition), a devaluation can improve the current-account permanently through an increase in net exports. Second, higher income elasticity of demand for imports may worsen the current account balance. The long-term growth rate y is therefore constrained by the growth rate of exports x relative to the income elasticity of demand for imports p, or $y = x/p$. Called the dynamic Harrod foreign trade multiplier by McCombie and Thirlwall (1994), this equation is equivalent to equation 7.4 (in chapter 7), assuming relative prices measured in a common currency do not change over time and there are no capital flows. Given demand stimulates investment and innovation, a growth-oriented strategy would focus on creating a competitive advantage through export promotion and reducing the income elasticity of demand for imports through import substitution. But as Landesmann and Pöschl point out in chapter 7, the long-term growth rate and catching-up also depends in general on the development of the real exchange rate, the scale of net capital imports, and how quickly the income and price elasticities change. Technology policy can speed up the change in the structural parameters and foreign direct investment can reduce the current account deficit directly and indirectly if technological learning occurs. Although both can facilitate the growth process by relaxing the balance-of-payments constraint, technology policies aimed directly at building technological and organizational capabilities were important in almost all instances of catching up since the 19th century.

5   Convergence and divergence in economic theory

Falling behind is a much more frequent phenomenon than catching up. The most prominent examples of catching up include Western and Central Europe in the 19th century, Scandinavia and Italy in the early 20th century, and East Asia in the late 20th century (Dosi et al., 1994). Although growth of the world economy does have an important influence on the growth of individual countries, long periods of growth appear to be country specific and dependent on technical and institutional change. Whether Eastern Europe can catch up with the West depends to a large extent on whether the creation of new institutions and capabilities put these countries on a growth path leading to convergence. By endogenizing the sources of economic growth, endogenous growth models can explain why falling behind is more likely to happen than catching up.

Neoclassical growth theory cannot explain why some countries grow at a faster rate than others. Solow (1956) developed a growth model using the standard assumptions to demonstrate that competitive markets (with substitution and flexible wages) result in the full employment of labour and capital and not escalating unemployment as suggested by the Harrod-Domar model. Given a constant returns production function with labour and capital as its arguments, the economy gravitates to a balanced growth path with no growth in per capita income. Policies to improve growth have only a transitory effect during the transitional process. Unless there is labour augmenting technical progress, growth in the productivity of labour is constrained by diminishing marginal returns on capital. Since technical knowledge is exogenous and assumed to be a public good that is costless to obtain and freely available, the model suggests that the capital–labour ratio, the real wage and the level of income per capita would converge over time if every country has the same savings rate. Starting from different initial conditions, countries with a lower capital–labour ratio and incomes per capita converge to the advanced market economies as a higher profit rate leads to higher capital accumulation and foreign direct investment. Yet this model cannot explain how the accumulation of capital and knowledge induces growth, why diverging patterns of technological accumulation persist within Europe, or why these patterns do not correspond to the inverse relationship between the capital–labour ratio and the rate of profit implied in the model.

By modifying the standard assumptions, endogenous growth theory avoids some of the problems in Solow's growth model by endogenizing technical change and technological learning. While these models are novel to neoclassical theory, the idea of endogenous technological progress was present in classical theory, Schumpeter and Kaldor. Adam Smith developed a theory of endogenous growth and technical change by combining a theory of capital accumulation with technological learning. John Stuart Mill observed that comparative advantage comes not only from natural resources, but also from 'superior capability, either natural or acquired, in the labourers better division of labour, and better tools or machinery'. Karl Marx and Joseph Schumpeter observed that technological competition is important for innovation and the diffusion of technology. While neoclassical assumptions held back Alfred Marshall from developing an actual endogenous theory of growth, he recognized that knowledge is the main source of growth. Piero Sraffa showed in 1926 that variable returns were inconsistent with the competitive partial equilibrium analysis of Marshall, leading to the revival of Smith's idea of technological learning by Allyn Young. In the 1950s and 1960s Nicholas Kaldor developed models of endogenous growth that integrated the insights of Smith and Young with the principle of effective demand.

Kaldor rejected the standard neoclassical assumption of decreasing returns and instead argued that increasing returns are important in industry. These positive feedbacks explain why diverging patterns of technological accumulation appear instead of the simple stabilizing forces found in the neoclassical growth model. Kaldor (1957) replaced the production function with a technological progress function that interrelated investment with technical change and technological learning. He subsequently showed in the 1960s that growing domestic and international markets engender a process of cumulative causation in which manufacturing growth generates new types of knowledge through various learning activities and hence a higher rate of productivity growth and GDP growth for the economy as a whole. This implies that technical change and technological learning are self-generating as output increases through the foreign trade and investment multipliers. Sustainable growth and structural adjustment therefore depend on national and regional technological and organizational capabilities. These capabilities are implied in income and price elasticities of demand used by Landesmann and Pöschl and reflect the competitive advantage of the CEECs. The speed of economic transformation in Eastern Europe therefore depends on how quickly these elasticities change. Kaldor explained the diverging patterns of technological accumulation in terms of high export growth and low import penetration. Increasing external demand improves the prospect of economic growth by relaxing the balance-of-payments constraint by increasing labour productivity and strengthening competitiveness.

Neoclassical models of endogenous growth focus on the production and use of new knowledge in the presence of increasing returns, non-convexities and monopoly power (Amable, 1994). The early models of Romer (1986) and Lucas (1988) suggest that growth rates differ because of positive feedbacks generated by technological learning external to the firm (diffusion) may exceed the negative feedbacks engendered by diminishing marginal returns internal to the firm. Subsequent models by Romer (1990), Grossman and Helpman (1991) and Aghion and Howitt (1993) recognize explicitly the role of monopolistic market structures in the production and distribution of knowledge. Romer developed a model that assumed technical knowledge can either be public (or nonrival) or private (rival) and at least partly excludable. While tacit knowledge is private and excludable, codified knowledge is essentially a public good requiring certain rights (partly excludable) to access it, allowing firms to gain monopoly profits to offset R&D costs. Differences in trade and growth performance appear because of the different character of public and private knowledge. In these models, positive feedbacks occur as the diffusion of public knowledge generates new products and processes and compensates for the negative feedbacks engendered by the decreasing productivity of new investments. A strategy to close the technology gap in Europe should focus on investment and education to accelerate the growth rate. The potential for convergence therefore depends on whether Eastern Europe can develop the 'social capability' to mobilize resources for infrastructural investment in education, training and R&D.

While the neoclassical endogenous growth models depart from the standard assumptions in some important ways and provide theoretical justification for the use of public policy, these models have limited scope for practical policy analysis (see Verspagen, 1992; Gligorov and Sundström, chapter 8 in this volume). By modifying the basic assumptions to include the effects of externalities (increasing returns) and monopoly power on technological progress, a wide range of dynamic behaviours and multiple equilibria are possible, opening up the possibility of policy intervention. All of these models question the ability of markets to ensure optimal growth and suggest that technology policy (subsidies and taxes) and trade policy (tariffs and subsidies) could compensate for the externalities and monopolistic distortions. Aghion and Howitt take a rather different view (based on Schumpeter) and suggest taxing innovators when excessive technological competition induces overinvestment in R&D (using monopoly profits), causing the destruction of more knowledge than it creates. Yet, there is a tendency to stress the static dimension (welfare effects) of public policy and overlook the dynamic dimension (knowledge, change and evolution) because these models place strong emphasis on the optimality conditions and neglect the role of institutions and institutional change in promoting growth and innovation. Kožul-Wright and Rayment explore the economics of public policy and institution-building from an evolutionary perspective and the conditions necessary for generating endogenous growth in Eastern Europe.[10]

The evolutionary approach to technical change contains the dynamic dimension of public policy (see chapter 9 by Radošević). In this perspective, public policy is an important impetus for building production capacity *and* technological capabilities. Bell and Pavitt (1993) define technological capabilities as the 'resources needed to generate and manage technical change, including skills, knowledge and experience, and institutional structures and linkages'. Technological learning is a cumulative, path-dependent activity that provides the basis for building these capabilities and hence generating technical change and investment in new capacity. Learning is also a complex and diverse activity that takes place between users and producers and between firms and organizations, engendering different patterns of technological accumulation and innovation depending on the learning structure. The incentive structures and competences of institutions support and sustain the rate and direction of technological learning providing a role for public policy to influence the innovation process (Patel and Pavitt, 1994). Sustainable growth depends therefore on the link between technical change and technological learning and the role given to public policy.

A primary concern of the evolutionary perspective is building an economic environment, inclusive of the institutional context and public policy, that is conducive to entrepreneurship and innovation. Metcalfe (1994) identifies two processes that are important to this perspective: the variety of process and product innovation and the selection of competing alternatives. These complex behavioural processes are driven by a dynamic competitive process quite different from the imperfectly competitive environment in which market failures (missing markets) impede the optimizing behaviour of (neoclassical) economic agents. In the evolutionary environment variety and selection are interrelated in a way that variety induces selection and selection creates variety through positive and negative feedbacks. It is in this context that behavioural diversity plays an important role. Kožul-Wright and Rayment recognize this role in the risk-taking and profit-seeking behaviour of entrepreneurs and equate entrepreneurship with the creation of new knowledge and the accumulation of technological capabilities. The process of creative destruction implies a wide range of entrepreneurial behaviours that are continually changing as they develop new capabilities to reduce the costs of risk-taking and increase profits. Behavioural diversity also implies that there is a wide variety of selection mechanisms present in the economy. The most obvious one is the market selection process (entry and exit). The diffusion process is another kind of selection process. Since all selection processes contain positive and negative feedbacks, policy plays an important role. For example, missing state institutions and other institutional rigidities may put up barriers to technological entry that can impair the market selection process through the creation of unproductive and destructive entrepreneurship. Path dependence of the diffusion (selection) process also affects the learning process and hence the technological opportunities. Policies should therefore take into account the co-evolution of technology and institutions and concentrate on creating incentives to increase variety while ensuring that the selection process does not hinder the process of generating variety.

The evolutionary perspective stresses the importance of institution-building in creating a market economy. While the spontaneous order of the market plays an important role in generating change, institutions are, as North (1994) mentioned, 'humanly devised constraints that structure human interaction'. These constraints can be either formal such as laws and constitutions or informal such as social norms and conventions and define the behaviour of individuals and organizations, such as firms and the government. The process of selection, therefore, is not spontaneous as suggested by Hayek, but the deliberate action of individuals, firms and governments. There are countless examples of institution-building in economic history, the most recent being the European Union. Kožul-Wright and Rayment stress the importance of institution-building to create an environment conducive to productive entrepreneurship and innovation. These institutions may include property rights, the Keynesian institutions of demand management, institutions of the labour market policy, institutions of science and technology policy, etc.

6 Is Eastern Europe catching up?

Catching up to the levels of technology and productivity in Western Europe is neither automatic nor easy for Eastern Europe. Evidence suggests that there has been no productivity convergence in the OECD countries since the end of the 1970s (Soete and Verspagen, 1993). Despite efforts to bring about real convergence in Europe, technology gaps continue, making it especially important to implement the kind of policies that stimulate technological learning. Closing the technology and productivity gap requires a clear technology policy that focuses on building national technological capabilities by improving the learning processes in firms and other organizations (Metcalfe, 1994).

It is perhaps too early to know whether the higher-than-average growth rates observed in the five most advanced CEECs is sustainable. Evidence suggests that high export growth in 1994 and 1995 may have set in motion a Kaldorian cumulative process in which export growth increases the growth of manufacturing, the productivity growth of labour, and finally domestic demand. Investment is rising in most of the CEECs, but it is not clear how much technological accumulation is taking place because the new private sector, especially in Poland, may conceal profits by reporting investment as current costs. Foreign direct investment (FDI) doubled in 1995 in the most advanced CEECs, but it is not clear whether it will improve the prospect of economic growth unless the CEECs introduce more comprehensive industrial policies (see chapter 10 by Kožul-Wright and Rayment). Improving terms of trade, along with exports of goods rising faster than imports in most of the CEECs, indicate some improvement in their competitive advantage. As growth accelerates, however, it becomes more likely that these countries will encounter the balance-of-payments constraint, putting a damper on future growth and the likelihood of catching up (see chapter 7 by Landesmann and Pöschl). There is evidence that some exports from Poland and Hungary to the EU have been more technology-intensive after 1989, but there is a visible shift away from capital- and technology-intensive exports from the CEECs towards more labour- and energy-intensive goods following the liberalization of trade (Landesmann, 1995). Together, these trends suggest an erosion of certain technological and organizational capabilities with no clear pattern of technological accumulation to facilitate the catching-up process.

Table 1.3 R&D intensity in Eastern Europe, 1990–94

	1990	1991	1992	1993	1994
Czech Republic	1.90	1.88	1.52	1.22	1.08
Hungary	1.60	1.08	1.07	0.99	0.90
Poland	...	1.05	0.83	0.83	0.84
Slovak Republic	1.89	2.93	2.03	1.66	1.12
Russia	2.03	1.54	0.78	0.81	...

Source: OECD Directorate for Science, Technology and Industry, and various statistical yearbooks.

Innovation surveys taken in some of the CEECs in the early 1990s indicate that product and process innovation is taking place, but it is not clear whether there is any significant improvement over the previous innovation system. Surveys taken in Poland suggest that the rate of product and process innovation did not improve between 1990 and 1992 over the 1980s, especially in small firms.[11] Statistics on gross expenditures in R&D and patents confirm this view. Table 1.3 shows that the percentage of GDP spent on R&D has been falling since the transition to the market economy. This suggests that the rate of technological accumulation has declined significantly in Eastern Europe, especially when considering the declines in GDP during this period. Table 1.4 shows recent trends in patenting in the US by Eastern Europe. Again these statistics suggest that there has been a significant erosion of technical knowledge since 1980 in most of the countries. Radošević also provides statistics confirming these trends in chapter 9.

Table 1.4 Number of Eastern European patents granted in the United States, 1975–93

	1975	1980	1985	1990	1991	1992	1993
Bulgaria	24	24	21	26	10	5	4
Czechoslovakia	120	55	54	38	28	18	12
Hungary	52	87	108	94	86	86	52
Poland	37	38	10	19	11	7	8
Romania	17	14	3	1	1	0	3
USSR	421	463	148	176	178	69	59

Source: Computer Horizon and OECD.

Despite an average growth rate exceeding the European Union average in 1994 and 1995, the long-term prospect of catching up is unclear. Raising the standard of living of Eastern Europeans to the level of EU requires the creation of institutional and organizational capabilities that put the economy on to a higher growth path. To jump to the conclusion that these countries are catching up to the EU would be premature. While the market selection process plays a central role in generating technical change and technological learning, it may produce negative consequences such as unproductive and destructive entrepreneurship. The market economy also contains many other selection mechanisms that can actuate the innovation process. Simple policy prescriptions derived from neoclassical economic theory might be misleading because the analysis leaves out many of the behaviours and selection mechanisms important to the growth and innovation process. Thus policy in Eastern Europe should take into account the complex forces behind the process of growth and restructuring.

Notes

I would like to thank Michael Landesmann, Friedrich Levcik, Josef Pöschl, and Leon Podkaminer for their insights into some of the issues discussed in this chapter.

1. Levcik (1990) also observes that since the mid-1970s export of investment goods by the OECD countries to the European CMEA was much higher than the respective import share.
2. Scholars did not anticipate the collapse of the centrally planned economy. Kalecki and Kornai advanced theories explaining why extensive growth predominated in the centrally planned economy. Using a growth model similar to Harrod, Kalecki (1993) argued that the Soviet growth strategy would lead to a rising capital–output ratio and a falling growth rate. Kornai (1992) developed the idea of the 'soft-budget' constraint to explain how unenforceable contracts led to chronic consumer and producer good shortages.

22 *Mark Knell*

3. In reality the dependence worked both ways. Firms learned to cheat the authorities and to manipulate them to obtain preferential conditions such as better access to investment goods.
4. Commission of the European Communities, (1988), *European Economy*, November. Quoted in Oughton (1993). Oughton suggests that the two poorest countries of the EU are likely to fall behind the EU average.
5. Comparing and contrasting the different innovation systems in Europe could provide some valuable lessons for Eastern Europe (see Nelson, 1993). In Austria, for example, demand management policies were mixed with industrial policies. To reduce unemployment, state firms created subsidiaries and joint ventures that were eventually sold off. This included the creation of some technology firms that are now the most competitive in Europe.
6. Contrary to the view of Sachs and Woo (1994), the lessons from the Chinese example for an economics of transition do not arise from the fact that it is still a relatively backward agricultural country. The existence of a large surplus labour force explains why China has a potentially higher growth rate than Eastern Europe, but not why technological accumulation has been sustainable since 1978.
7. In 1990, Poland expected a 3.1 per cent decline in GDP and a 5 per cent decline in industrial output, but observed declines of 11.6 per cent and 24.2 per cent respectively.
8. Taylor (1991) lists three recurring controversies in monetary theory: (1) whether prices or outputs accommodate to the money supply; (2) whether money is endogenous or exogenous; and (3) whether banking system assets (credit) are more important than liabilities (money).
9. Although controversial, innovation surveys are one of the best ways to capture some of the qualitative aspects of the innovation process. Surveys were done in several Eastern European countries. Surveys taken in the late 1980s and early 1990s in Russia and Eastern Germany are summarized by Elena G. Zhuravskaya and Maria V. Gracheva, *Innovation Activities of Industrial Enterprise in Market and Transition Economies*, IIASA working paper WP-94-001, January 1994. Hungarian survey results taken from 1990 to 1993 are summarized in Annamaria Inzelt, *For a Better Understanding of the Innovation Process in Hungary*, presented at the Six Countries Programme Conference 'Research Co-operation with Countries in Transition', 1–2 December, 1994. A summary of the 1993 survey of Poland taken by J. Baruk is in issues 2, 5, 6, and 7 of *Wiadomosci Statystyczne* in 1994. There was also an innovation survey taken in Czechoslovakia during the early 1990s.
10. See Chang (1994) for a survey of the literature on industrial policy.
11. The Polish innovation survey indicates that systemic changes have not improved innovation in 2430 public and private enterprises in any significant way. Ironically, state enterprises were almost twice as likely to introduce new products and processes than private ones. See Jerzy Baruk, 'Przyczyny pasywnosci innowacyjnej', *Wiadomosci Statystyczne* 7, 1994, 10–14.

References

Aghion, P. and P. Howitt (1993), 'A model of growth through creative destruction', in D. Foray and C. Freeman, *Technology and the Wealth of Nations*, London: Pinter Publishers.
Amable, B. (1994), 'Endogenous Growth Theory, Convergence and Divergence', in G. Silverberg and L. Soete (eds), *The Economics of Growth and Technical Change*, Aldershot: Edward Elgar.
Baumol, W. (1993), *Entrepreneurship, Management, and the Structure of Payoffs*, Cambridge: MIT Press.
Bhaduri, A. (1992), 'Conventional Stabilization and the East European Transition', in Sándor Richter (ed.), *The Transition from Command to Market Economies in East-Central Europe*, Boulder: Westview Press.

Bell, M. and K. Pavitt (1993), 'Technological accumulation and industrial growth: Contrasts between developed and developing countries', *Industrial and Corporate Change*, 157–210.

Blanchard, O.J., K. Froot and J.D. Sachs (eds) (1994), *The Transition in Eastern Europe*, 2 vols., University of Chicago Press.

Brus, W. and K. Laski (1989), *From Marx to the Market*, Oxford University Press.

Chang, H.J. (1994), *The Political Economy of Industrial Policy*, London: Macmillan.

Dosi, G., C. Freeman and S. Fabiani (1994), 'The process of economic development: Introducing somes stylized facts and theories on technologies, firms and institutions', *Industrial and Corporate Change*, vol. 3, 1–45.

ECE (1992), *Economic Survey of Europe in 1991–1992*, United Nations, New York.

Fagerberg, J. (1994). 'Technology and International Growth Rates', *Journal of Economic Literature*, 32, September, 1147–75.

Foray, D. and C. Freeman (1993), *Technology and the Wealth of Nations*, London: Pinter Publishers.

Freeman, C. (1995), 'The "National System of Innovation" in historical perspective', *Cambridge Journal of Economics*, 19, 5–24.

Grossman, G. and E. Helpman (1991), *Innovation and growth*, Cambridge, MIT Press.

Gylfason, T. (1995), *The Path of Output from Plan to Market*, East European Series number 19, Institute for Advanced Studies, Vienna.

Hanson, P. and K. Pavitt (1987), *The Comparative Economics of Research Development and Innovation in East and West: A Survey*, New York: Harwood Academic Publishers.

IMF (1987), *Theoretical Aspects of the Design of Fund-Supported Adjustment Programs*, Occasional Paper 55, International Monetary Fund, Washington, D.C.

Kaldor, N. (1957), 'A Model of Economic Growth', *Economic Journal* 67, 591–624.

Kaldor, N. (1978), *Further Essays on Economic Theory*, London: Duckworth.

Kaldor, N. (1989), *Further Essays on Economic Theory and Policy*, London: Duckworth, edited by F. Targetti and A.P. Thirlwall.

Kalecki, M. (1993), *Collected Works*, ed. by J. Osiatyński, vols. 3 and 4, Oxford: Oxford University Press.

Knell, M. (1993), 'The Political Economy of Transitions to Market Economies', in I. Rima (ed.), *The Political Economy of Restructuring*, Aldershot: Edward Elgar.

Kornai, J. (1992), *The Socialist System*, Princeton University Press.

Landesmann, M.A. (1995), 'The Pattern of East-West European Integration: Catching Up or Falling Behind', *WIIW Research Reports*, no. 212.

Laski, K. et al. (1993), 'Transition from the Command to the Market System: what went wrong and what to do now?', *WIIW Working Papers*, no. 1, Vienna.

Levcik, F. (1990), 'The Technological Gap in the CMEA Countries: Missing Incentives', in K. Dopfer and K.F. Raible, *The Evolution of Economic Systems*, New York: St. Martin's Press.

Lipton, D. and J.D. Sachs (1990), 'Creating a Market Economy in Eastern Europe: The Case of Poland', *Brookings Papers on Economic Activity*.

Lucas, R.E. (1988), 'On the Mechanics of Economic Development', *Journal of Monetary Economics* 22, 3–42.

McCombie, J. S. L. and A.P. Thirlwall (1994), *Economic Growth and the Balance-of-Payments Constraint*, London: Macmillan.

Metcalfe, S. (1994), 'Evolutionary Economics and Technology Policy', *Economic Journal* 104, 931–44.

Mills, C.A. and R. Nallari (1992), *Analytical Approaches to Stabilization and Adjustment Programs*, Economic Development Institute of the World Bank, EDI seminar paper number 44, Washington, D. C.

Murrell, P. (1991), 'Can Neoclassical Economics Underpin the Reform of Centrally Planned Economies?', *Journal of Economic Perspectives* 5, 59–76.

Murrell, P. (1995), 'The Transition According to Cambridge, Mass', *Journal of Economic Literature* 33, 164–78.

Nelson, R.R. and S. Winter (1982), *An Evolutionary Theory of Economic Change*, Harvard University Press.

Nelson, R.R. (ed.) (1993), *National Innovation Systems: A Comparative Analysis*, Oxford: Oxford University Press.

Oughton, C. (1993), 'Growth, Structural Change and real convergence in the EC', in K.S. Hughes (ed.), *European Competitiveness*, Cambridge University Press.

Patel, P. and K. Pavitt (1994), 'Uneven (and Divergent) Technological Accumulation among Advanced Countries: Evidence and a Framework of Explanation', *Industrial and Corporate Change*, 759–87.

Romer, P.M. (1986), 'Increasing Returns and Long-Run Growth', *Journal of Political Economy* 94, 1002–37.

Romer, P.M. (1990), 'Endogenous technological change', *Journal of Political Economy* 98, S71–S102.

Sachs, J. and Woo, W.T. (1994), 'Structural Factors in the Economic Reforms of China, Eastern Europe, and the former Soviet Union', *Economic Policy* 18, 102–31.

Soete, L. and B. Verspagen (1993), 'Technology and Growth: The Complex Dynamics of Catching Up, Falling Behind and Taking Over', in A. Szirmai, B. van Ark and D. Pilat (eds), *Explaining Economic Growth*, Amsterdam: Elsevier.

Solow, R. (1956), 'A Contribution to the Theory of Economic Growth', *Quarterly Journal of Economics* 70, 65–94.

Stiglitz, J.E. (1994), *Whither Socialism?*, MIT Press, Cambridge.

Tarp, F. (1993), *Stabilization and Structural Adjustment*, Routledge, London.

Taylor, L. (1991), *Income Distribution, Inflation, and Growth*, MIT Press.

Verspagen, B. (1992), 'Endogenous Innovation in Neo-classical Growth Models: A survey', *Journal of Macroeconomics* 14, 631–62.

2 Stabilization and Prospects for Sustainable Growth in the Transition Economies

Peter Havlik

1 Introduction

Economic performance in the transition economies continues to show widely diverging trends. Bulgaria, the Czech Republic, Hungary, Poland, the Slovak Republic, Slovenia, Romania, Russia and Ukraine have all made considerable progress in the transition to a market economy. However, the prospects for sustainable growth remain extremely uneven as they depend on stabilization and structural adjustment, for example privatization, liberalization and institution-building. All of these countries dismantled the co-ordination mechanisms of the command economy with surprising speed. But difficulties in creating new institutions resulted in a slower and more painful transition than most analysts had expected in early 1990. The relative success of Central and Eastern Europe sharply contrasts with the desperate situation in most republics of the former Soviet Union. The heritage of communism remains important in all these countries. This is especially true of the CIS republics where the 'collective memory' of market economy and democracy is very faint, but is also present in such countries as the Czech Republic and Slovenia who have 'western' democratic traditions. Moreover, in some of the newly independent countries, such as the Slovak Republic and Ukraine, the need for nation-building complicates the economic transition. Any attempt to assess the current state and economic prospects of the region must take into account the political, cultural and economic dimensions.

The growing differentiation in the region makes generalizations extremely difficult. A common feature to all transition countries is that the economic and social costs greatly exceeded those originally anticipated following the political revolutions and the initial economic reforms. Table 2.1 shows that by the end of 1995 most of the transition economies were still significantly behind their pre-reform GDP levels.[1]

Open unemployment rose from a negligible amount to double-digit rates. Income differentiation has increased, while average consumption, social security and welfare have generally declined. At the same time, individual political freedoms have broadened enormously, allowing citizens freely to cross national borders and to pursue private initiative and entrepreneurship. The private sector, virtually non-existent in most communist countries, now accounts for a significant part of economic activity. Besides Hungary and Poland, the most striking examples are the Czech Republic and Russia, where private and non-state firms generated about 70 per cent of GDP in 1995.

Table 2.1   Real GDP in Eastern Europe, 1990–95

	Average annual growth rate (%)						Index 1989 = 100
	1990	1991	1992	1993	1994	1995[a]	1995[a]
Czech Republic	−1.2	−14.2	−6.4	−0.9	2.6	5.2	84.8
Hungary	−3.5	−11.9	−3.0	−0.8	2.9	2.0	85.9
Poland	−11.6	−7.0	2.6	3.8	5.2	7.0	98.6
Slovak Republic	−2.5	−14.5	−6.5	−3.7	4.9	7.4	84.6
Slovenia	−4.7	−8.1	−5.4	1.3	5.3	4.0	91.9
CEEC-5[b]	*−6.8*	*−10.1*	*−1.5*	*1.2*	*4.2*	*5.7*	*92.0*
Bulgaria	−9.1	−11.7	−7.3	−2.4	1.4	2.5	75.6
Romania	−5.6	−12.9	−8.7	1.4	4.0	6.9	84.6
CEEC-7[b]	*−6.8*	*−10.7*	*−3.2*	*1.0*	*4.0*	*5.6*	*89.4*
Russia	−3.0	−5.0	−14.5	−8.7	−12.6	−4.0	60.3
Ukraine	−2.6	−11.6	−13.7	−14.2	−23.0	−11.8	43.3

Note: [a]Preliminary. [b]WIIW estimate.
Source: National statistics (March 1996).

Unfortunately, in most transition countries this increase in individual freedoms has brought not only new opportunities, but also a general disregard of state authority. The discrediting of the traditional authoritarian state contributed not only to problems related to tax collection but also to an upsurge of crime and, more controversially, to the growth of a shadow or illegal economy. In the political and military spheres the artificial internationalism of the communist era has variously turned into nationalist xenophobia. In some instances, especially in parts of the former Yugoslavia and the former Soviet Union, nationalist feelings have escalated into violent conflicts, with serious economic consequences. The initial swing to the right in politics has largely evaporated; in many countries the successors of former communist parties were democratically re-elected. Nevertheless, a resurrection of the old system is nowhere on the agenda. In addition, the West, being preoccupied with its own problems, is now more cautious in accepting Central and Eastern Europe into the European Union and will probably delay integration until the next century.

From the perspective of systemic transformation, current economic performance and future growth prospects, it is useful to divide the transition economies into three regions, the boundaries approximately following the west–east and east–south axes. The Czech Republic, Hungary, Poland, the Slovak Republic and Slovenia belong to the first, more advanced 'western' group of transition countries (CEEC-5). This group has been showing encouraging signs of recovery since 1993 (Poland has been growing since 1992), with a booming private sector and declining inflation – though the latter is still rather high by Western standards. Table 2.1 shows that growth prospects in the CEEC-5 group look relatively favourable with GDP growth of more than 5 per cent achieved in 1995. Inflation decreased, though only in the Czech Republic and Slovenia it dropped below 10 per in 1995.

Bulgaria and Romania make up the second group. Bordering the south-east, this group is much less advanced, struggling either with political instability or lack of support for reform. There are few signs of a solid recovery: these countries' economies remain fragile in 1995, though Romania achieved strong GDP growth. High inflation, perhaps around 40 per cent annually, and slow structural reforms characterize these economies. Nevertheless, the transformational recession appears to have ended in 1994 as all countries in this region, designated CEEC-7, experienced growth for the first time since the transition process began.[2]

Lastly, Russia, Ukraine and the other CIS republics make up the third, 'eastern' group of transition countries.[3] Here, progress with reform has been meagre, confined to largely spontaneous 'stroke-of-the-pen' price liberalization and privatization. A highly unstable political situation, distorted economic structures, very weak democratic traditions and the extra complications of nation-building make transition extremely difficult. The CIS economies have been disintegrating rapidly, with mutual trade in near collapse and output in almost a free fall. Financial stabilization has been largely unsuccessful so far. In sharp contrast to the CEEC region, prospects for the CIS are still accordingly bleak, with no expectation of growth before 1997. High two-digit annual inflation is likely to persist. Nevertheless, there are also considerable internal differences within the three groups defined above as will become apparent in the following section.[4]

2 Trends in output, productivity and employment

Poland, Slovenia, the Czech Republic and, perhaps surprisingly, the Slovak Republic and Romania have all shown the clearest signs of economic recovery and growth since 1994. The Polish economy had been growing since 1992, and its performance was strong especially in industry; in 1995 industrial sales rose by almost 10 per cent (manufacturing exports performed even better). Table 2.3 shows that falling industrial employment induced double digit growth in labour productivity. In Hungary, industrial output has been increasing since 1993, and grew by 7 per cent in 1995. This was largely due to

Table 2.2   Industrial production in Eastern Europe, 1990–95

	Average annual growth rate (%)					
	1990	1991	1992	1993	1994	1995[a]
Czech Republic	−3.3	−24.4	−7.9	−5.3	2.1	9.5
Hungary	−10.2	−16.6	−9.7	4.0	9.6	7.0
Poland[b]	−24.2	−8.0	2.8	6.4	12.1	9.4
Slovak Republic	−4.0	−19.4	−9.0	−3.8	4.9	8.3
Slovenia	−10.5	−12.4	−13.2	−2.8	6.4	2.0
CEEC-5[c]	*−15.0*	*−14.3*	*−3.1*	*1.9*	*8.4*	*8.4*
Bulgaria	−16.7	−22.2	−15.9	−10.3	8.5	4.6
Romania	−19.0	−22.8	−21.9	1.3	3.3	9.4
CEEC-7[c]	*−15.9*	*−16.3*	*−7.4*	*1.1*	*7.4*	*8.3*
Russia	−0.1	−8.0	−18.0	−14.1	−20.9	−10.1
Ukraine	−0.1	−4.8	−6.4	−8.0	−27.3	−11.5

Notes: [a]Preliminary. [B]Sales. [c]WIIW estimate.
Source: National statistics (March 1996).

manufacturing as in Poland. Also the increase in labour productivity reached 15.7 per cent in 1994, and more than 10 per cent in 1995. Slovenia's recovery started in the second half of 1993 and further strengthened in 1994 with a 5 per cent growth rate of GDP. Industrial output increased 6.4 per cent, somewhat slower than in both Poland and Hungary. However, the increase in industrial labour productivity was 13.2 per cent.

In the Slovak Republic, the 5 per cent increase in GDP during 1994 came as a surprise, as political tensions and the effect of the split from the Czech Republic had detrimental effects on the economy. Here, too, industrial production and the labour productivity in industry expanded quite strongly. In the Czech Republic, GDP growth was 2.6 per cent in 1994 and started to accelerate only in 1995.[5] The poor Czech performance in manufacturing and the somewhat slower productivity growth of 5.1 per cent in 1994 might be an indication of the delayed restructuring of big enterprises, despite nominally rapid privatization. The Czech recovery was until recently confined mostly to trade, services and construction.

Table 2.3 Labour productivity in industry in Eastern Europe, 1990–95

	Average annual growth rate (%)					
	1990	1991	1992	1993	1994	1995[a]
Czech Republic[b]	−0.3	−14.4	−2.2	−1.2	5.1	10.5
Hungary[c]	−5.0	−6.2	3.8	13.4	15.7	10.5
Poland	−20.3	−3.0	14.3	12.6	15.5	13.1
Slovak Republic[b]	1.6	−22.5	−8.3	−4.7	7.0	4.1
Slovenia	−7.5	−1.4	−3.3	6.4	13.2	6.3
Bulgaria[d]	−12.1	−5.6	−1.9	0.0	12.2	8.9
Romania	−19.4	−15.0	−13.4	9.0	14.7	15.6
Russia	2.6	−4.1	−15.0	−12.0	−13.3	. . .
Ukraine	1.7	−2.0	−4.1	−3.2	−20.3	−8.8

Notes: [a]Preliminary. [b]Enterprises with more than 100 employees, from 1992 to 1994 with more than 25 employees. [c]From 1993 to 1994 enterprises with more than 20 employees, from 1995 with more than 10 employees. [d]Estimate for public sector only.
Source: National statistics (March 1996).

Bulgaria's GDP grew by only 2.5 per cent whereas state-owned and co-operative enterprises reported a growth of industrial sales by less than 5 per cent. In Romania GDP and industrial production increased by about 7–9 per cent in 1995. Political stalemate and the absence of parliamentary support for more consistent reform policies supporting enterprise restructuring and privatization may be the main reason for slow growth in both countries. Nevertheless, Table 2.12 shows that Bulgaria and Romania performed very well as compared to the performance of the CIS republics. Russia, Ukraine and most other CIS republics still observed output declines in 1995. Almost everywhere in the CIS, except in Armenia and Uzbekistan, industrial production declined, with many enterprises idle due to the attempted credit squeeze and lack of orders.

After a huge decline, labour productivity in industry stagnated in Russia and continued to decline in Ukraine.

Services have grown rapidly in all transition countries, except for personal services in the CIS. Otherwise the performance of other economic sectors was mixed. Construction boomed in the Czech Republic, Hungary and Romania, although housing construction mostly declined. Agriculture recovered in Hungary, the Slovak Republic and Slovenia, but in Russia and Ukraine grain harvests were the worst in years, increasing the need to import grain.

Table 2.4   Registered unemployment in Eastern Europe, 1992–95

	(end of period), in 1000 persons (A) and rate in % (B)[a]							
	1992 A	1992 B	1993 A	1993 B	1994 A	1994 B	1995 A	1995 B
Czech Republic	135	2.6	185	3.5	167	3.2	153	2.9
Hungary	663	13.2	632	13.3	520	10.9	496	10.4
Poland	2509	13.6	2890	16.4	2838	16.0	2629	14.9
Slovak Republic	260	10.4	368	14.4	371	14.8	333	13.1
Slovenia	118	13.4	137	15.5	124	14.2	127	14.4
CEEC-5[b]	*3685*	*11.5*	*4212*	*13.5*	*4020*	*12.9*	*3738*	*12.0*
Bulgaria	577	15.2	626	16.4	488	12.8	424	11.1
Romania	929	8.4	1165	10.4	1224	10.9	998	8.9
CEEC-7[b]	*5191*	*11.1*	*6003*	*13.0*	*5732*	*12.4*	*5160*	*11.2*
Russia	578	0.8	836	1.2	1637	2.2	2327	3.2
Ukraine	71	0.3	84	0.4	82	0.3	127	0.6

Notes: [a]Share of unemployed in % of economically active persons; figures for Croatia are the % of unemployed persons plus employees. [b]WIIW estimate.
Source: National statistics and WIIW (March 1996).

Unemployment is no longer rising in the CEECs, but it also appears that there are no significant declines in those countries observing strong output growth. Except for the Czech Republic,[6] Table 2.4 shows that all of the CEECs suffer from high unemployment rates. Despite a decline of more than one percentage point in 1995, more than 5 million persons were unemployed in the CEEC-7 region. At the end of 1995 the average unemployment rate of 11.2 per cent observed in the CEEC-7 was about the same as that observed in the European Union. CEEC unemployment remains high, despite growing output. Even in Hungary, Poland, the Slovak Republic and to some extent in Slovenia, the resumption of economic growth has not led to a larger-scale creation of new jobs, but rather to (urgently needed) productivity increases. Firms were thus able to improve profitability and to restore some of the efficiency losses incurred during the first reform years. In Russia and Ukraine open (registered) unemployment still hardly exists. Table 2.4 shows the official unemployment rate at the end of 1995 was 3.2 per cent in Russia and about 0.6 per cent in Ukraine. The actual unemployment levels in both countries were several times higher, with estimates ranging between 10 and 20 per cent of the labour force. Reliable figures are scarce. Low benefits discourage many jobless from registering, and enterprises, which often also fulfil various social functions, have so far been reluctant to dismiss redundant workers. The situation in most of the (nominally) privatized firms is not much better.

3 Consumption and investment recovering in the CEECs

Consumption and investment follow a similar trend as production and employment, with differences distinguishable among the three country groups.[7] In the CEEC-7, there are encouraging signs of recovery in private consumption and, most importantly, investment since 1994. Statistics are often only available for proxies such as wages or retail trade turnover and investment statistics are not fully comparable. Nevertheless, the evidence suggests that public consumption either declined or stagnated in most countries providing little or no stimulus for increasing final demand. In Poland private consumption grew by 5 per cent in 1994, wages increased by 3.4 per cent in real terms and retail sales grew by 2.3 per cent. More importantly, investment outlays, especially purchases of machinery and equipment, have been expanding rapidly, indicating significantly improved expectations of firms. In Hungary overall gross fixed investment stagnated, but investment in the private sector increased. As the result of the stabilization package from March 1995, real wages and retail trade turnover declined significantly (by 12.2 and 7.8 per cent, respectively).

In the Czech Republic both private consumption and gross fixed investment started growing in 1992, implying a decline in public consumption and the export surplus. Slovenia provides a similar picture, with gross wages increasing by about 5 per cent in 1995,[8] retail sales growing by almost 4 per cent, and gross fixed investment increasing by 15 per cent. The Slovak recovery rests on the weakest foundations as it appears that growing consumption at increasing wages and retail trade are sources of growth, while investment remains sluggish.

In the remaining transition countries domestic demand remains depressed, though the evidence is even more incomplete and controversial. In Bulgaria, there are no statistics on consumption (average real wages dropped by more than 6 per cent); the officially reported retail sales grew in 1995 by about 3 per cent, the same growth as in 1994.[9] However, the economic environment in Bulgaria does not encourage investment as the construction statistics seem to indicate. Romania observed a 16 per cent growth in real wages in 1995, but also observed strong growth of both retail trade and gross fixed investment (by 25 and 10 per cent, respectively). Private consumption and overall domestic demand remain depressed. In Russia, real money incomes fell by approximately 15 per cent in 1995, but wages declined by more than 25 per cent and retail trade contracted by some 7 per cent. Gross fixed investment fell by another 13 per cent. The situation looked even bleaker in Ukraine where investment dropped by approximately 35 per cent and registered retail sales declined by 13 per cent in 1995. As in Russia, the economy lives on stocks and people are spending more time on self-supply and barter exchange of services in order to get by.

Table 2.5 Real gross fixed investment in Eastern Europe, 1990–95

| | Average annual growth rate (%) | | | | | | Index 1989=100 |
	1990	1991	1992	1993	1994	1995[a]	1995[a]
Czech Republic	6.5	−32.5	16.6	8.0	16.9	15.7	105.9
Hungary	−9.6	−12.1	−1.5	2.5	12.3	0.0	90.1
Poland[b]	−10.1	−4.1	0.4	2.3	8.2	18.6	95.8
Slovak Republic	4.8	−27.3	9.2	13.1	2.1	9.2	96.1
Slovenia[c]	...	−14.8	−14.9	15.0	18.3	15.5	89.8
Bulgaria[c]	−18.5	−19.9	13.7	−24.5	−11.9	...	49.4
Românìa	−38.3	−25.8	−1.1	8.4	26.4	10.5	62.1
Russia	0.1	−15.5	−39.7	−11.6	−24.0	−13.0	34.3
Ukraine	1.9	−7.1	−36.9	−10.3	−23.0	−35.0	41.2

Notes: [a]Preliminary. [b]Investment outlays. [c]GDP coverage.
Source: National statistics (March 1996).

The growth in gross fixed investment in most CEECs confirms our earlier growth projections, increasing the prospects for a more sustained recovery in the future. Nevertheless, Table 2.5 shows that, except in the Czech Republic, investment still remains below its pre-reform levels. This may be a problem especially given the need to build new capacity in the export industries, to improve the crumbling and inadequate infrastructure, and to modernise the existing capital stock. Unfavourable tax laws, high real interest rates, and the reluctance of domestic banks to lend are hindering the necessary investment expansion.[10] Table 2.9 suggests, except for Hungary, and to some extent also the Czech Republic and Poland, that the contribution of foreign investments has so far been disappointing.

4 The dilemma of price stabilization versus growth

One of the main targets of economic policy in all transition countries has been to reduce inflation. Table 2.6 shows that Russia and Ukraine continue to have high inflation while annual inflation rates in most of the CEECs fell to moderately low levels. Producer prices have usually risen more slowly than consumer prices in the CEEC-7, but not in Russia, Ukraine and most other CIS republics where the budgets of enterprises have been soft and price distortions much greater. The CEEC-5 was most successful in reducing inflation; the Czech Republic had the lowest inflation rate, while Hungary and Poland had the highest. Inflation in the CIS republics has been high and volatile and combined with declined output. There were some signs of improvement as the monthly inflation rates fell below 5 per cent in Russia in late 1995, but this may be only temporary.

Table 2.6   Consumer price inflation in Eastern Europe, 1990–95

	Average annual growth rate (%)					
	1990	1991	1992	1993	1994	1995[a]
Czech Republic	9.9	56.7	11.1	20.8	10.0	9.1
Hungary	28.9	35.0	23.0	22.5	18.8	28.2
Poland	585.8	70.3	43.0	35.3	32.2	27.8
Slovak Republic	10.6	61.2	10.0	23.2	13.4	9.9
Slovenia[b]	549.7	117.7	201.3	32.3	19.8	12.6
Bulgaria	23.8	338.5	91.3	72.9	96.2	62.2
Romania	5.1	170.2	210.4	256.1	136.8	32.3
Russia	5.3	92.6	1526.0	875.0	307.0	198.0
Ukraine	4.8	91.2	1210.0	5371.0	891.0	377.0

Notes: [a]Preliminary. [b]Retail prices.
Source: National statistics and WIIW (March 1996).

Historical experience suggests that it will be difficult to reduce inflation in the CEEC-5 to single-digit annual rates. Inflation remains high in Bulgaria and Romania and continues at a moderately high level in Poland and Hungary. Although there is virtually complete price liberalization in the CEEC-5, price controls on some services and basic items for households in Poland and the Czech and Slovak Republics remain. Moreover, fiscal and credit policies are neutral or even slightly restrictive and real exchange rates have appreciated in most cases. Inflationary pressures might come from attempts to restore export competitiveness through exchange rate devaluation as in Hungary, Poland, and Bulgaria. Or they could come from the expanding money supply caused by capital inflows, as in the Czech Republic, Poland and Slovenia. In the CEECs, budget deficits did not increase during 1995 except in Bulgaria and Romania. Fiscal problems of a different magnitude resulted in budget deficits of about 5-10 per cent of GDP in Russia and Ukraine. Poland and Hungary had fiscal deficits of less than 3 per cent, but both had a primary (noninterest) budget surplus.[11] The Czech Republic and Slovenia achieved a budgetary surplus of almost 1 per cent of GDP.

The CEEC-5 countries now face an important dilemma over whether inflation and growth are contradictory or complementary policy objectives. An important issue in the debate over the relationship between growth and inflation is the level of capacity utilization and the labour market. Some of the production capacity inherited from the old system is not competitive in world markets and some military production capacity was phased out.[12] Nevertheless, there is the possibility of using under-utilized capacities more efficiently, such as housing construction. Poland, Hungary and Slovenia initially expanded production largely without any addition of new production capacities. Yet, after 1994 investment in new or modernized capacity increased in most of the CEECs (Table 2.5), causing unemployment to fall slightly.[13]

The increase in the utilization of production capacity and the employment of labour recently played a more important role than the addition of new capacity in increasing output and labour productivity. The existence of falling inflation rates and under-utilized capacity in a growing economy suggests that inflation and growth are not contradictory policy targets. Instead it appears that increasing demand is not the cause of inflation in the CEEC-5, but spiralling distributional conflict and increasing capital costs. The desire of workers, pensioners and managers to maintain or increase their standard of living in an inflationary economy strengthens the distributional conflict. Growing disillusionment of workers, following substantial wage cuts at the beginning of the transition process, may also be strengthening the inflationary spiral in the CEEC-5. Conventional stabilization tools of restrictive monetary and fiscal policies cannot counter this type of inflation. Instead an incomes policy that reduces the distributional conflict might be more effective in keeping money wages from growing faster than labour productivity. What is crucial in this context is that the impact of economic growth on labour productivity is positive, reducing the pressure on costs.[14] This requires *inter alia* the convergence of consumer and producer price indices. The Appendix shows that in all CEEC-7 countries the consumer price index (CPI) has been rising faster than the producer price index (PPI). This fact suggests that services are increasing as a share of GDP and/or there are greater price increases in the basket items included only in the CPI, such as rents, public utilities, etc. Under these conditions there is a coincidence between falling real consumer wages and increasing real product wages. This will be the case if the CPI rises more quickly than money wages and the PPI rises more quickly than the difference between money wages and labour productivity.

Great differences between both price indices were observed especially in Bulgaria, Hungary, Poland and Slovenia. The Czech and the Slovak Republics observed small price differences that were probably due to a more cautious approach of governments to administrative price increases. From this point of view the wage and price policies in these two countries appear more successful in controlling cost-related inflation. Nevertheless, it is necessary to complement incomes policies with tax policies on profits, investment, depreciation, interest rates and exchange rates.

5 Foreign trade and trade financing: constraints on growth?

Foreign trade in the transition countries has recently also gone through turbulent times. The collapse of the CMEA (the Council for Mutual Economic Assistance) in 1990, coupled with trade liberalization measures, led to a massive decline in intra-regional trade and a reorientation of trade to markets in the West, especially in the European Union (EU). In 1989, trade with the European Community (EC) accounted for between 5 per cent (Bulgaria) and 32 per cent (Poland) of CEEC exports.[15] By 1995 these shares had jumped to more than 30 per cent and 60 per cent, respectively. Similar trade shifts occurred in imports, and currently between 30 per cent (Bulgaria) and about 60 per cent (Poland and Slovenia) of CEEC imports come from the EU. The EU is now the major trading partner of Central and Eastern Europe. From the perspective of the EU, the transition economies are of only marginal importance. In 1994 only 6 per cent of total EU exports went to the CEEC-7. This asymmetry implies that trade policies will have a disproportionately greater impact on the CEECs than on the EU

Table 2.7   Foreign trade in Eastern Europe, 1990–95

		value in million US dollars						growth rates	
		1990	1991	1992	1993	1994	1995[a]	1994	1995[a]
Czech	Exports	9052	7924	8779	13205	14255	17054	8.0	19.6
Republic[a]	Imports	9815	7082	10382	12859	14971	20885	16.4	39.5
	Balance	−764	842	−1603	346	−716	−3831	...	...
Hungary	Exports	9551	10216	10678	8908	10775	12861	21.0	21.5
	Imports	8622	11438	11120	12630	14673	15466	16.2	7.0
	Balance	929	−1221	−442	−3722	−3898	−2605	...	...
Poland	Exports	14322	14903	13187	14143	17240	22450	21.9	30.2
	Imports	9528	15522	15913	18834	21569	28400	14.5	31.7
	Balance	4794	−618	−2726	−4691	−4329	−5950	...	...
Slovak	Exports	2875	3284	3712	5447	6691	8545	22.8	27.7
Republic[c]	Imports	3217	3608	3837	6334	6611	8484	4.4	28.3
	Balance	−342	−324	−124	−887	80	60	...	...
Slovenia	Exports	4118	3874	6681	6083	6828	8286	12.2	21.4
	Imports	4727	4131	6141	6501	7304	9451	12.4	29.4
	Balance	−609	−257	540	−418	−476	−1165	...	...
CEEC-5	Exports	39917	40201	43037	47783	55789	69195	16.7	24.5
	Imports	35909	41780	47393	57156	65128	82686	13.9	27.4
	Balance	4008	−1579	−4356	−9372	−9339	−13491	...	...
Bulgaria	Exports	13440	3433	3922	3721	3985	4731	7.1	18.7
	Imports	13128	2700	4468	4757	4185	4743	-12.0	13.3
	Balance	311	732	−546	−1036	−199	−12	...	...
Romania	Exports	5776	4266	4363	4892	6151	7520	25.7	22.2
	Imports	9203	5793	6260	6522	7109	9410	9.0	32.4
	Balance	−3427	−1528	−1896	−1630	−958	−1891	...	...
CEEC-7	Exports	59133	47899	51323	56399	65926	81446	16.9	23.6
	Imports	58240	50274	58121	68437	76421	96839	11.7	26.8
	Balance	892	−2375	−6798	−12038	−10498	−15394	...	...
Russia[d]	Exports	71148	50911	42376	44297	51450	64344	16.1	25.1
	Imports	81751	44473	36984	26807	28337	33266	5.7	17.4
	Balance	−10603	6438	5392	17490	23113	31078	...	...
Ukraine[d]	Exports	13500	4800	3774	3226	4686	5531	45.4	18.0
	Imports	16600	6600	2219	2652	2908	3861	9.7	32.8
	Balance	−3100	−1800	1555	571	1778	1670	...	...

Notes: [a]Preliminary. [b]From 1993 including trade with Slovakia. [c]From 1993 including trade with the Czech Republic. [d]Russian and Ukrainian trade without CIS.

Sources: National statistics and WIIW estimates (March 1996).

economies. Another distinctive feature of the transition countries' trade has been the asymmetry in the adjustment of export and import structures. Detailed analyses for manufacturing industry trade show that while the composition of CEEC imports changed dramatically after trade liberalization, the structure of exports from the CEECs to the EU remained fairly stable. Moreover, the composition of exports is quite different from what the EU generally imports from the rest of the world. Besides, the CEECs compete on EU markets with rather similar, usually labour- and raw material-intensive products.[16]

Statistical problems hinder an analysis of foreign trade in Eastern Europe. These problems include changes in exchange-rate regimes, switching to customs-statistics reporting and the dissolution of countries like the CSFR, Yugoslavia and the Soviet Union. The summary of recent developments presented in Table 2.7 therefore does not give a complete trade picture. In particular it is not possible to observe the substantial mutual trade within the CIS. Since 1991, the CEECs recorded sizeable and growing trade deficits, especially Hungary, Poland and recently also the Czech Republic. On the other hand, Russia, Ukraine and most other CIS states enjoy considerable trade surpluses that may, however, reflect significant under-reporting of both exports and especially of imports.[17] Another interesting feature of recent trade developments is that the combined CEEC-5 exports are of a similar magnitude as Russia's, though the population is about half as much.

Foreign trade of Eastern Europe improved considerably in 1994–95, after a rather poor year in which total CEEC exports stagnated in current dollar terms. Hungarian, Slovenian, Slovak and Bulgarian exports recovered, Polish and Romanian exports accelerated, and CEEC-7 exports expanded by about 20 per cent on annual average. Exports to the EU grew faster than average and the share of the EU in total CEEC exports increased further. Imports have been growing strongly as well (except for Bulgaria, and in 1995 also Hungary) and the trade deficits mostly persisted. In Bulgaria, a severe exchange rate crisis led to deep import cuts. The Slovak Republic, on the other hand, managed to curb its import demand by import restrictions. The Czech Republic reported relatively slow growth of exports and disturbingly high growth of imports, presumably related to the beginning economic recovery and an appreciating currency. Contrary to conventional economic reasoning, Russia managed to expand exports by 25 per cent, despite its huge real currency appreciation and declining output.

A major obstacle to sustained economic recovery in the transition countries are the high, and potentially widening, trade and current-account deficits.[18] Table 2.8 shows that most CEEC-7 countries reported negative current-account balances in 1995; financing these deficits might be potentially problematic. Several issues, besides the growing import demand that comes with economic recovery, are causes for concern of policy-makers. First, all transition countries have low dollar wages because of the initial devaluation that followed trade liberalization and the introduction of internal currency convertibility.[19] This gives them an important competitive edge especially in labour-intensive industries, but is also eroding with currency appreciation and rising unit labour costs (see appendix). Due to the large current gaps, unit labour costs are 25 to 35 per cent of the Austrian level, except for Slovenia, where they were about 60 per cent of the Austrian level in 1995. East European labour costs will remain significantly below West European levels in the future, creating a pretext for protectionist measures by the EU.

Table 2.8   Current-account balances of Eastern Europe, 1990–95

	in millions of US dollars					
	1990	1991	1992	1993	1994	1995[a]
Czech Republic	-338	1143	-305	115	−50	−1900
Hungary	127	267	324	−3455	−3911	−2480
Poland	716	-1359	-269	−2329	−944	−2101
Slovak Republic	...	...	...	−601	665	646
Slovenia	518	129	926	150	459	23
CEEC-5	...	...	...	*−6120*	*−3781*	*−5512*
Bulgaria	-1152	-77	-360	−1098	−25	200
Romania	-1656	-1187	-1564	−1170	−428	−1323
CEEC-7	...	...	...	*−8388*	*−4234*	*−6635*
Russia	-4300	7100	4179	6231	4836	10400
Ukraine	...	...	...	−849	−1395	−1380

Note: [a]Preliminary.
Source: WIIW (March 1996).

   Second, real exchange rates have been appreciating despite nominal devaluation, causing export competitiveness to deteriorate. In the CEEC-5, the real value of domestic currency in dollars in 1995 is higher than in 1989 (even if measured by changes in producer prices). Even in the Czech and Slovak Republics currency appreciation already wiped out the initially strong devaluation effect of 1990/91. After 1992, a process of rapid currency appreciation began in Russia and in Ukraine. Only Slovenia seems reasonably consistent in following its policy of real depreciation, though the Slovenian currency, the tolar, also appreciated in 1995. The appendix shows that the real currency appreciation is also clearly visible in the trends of the Exchange Rate Deviation Indexes (ERDI).[20] Given the current export performance and propensity to import, most transition countries, except perhaps Slovenia, might face serious balance-of-trade problems if the ERDI drops below 2 (see Hungary, Poland and recently also the Czech Republic).

Rising labour productivity and quality improvements are necessary for sustainable economic growth. Better capacity utilization improves labour productivity, but the ability to imitate more advanced technologies and to improve existing ones is imperative for sustainable growth. However, it takes time to derive productivity gains from the technology transfer and producers must learn how to use new technologies to their advantage. Without investment, the creation of new export capacities, and access to new markets, sustainable productivity increases are not possible. Without product and process innovation, and new export capacities and marketing abilities, Eastern Europe will not be able to compete in EU markets, reducing the chance of a sustainable economic recovery.

While income from services, including tourism transfers and foreign direct investment, eased the balance-of-payments constraint in some countries, the external financial position of most of the transition countries was rather tight. Thanks to restrictive measures such as devaluation and the introduction of temporary import surcharge in early 1995, the Hungarian current-account deficit (more than $3.9 billion in 1994) dropped below $2.5 billion by the end of 1995.

Bulgaria, Poland and Russia have not been able to service their foreign debt obligations, and were forced to reschedule both official and commercial debts. Bulgaria reached a deal with Paris and London Club creditors in April and June 1994, respectively. The Polish debt to official creditors has come down from $33 billion to $25.4 billion since April 1991. Effectively, Poland paid only 20 per cent of interest due ($1.8 billion), leaving the creditors to write off the $6.1 billion in unpaid interest. The second stage of the Paris Club debt reduction scheme provides for further concessions. Until 2001 the annual interest service will amount to $600–700 million, with only nominal paybacks of principal. Significant principal repayments are to start only in 2001 and will reach their peak ($4 billion) in 2008. Poland's generally 'good conduct' (and tough negotiating) has produced success also concerning commercial debts (London Club). The first accord on this debt ($12.3 billion) stipulates a 45 per cent debt reduction and very favourable terms for the servicing of the remaining portion of the debt. Table 2.9 reflects falling gross debt and rising reserves resulting from Bulgarian and Polish debt rescheduling.

Russia has been continuing its roll-over policy for its debts (mainly those inherited from the former Soviet Union estimated at more than $100 billion). The agreement with the Paris Club in June 1994 grants a three-years grace period and reschedules $7 billion of official debt service due in 1994 for 15 years.[21] Total debt service in 1994 was about $29 billion and included $17–19 billion owed to commercial banks. The debt service will peak in 1996–97 with about $15 billion per year, and Russia seeks a deal with both official and commercial creditors to reschedule the debt for at least 25 years. Russia has paid only a fraction of outstanding debt service and earmarked only about $6 billion for total debt service in 1995. During 1995, Russia received substantial new credits, mainly from the IMF and the World Bank, to cover the budget deficit and a rescheduling agreement with the London Club was reached in late 1995. In March 1996, the granting of a $12.1 billion IMF credit opened the way for a long-term rescheduling of official debts as well.

Table 2.9   Foreign financial position of Eastern Europe, 1993–95

	million dollars, end of period								
	Gross debt[a]			Reserves of National Bank[b]			Foreign direct investment[c]		
	1993	1994	1995	1993	1994	1995	1993	1994	1995
Czech Republic	8496	10694	...	3872	6243	13900	2153	3191	5917
Hungary	24560	28521	31655	6691	6727	11967	5576	7087	11919
Poland	47200	42174	41400	4281	6029	14963	979	1521	...
Slovak Republic	3626	4310	4800	450	1745	3400	323	531	728
Slovenia[d]	1873	2258	2956	788	1499	1821	294	378	528
Bulgaria	12472	10363	9700	655	1002	1236	141	247	...
Romania[e]	3357	4543	5305	42	592	334	211	552	970
Russia[f]	80000	112800	120000	4528	2300	11000	2858	3496	4637
Ukraine[g]	4214	7167	8143	133	646	1096	...	...	...

Notes: [a]In convertible currencies; total for the Slovak Republic, Slovenia, Croatia, Russia, and Ukraine. [b]Including gold for the Czech Republic, Slovakia, Poland. Figures for Hungary correspond to total reserves of the country. [c]Based on BOP inflows cumulated, FDI net for Poland and Bulgaria. [d]Excluding portion of debt of the former Yugoslav Federation. [e]Medium- and long-term. [f]Assumes responsibility for all old Soviet debts. [g]Excluding share of FSU debt.
Source: National statistics.

6 Economic outlook and possible time horizons for catching up

Economic performance improved considerably in 1994–95 in the CEEC-7 region, improving the prospects for sustainable economic

Table 2.10   GDP per capita at current dollar PPPs, 1990–2010

	1990	1991	1992	1993	1994	1995	2000	2005	2010
								projection	
Czech Rep.	9374	8285	8333	8476	8946	9635	12297	15694	20030
Hungary	5795	5661	5918	6057	6435	6733	8593	10968	13998
Poland	4222	4011	4412	4701	5080	5551	7085	9042	11540
Slovak Rep.	6214	5460	6206	6110	6629	7262	9268	11829	15097
Slovenia	9246	8701	8874	9272	10056	10697	13652	17424	22238
Bulgaria	4675	4256	4296	4330	4535	4781	6102	7787	9939
Romania	4053	3623	3616	3778	4046	4434	5659	7223	9219
Russia	5706	5565	5120	4815	4337	4263	5441	6944	8862
Ukraine	4407	3967	3663	3241	2588	2349	2998	3826	4883
Austria	16623	17342	18744	19128	19664	20057	22144	24449	26994
Germany	15779	16993	18649	18510	18936	19314	21325	23544	25995
Greece	7424	7764	8556	8797	8885	9063	10006	11047	12197
Portugal	9363	10404	11499	11953	12073	12314	13596	15011	16573
Spain	11755	12705	13278	13311	13537	13808	15245	16832	18584
USA	21965	22385	23228	24302	25250	25755	28435	31395	34663
EU (12)	15248	15974	17175	17089	17516	17867	19726	21779	24046

European Union (12) average = 100

	1990	1991	1992	1993	1994	1995	2000	2005	2010
Czech Rep.	61	52	49	50	51	54	62	72	83
Hungary	38	35	34	35	37	38	44	50	58
Poland	28	25	26	28	29	31	36	42	48
Slovak Rep.	41	34	36	36	38	41	47	54	63
Slovenia	61	54	52	54	57	60	69	80	92
Bulgaria	31	27	25	25	26	27	31	36	41
Romania	27	23	21	22	23	25	29	33	38
Russia	37	35	30	28	25	24	28	32	37
Ukraine	29	25	21	19	15	13	15	18	20
Austria	109	109	109	112	112	112	112	112	112
Germany	103	106	109	108	108	108	108	108	108
Greece	49	49	50	51	51	51	51	51	51
Portugal	61	65	67	70	69	69	69	69	69
Spain	77	80	77	78	77	77	77	77	77
USA	144	140	135	142	144	144	144	144	144

Notes: Benchmark PPPs for 1993. Projection assumes no population growth, 5% GDP growth in Eastern Europe and 2% growth in the European Union and USA.

growth. The strong growth of about 5 per cent per year should continue in 1996 and 1997, except in Hungary where the restrictive policies may depress GDP growth below 3 per cent. However, inflation will probably not drop significantly below 10 per cent per year anywhere, including the CEEC-5 region. In Bulgaria and in Romania it should remain at high double-digit annual rates. Unfortunately, the expected GDP growth will not be strong enough to reduce unemployment substantially. Unemployment rates may remain high – especially in Poland and the Slovak Republic. Unemployment should also rise in the Czech Republic since lay-offs following industrial restructuring may not be compensated by the existing job possibilities (mainly in the service sector). Investment should expand in the CEEC-5, especially in the Czech Republic, Hungary, Poland and Slovenia. Domestic savings will have to increase to finance these new investments and the possible increase in imports.

After disastrous declines in 1994, Russia, Ukraine and the other CIS republics might bottom-out of the recession during 1996–97. Inflation in the CIS should remain high despite recent temporary successes and the likely policy changes may result in even higher price increases. The investment decline might slowly end, if only because of the extremely low current level of investment. Russia will not meet interest payments on external debts and the current account will remain in surplus as imports remain low. The prospects for most other CIS republics are even worse, due to their generally much weaker commitment to reforms, lack of state identity and Russian economic and political pressures. Ukraine is in a desperate situation and may (like Belarus and Kazakhstan) consider a 're-integration option'.

The current economic recovery in the CEEC-7 and forecasts to 2000 indicate that the CEEC-7 will grow faster than the expected EU average growth rate. A rather optimistic scenario would be to assume a growth rate differential in real per capita GDP of 3 per cent between the CEEC-7 and the EU average. The real per capita GDPs in Slovenia and the Czech Republic were in 1995 about 50–60 per cent of the average EU level of about $17,900.[22] Table 2.11 shows that in 2000, real per capita GDPs of Slovenia and the Czech Republic will still be less than 70 per cent of the EU average. Hungary, Poland, and the Slovak Republic will still be less than 50 per cent of the EU average. A more likely possibility is for the CEEC-7 to catch up with the less prosperous European countries (Greece, Ireland, Portugal and Spain). Even under the optimistic scenario, convergence between the two most advanced CEEC countries and Spain (75 per cent of the EU average GDP per capita) could not happen before 2005. For the other CEECs to converge to the EU average

Table 2.11 The CIS economies: 1995 over 1994 (average annual growth rates and values in million US dollars)

	GDP	Gross industrial production	Consumer prices	Industrial producer prices	Retail trade turnover	Freight transport [a]	Foreign trade excl. CIS, mn USD Exports	Foreign trade excl. CIS, mn USD Imports	Average wages USD, Dec
Russia	−4	−3	196	240	−7	−12 [d]	64344	33266	115.3
Ukraine	−12	−11.5	180 [c]	180 [c]	−13.2 [e]	−20	5531	3861	45.3
Belarus	−10	−11.5	710	500	−25.3	−26	1662	1406	65.2
Moldova	−3	−6	30	50	−4.2 [e]	−15	274	271	32.2
Kazakhstan	−8.9	−7.9	180	140	−9	−27	2380	1209	79.9
Armenia	5 [b]	2.4	180	280	54	−2	103	334	16.8
Georgia	...	−9.8	60 [c]	...	155 [e]	...	65	140	...
Azerbaijan	−17.2	−21.4	410	1770	3	−30	335	443	13
Turkmenistan	...	−6.9	...	...	...	...	594	96	42.5
Uzbekistan	−1	0.2	320	830	−7.8	−1	1825	1650	29.5
Kyrgyzstan	−6.2	−12.5	50	40	−8.7	−31	128	152	33.9
Tajikistan	−12.4	−5.1	400	280	−76.3 [e]	−29	506	375	126.9
CIS	−5	−6	...	370	−10.5 [e]	−16	77747	43203	...

Notes: [a]Excluding pipelines. [b]January to November 1995 over same period in 1994. [c]December 1995 over same period in 1994. [d]December 1995 over December 1994. [d]Including private sector. [e]Officially reported trade.

Sources: Sodruzhestvo Nesavysimikh Gosudarstv v 1995 godu, CIS-STAT, Moscow, January 1996.

by 2010 would require a growth differential of more than 5 per cent, a highly unrealistic assumption. Without technological learning and institutional as well as technical change, chances of the CEECs' fast catching up to the EU are small. Realistically, substantial East–West income differences will prevail in the future.

Notes

1. There is a dispute over whether official statistics reflect actual developments properly. Clearly, there are activities, mainly in the emerging private sector and the unofficial economy, which are not covered by the data available. Nevertheless, a substantial decline in overall economic activity can hardly be disputed. For a more detailed discussion of statistical measurement problems see Bartholdy, K. (1994), 'Are the economies in Eastern Europe growing? Do demand and supply estimates give different answers?', *Economics of Transition*, vol. 2, no. 1, 111–16.
2. For the concept of transformational recession see Kornai, J. (1993), 'Transformational Recession. A General Phenomenon Examined Through the Example of Hungary's Development', *Economie Appliquée*, no. 2.
3. For an overview of the key economic developments in the CIS republics see Table 2.12.
4. The analysis is mostly based on information provided by WIIW country experts. The author would like to thank H. Boss, M. Knell, K. Laski, L. Podkaminer and J. Pöschl, as well as other colleagues at WIIW for valuable suggestions and comments on an earlier version. All remaining errors are, of course, the author's sole responsibility.
5. Slovak (and Czech) statistics must be interpreted with caution since the reported year-to-year growth rates for 1994 are probably affected by difficulties in the establishment of separate national accounts in 1993. Both the Czech and Slovak growth figures are affected by the low base of comparison one year earlier (effect of separation).
6. The extremely low unemployment rate in the Czech Republic (2.9 per cent at the end of 1995) can be explained mainly by a decrease in the labour force, the slow pace of industrial restructuring and, last but not least, by the expansion of the private sector and services – see J. Křovák (1994), 'Employment and Unemployment in the Czech Republic', *The Vienna Institute Monthly Report*, no. 5, 23–32.
7. Exports and imports are discussed separately in section 5.
8. Slovenia has the highest gross wages in the region at more than $900 per month.
9. Statistics on investment are very controversial as a recent revision of accounting methods changed the Bulgarian figures significantly.
10. Effective marginal tax rates on capital income are often more than 80 per cent. According to the BIS, bank credit to non-financial enterprises in the CEEC-7 actually declined in real terms (except in Slovenia and perhaps also the Czech Republic) – see Bank for International Settlements (1994), *64th Annual Report*, Basle, 13 June, p. 68.
11. For a discussion of fiscal deficits and economic growth see Oblath, G. (1995), 'Economic Growth and Fiscal Crisis in Central and Eastern Europe', *WIIW Research Reports*, no. 218, The Vienna Institute for Comparative Economic Studies, May.
12. Though the latter is reversible as examples in the Czech and the Slovak Republics and in Russia and Ukraine have shown.
13. In Hungary the automobile producers Suzuki and Opel added new capacity.
14. If labour productivity increases – as was recently the case in most CEECs (see Table 2.3) – then the rise in money wages will not cause any cost–push inflation, provided that growth in money wages lags behind growth in labour productivity. The latter, however, was mostly not the case and unit labour costs have been increasing – Table 2.7.
15. The exception was Slovenia, which traditionally had a large share of trade with the EU – more than 50 per cent of exports in 1989.

16. Dobrinsky, R. and M. Landesmann (1995), 'Transforming Economies and European Integration', Aldershot: Edward Elgar, as well as Landesmann, M., 'The Pattern of East-West European Integration: Catching Up or Falling Behind?', *WIIW Research Reports*, no. 212, The Vienna Institute for Comparative Economic Studies, January.
17. Moreover, Ukraine has a substantial trade deficit with Russia.
18. See, for instance, Bank for International Settlements, op. cit., p. 68; Wissels, R. (1994), 'Prospects for growth in Eastern Europe', *Working Paper*, no. 15, Austrian National Bank, Vienna; and chapter 7 by Landesmann and Pöschl in this volume.
19. Note that the Czech dollar wages are still lower than those in Slovenia and Hungary, not to speak of neighbouring Western partners.
20. Higher ERDI values are usually associated with lower productivity levels. However, East European ERDIs have been much lower than warranted by their productivity levels as measured e.g. by their real per capita GDP. Thus, for instance, the ERDI of Turkey was 1.75 in 1990 (Portugal: 1.37, Greece: 1.13) – see OECD as quoted in *WIFO Monatsberichte (Statistische Übersichten)* (1994), no. 5, i.e. much lower than the current ERDI levels in most CEECs. One must also take into account that since the currencies of major European trading partners (e.g. Germany and Austria) were overvalued with respect to the dollar (ERDI less than 1), the undervaluation of East European currencies with respect to DM and ATS was even more pronounced. Note that Hungary was forced to devalue at the beginning of 1995.
21. In 1993 the official debt amounting to $15 billion was rescheduled for ten years as Russia took over responsibility for Soviet debts.
22. Our rough estimates based on extrapolated PPP benchmarks for 1993 from the European Comparison Project as published in *Statistische Nachrichten* (1995), nos. 7, 9 and 10, Austrian Statistical Office, Vienna. Benchmark PPPs in ATS were linked to USD assuming PPP ATS/USD = 13.9. Benchmark PPPs extrapolated with GDP price deflators. GDP per capita for OECD countries according to OECD as published in *WIFO Monatsberichte (Statistische Übersichten)* (1996), no. 2.

Appendix   *Table 2A: Prices, exchange rates and unit labour costs, 1989–95*

	Annual averages and index 1989 = 100						
	1989	1990	1991	1992	1993	1994	1995
Czech Republic							
Producer price index	100	102.5	174.7	192.0	217.1	228.5	245.9
Consumer price index	100	109.9	172.2	191.3	231.1	254.3	277.4
GDP deflator	100	109.5	161.2	190.1	220.9	245.3	269.7
Exchange rate (ER), CZK/USD	15.05	17.95	29.48	28.26	29.15	28.78	26.54
ER nominal index	100	119.3	195.9	187.8	193.7	191.2	176.3
Real ER (CPI-based) index	100	113.1	122.6	108.5	94.4	86.5	74.8
Real ER (PPI-based) index	100	121.2	120.9	108.1	100.5	96.2	84.4
PPP, CZK/USD	5.56	5.84	8.39	9.20	10.40	11.22	12.06
ERDI (USD)	2.71	3.07	3.51	3.07	2.80	2.57	2.20
Average annual wages, CZK	38040	39432	45504	55728	69804	82728	98040
GDP nominal, bn CZK	524.5	567.3	716.6	791.0	910.6	1037.5	1200
Employment, thousands	5403.0	5351.0	5058.6	4927.1	4848.3	4884.8	4995
GDP per worker, CZK	97076	106018	141659	160540	187819	212396	240240
Unit labour costs index	100	103.9	132.1	168.4	209.5	243.8	280.9
Unit labour costs, Austria=100	27.50	20.03	15.09	18.00	22.20	25.63	27.87
Hungary							
Producer price index	100	122.0	161.8	180.3	199.8	222.4	286.7
Consumer price index	100	128.9	174.0	214.0	262.1	311.4	399.3
GDP deflator	100	125.7	157.6	191.4	232.6	278.0	350.7
Exchange rate (ER), HUF/USD	59.10	63.20	74.81	79.00	92.04	104.75	125.60
ER, nominal index	100	106.9	126.6	133.7	155.7	177.2	212.5
Real ER (CPI-based) index	100	86.5	78.4	69.0	66.9	65.4	62.6
Real ER (PPI-based) index	100	91.3	84.4	81.9	87.8	91.7	87.2
PPP, HUF/USD	28.86	34.82	42.58	48.10	56.83	65.99	81.38
ERDI (USD)	2.05	1.82	1.76	1.64	1.62	1.59	1.54
Average annual wages, HUF	126852	161352	215208	267528	326076	399708	466800
GDP nominal, bn HUF	1722.8	2089.3	2491.7	2935.1	3537.8	4350.9	5600
Employment, thousands	5488.5	5385.8	5048.0	4574.1	4244.2	4108.0	4070
GDP per worker, HUF	313896	387928	493606	641678	833561	1059129	1375921
Unit labour costs index	100	129.4	170.1	197.5	225.2	259.6	294.4
Unit labour costs, Austria=100	34.76	35.14	37.99	37.47	37.51	37.21	30.63
Poland (new zloty)							
Producer price index	100	722.4	1069.9	1374.7	1813.2	2271.9	2849.0
Consumer price index	100	685.8	1167.9	1670.1	2259.9	2987.6	3818.1
GDP deflator	100	580.1	900.9	1247.8	1628.9	2091.3	2609.9
Exchange rate (ER), PLZ/USD	0.145	0.950	1.058	1.363	1.815	2.273	2.41
ER, nominal	100	656.8	731.7	942.5	1254.6	1571.4	1666.3
Real ER (CPI-based) index	100	99.8	67.5	62.4	62.5	60.5	51.3
Real ER (PPI-based) index	100	94.7	73.7	75.8	77.9	79.5	68.8
PPP, PLZ/USD	0.06242	0.34753	0.52635	0.67819	0.86057	1.07362	1.30976
ERDI (USD based)	2.32	2.73	2.01	2.01	2.11	2.12	1.84
Average annual wages, PLZ	248	1236	2108	3477	4685	6394	8496
GDP nominal, bn PLZ	11.8	56.0	80.9	114.9	155.8	210.4	281.0
Employment, thousands	17001.8	16280.0	15326.4	14676.6	14330.1	14474.5	14590
GDP per worker, PLZ	696	3441	5277	7832	10871	14536	19260
Unit labour costs index	100	584.0	1008.9	1553.4	1968.7	2579.4	3228.6
Unit labour costs, Austria=100	29.26	21.74	32.82	35.18	34.26	35.09	36.06
Slovak Republic							
Producer price index	100	105.2	177.7	187.1	219.3	241.2	262.9
Consumer price index	100	110.6	178.3	196.1	241.6	274.0	301.1
GDP deflator index	100	106.7	143.5	160.3	185.8	209.3	228.8
Exchange rate (ER), SKK/USD	15.05	17.98	29.49	28.29	30.79	32.04	29.74
ER, nominal index	100	119.5	195.9	188.0	204.6	212.9	197.6
Real ER (CPI-based) index	100	112.56	118.47	105.92	95.35	89.35	77.20

	Annual averages and index 1989 = 100						
	1989	1990	1991	1992	1993	1994	1995

Slovak Republic (cont.)

Real ER (PPI-based) index	100	118.33	118.87	111.02	105.04	101.50	88.42
PPP, SKK/USD	7.23	7.40	9.71	10.09	11.37	12.45	13.30
ERDI (USD based)	2.08	2.43	3.04	2.80	2.71	2.57	2.24
Average annual wages, SKK	37080	38604	45240	54516	64548	75528	86340
GDP nominal, bn SKK	234.2	243.6	280.1	332.3	369.9	441.3	518.0
Employment , thousands	2498.0	2478.0	2281.0	2013.4	2012.3	1976.9	2019.8
GDP per worker, SKK	93755	98305	122797	165044	183820	223228	256461
Unit labour costs index	100	105.9	133.7	133.9	164.9	179.1	194.8
Unit labour costs, Austria=100	36.10	26.75	20.03	18.76	21.72	22.19	22.63

Slovenia

Producer price index	100	490.4	1099.0	3469.6	4218.9	4965.8	5601.3
Consumer price index	100	651.6	1400.9	4305.1	5721.7	6923.3	7795.6
GDP deflator index	100	590.8	1141.7	3515.9	4893.1	5956.5	6538.7
Exchange rate (ER), SIT/USD	2.88	11.32	27.57	81.29	113.24	128.81	118.52
ER, nominal index	100	393.6	958.5	2826.0	3936.9	4478.1	4120.3
Real ER (CPI-based) index	100	62.94	73.76	72.53	77.48	74.38	62.18
Real ER (PPI-based) index	100	83.62	94.02	90.00	105.07	103.71	86.54
PPP, SIT/USD	1.88	10.65	20.06	57.48	77.75	91.98	98.70
ERDI (USD based)	1.53	1.06	1.37	1.41	1.46	1.40	1.20
Average annual wages, SIT	25452	122064	201984	612528	905184	1135416	1344252
GDP nominal, bn SIT	34.9	196.8	349.4	1018.0	1435.1	1839.6	2100.0
Employment , thousands	946.3	909.7	839.0	783.4	766.4	752.3	750.4
GDP per worker, HUF	36927	216283	416452	1299366	1872409	2445297	2798507
Unit labour costs index	100	483.8	803.4	2404.7	3432.0	4012.7	4556.9
Unit labour costs, Austria=100	85.55	87.88	58.33	53.11	55.66	56.02	60.18

Bulgaria

Producer price index	100	114.7	454.7	708.9	899.3	1573.9	2403.8
Consumer price index	100	123.8	542.9	1038.6	1795.7	3523.2	5714.6
GDP deflator index	100	126.2	427.0	681.7	1039.3	1862.7	2848.8
Exchange rate (ER), BGL/USD	0.84	0.79	16.68	23.34	27.65	54.25	67.13
ER, nominal index	100	93.2	1978.4	2768.6	3279.7	6435.0	7963.0
Real ER (CPI-based) index	100	78.5	392.8	294.6	205.7	210.0	163.9
Real ER (PPI-based) index	100	84.7	469.1	431.6	410.6	470.2	389.7
PPP, BGL/USD	0.93	1.12	3.71	5.51	8.16	14.22	21.26
ERDI (USD based)	0.91	0.70	4.50	4.24	3.39	3.82	3.16
Average annual wages, BGL	3292	4536	12144	24564	38772	57864	87808
GDP nominal, bn BGL	39.6	45.4	135.7	200.8	298.9	543.5	852.0
Employment , thousands	4365.0	4096.8	3564.0	3273.7	3221.8	3157.9	3038.0
GDP per worker, BGL	9067	11079	38078	61348	92784	172100	280448
Unit labour costs index	100	142.3	375.1	751.9	1196.4	1725.3	2457.1
Unit labour costs, Austria=100	75.72	96.56	11.68	15.00	20.61	14.83	14.86

Romania

Producer price index	100	126.9	406.2	1156.8	3065.5	7372.6	9960.4
Consumer price index	100	105.1	283.9	881.5	3138.9	7431.5	9831.8
GDP deflator index	100	113.6	335.0	1004.0	3293.1	7865.8	10673.9
Exchange rate (ER), ROL/USD	14.92	24.43	76.39	307.95	760.05	1655.09	2033.26
ER, nominal index	100	163.7	512.0	2064.0	5094.2	11093.1	13627.7
Real ER (CPI-based) index	100	162.4	194.4	258.7	182.7	171.7	163.1
Real ER (PPI-based) index	100	134.4	135.9	197.2	187.1	173.0	161.0
PPP, ROL/USD	8.37	9.12	26.24	73.16	233.26	541.44	718.21
ERDI (USD based)	1.78	2.68	2.91	4.21	3.26	3.06	2.83
Average annual wages, ROL	36756	40572	110928	305124	940164	2180328	3375444
GDP nominal, bn ROL	800.0	857.9	2203.9	6029.2	20051.0	49794.8	72249.0
Employment , thousands	10875.6	10892.6	10812.7	10621.9	10260.0	10036.5	10015.0
GDP per worker, ROL	73563	78755	203827	567617	1954289	4961371	7214079
Unit labour costs index	100	117.1	364.8	1080.1	3170.6	6918.2	9995.4
Unit labour costs, Austria=100	53.27	31.83	30.88	20.34	24.74	24.28	24.85

Appendix   *Table 2A (continued)*

	1989	1990	1991	1992	1993	1994	1995
	Annual averages and index 1989=100						

Russia

	1989	1990	1991	1992	1993	1994	1995
Producer price index	100	103.0	245.1	5882.6	61767.3	271775.9	926755.8
Consumer price index	100	105.3	202.8	3297.5	32150.6	130852.9	389941.8
GDP deflator index	100	115.9	264.8	4210.7	41638.9	169624.9	479826.5
Exchange rate (ER), RUR/USD	0.63	0.59	1.75	192.50	932.15	2204.00	4554.00
ER, nominal index	100	92.9	277.1	30555.6	147960.3	349841.3	722857.1
Real ER (CPI-based) index	100	91.9	147.3	1023.9	518.2	307.5	218.1
Real ER (PPI-based) index	100	94.0	121.9	574.0	269.7	148.0	91.8
PPP, RUR/USD	0.68	0.76	1.69	24.97	240.06	950.30	2627.72
ERDI (USD based)	0.92	0.77	1.03	7.71	3.88	2.32	1.73
Average annual wages, RUR	3156	3636	6912	76620	771120	2910924	6420000
GDP nominal, bn RUR	573.1	644.2	1398.5	19005.5	171510.0	610993.0	1659000
Employment , thousands	75168.0	75325.0	73848.0	72071.0	70852.0	68484.0	67000
GDP per worker, RUR	7624	8552	18938	263705	2420680	8921690	24761194
Unit labour costs index	100	119.0	233.5	2955.5	32043.8	133700.7	300544.0
Unit labour costs, Austria=100	97.70	104.65	66.97	6.89	15.79	27.28	25.84

Ukraine

	1989	1990	1991	1992	1993	1994	1995
Producer price index	100	104.5	235.5	5747.5	273999.0	2742811.5	15167235
Consumer price index	100	104.8	200.4	2625.2	143625.0	1423324.0	6789255
GDP deflator index	100	111.3	225.6	4395.3	150951.9	1503695.1	7961039
Exchange rate (ER), UAK/USD	0.63	0.59	1.75	200.49	4795.75	31699.00	147281
ER, nominal index	100	92.9	277.1	31823.8	761230.2	5031587.3	23377857
Real ER (CPI-based) index	100	92.3	149.1	1339.5	596.8	406.5	405.1
Real ER (PPI-based) index	100	92.6	126.9	611.8	312.8	211.0	181.3
PPP, UAK/USD	0.69	0.73	1.45	26.30	878.03	8499.44	43987.02
ERDI (USD based)	0.92	0.80	1.20	7.62	5.46	3.73	3.35
Average annual wages, UAK	2612	3000	5712	76464	1861704	16505400	97597200
GDP nominal, bn UAK	154.1	167.1	299.4	5032.7	148300.0	1137794.0	5300000
Employment , thousands	25400.0	25277.3	24977.1	24485.0	23923.7	23025.0	22500
GDP per worker, UAK	6067	6611	11987	205542	6198874	49415592	235555556
Unit labour costs index	100	117.3	249.7	3797.5	105289.6	1166462.6	7660599.1
Unit labour costs, Austria=100	88.77	93.73	65.07	7.73	9.16	15.04	18.50

Notes: ER = Exchange Rate, PPP = Purchasing Power Parity, ERDI = Exchange Rate Deviation Index (all in terms of national currency per USD). Benchmark PPPs for 1993 were extrapolated with GDP price deflators.

Sources: Austrian Statistical Office (1995), *Statistische Nachrichten*, nos. 9 and 10; national statistics; OECD; WIIW.

3 Economics of Transition: Some Gaps and Illusions

Alec Nove

1 Introduction

The formerly communist-ruled countries of Eastern Europe differ widely among themselves, in resources, population, level of development, degree to which market-type reforms had already been introduced before 1989 and in the political and economic measures taken after that date. We will leave out of account here those ex-Soviet republics which devote most of their energies to fighting, e.g., Armenia, Azerbaijan, Georgia, and Moldova. Central Asia too would require separate treatment. The others, despite the differences mentioned above, have in common the high priority they all give to the creation of a market economy, to a transition from what was called socialism to some variety of capitalism. They also share in common a steep decline, in 1990–92, in GNP, industrial production, real wages, and investment, and this whether or not a 'shock therapy' strategy was pursued.

It is true that the scale of the decline may be incorrectly measured or wrongly interpreted. Thus Winiecki has pointed out[1] that, firstly, there is considerable private activity which is unrecorded; secondly that citizens do now have a wider choice and do not have to stand in line, and, thirdly, that useless, unsaleable production ought to have ceased to be produced. There is evidence for each of these propositions. However, the fact of decline is surely not in dispute. Let us now list its causes, while bearing in mind that the relative weight of the causes varies as between countries. We could then consider how far the decline was unavoidable (or even desirable), given the chosen 'transition' strategy, and also the relevance or otherwise of mainstream economic theory. Finally we can situate Western aid and investment as a factor, bearing in mind the role of Marshall aid in the postwar recovery of Western Europe. It is also worth noting the very different strategy being adopted in China.

2 Why the decline?

The following generalizations apply (in unequal measure) to all countries.

1. *The consequences of political disruption.* This includes the collapse of Comecon, which deprived some industries of markets and others of supplies. Thus, for example, Poland, Hungary, Czechoslovakia and Bulgaria depended greatly on the Soviet market. And the former Soviet Union depended on these countries for various industrial components, medical drugs and consumer goods. The disruption of the Soviet Union had similar deleterious effects in that national republics and even regions obstructed trade and payments, a process stimulated by the progressive devaluation (and non-convertibility, both domestically and internationally) of the rouble, and the role of barter deals.

2. *The consequences of institutional disruption.* Again in varying degrees, management (and bureaucrats) found themselves in a situation with which they were unfamiliar, with the disappearance of the system to which they had been accustomed. Market-type institutions were still in process of formation. Management had not developed marketing skills, the necessary information flows were missing or inadequate, the legal structure all too often ambiguous or confused, 'market culture' lacking (less lacking in Budapest, say, than in Kiev or Rostov). Commercial banks were inevitably run by men or women inexperienced in commercial banking. Management from countries which had retained the state monopoly of foreign trade lacked the skills of marketing their products abroad. In some countries underpaid bureaucrats turned to corruption on a large scale. All in all, the moral, institutional, and legal infrastructure of markets was still in process of formation. To these problems must be added the uncertainty engendered by change in ownership, what a Czech economist (Mertlík) has called 'privatization agony': management, no longer subject to control from above, had no long-term prospect, in that the enterprise could be privatized, on terms not yet clear. There will be much more to say later about the forms and effects of privatization. But it is only natural that this circumstance affects managerial behaviour.

3. *The consequences of inherited structural distortions.* Some economies were heavily 'slanted' toward the military-industrial complex, and the end of the arms race led to an immediate fall in output of military end-products and of inputs for these products, while 'conversion' required time and scarce resources. Nearly all these countries had an overdeveloped heavy-industry sector, sometimes based on artificially low-priced energy and materials, transported long distances (e.g.,

steelworks in Hungary and Poland). There were serious deficiencies in infrastructure. There were some of the world's worst cases of atmospheric pollution. This called for a major redistribution of resources to previously neglected sectors, but meanwhile output would fall in those sectors which were plainly uneconomic in the new circumstances (there were cases where, if evaluated in world prices, the net product was negative, i.e., the value of inputs exceeded the value of output). (The fall in oil output in Russia, which is having serious consequences, had other causes.)

4. *The effect of deflation on consumer demand.* Again in varying degrees, all countries have seen a decline in real incomes. This has had the effect of increasing the share of income devoted to food (Engels's law in reverse) and a corresponding fall in demand for manufactured consumer goods and durables. In Russia and Ukraine, and even Poland, there was also a fall in demand for the dearer foodstuffs, such as sausage. So the fall in consumption was due partly to the drop in output and in imports, and partly to the fall in purchasing power, which was also a cause of the drop in output. Price relativities have been greatly affected by the elimination of most subsidies. Thus in Russia the (official) prices of bread and meat multiplied a hundredfold between 1980 and the end of 1982, while average incomes rose roughly twenty-fold in the same period.

5. *The consequences of (premature?) currency convertibility and import liberalization.* Consumer goods production is seriously affected by the citizens' preference for goods imported from the West. This is noticeable in Poland and in the Czech and Slovak Republics, but in Russia it has even affected vodka (some prefer to buy Smirnoff!). The effect has been most shattering in East Germany, whose citizens have real German money to spend, and buy West German.

6. *The consequences of the collapse of investment.* As we shall see, investment has fallen very sharply in all these countries, despite the urgent need for restructuring and conversion, and this naturally is associated with a fall in demand for machinery, building materials and other investment goods. For reasons to be examined, foreign investment can only very partially fill the gap.

7. *The consequences of 'marketization' of formerly state-sponsored services.* For example, medical services, education, culture, crèches, holiday homes and scientific research have all been cut back or put on a commercial basis or both. Hence the steep decline in many of the 'services' components in GNP, especially in Russia.

All this must be seen in the context of the triumph of neo-classical economics in its 'Chicago' form, as represented in the attitude to the role of the state of such economists as Milton Friedman and Gary Becker, though the influences of the IMF and the World Bank are responsible too. Extremist neo-conservative think-tanks send missionaries to expound the gospel: roll back the state, do not copy Western Europe, or even the United States, where government remains on people's backs. Laissez-faire is seen as the answer, along with shock therapy to get the pain over more quickly.

They invoke Hayek's authority. However, they may have overlooked Hayek's warning in his *Road to Serfdom*. In 1944, looking forward to the desired postwar economic freedom, he wrote: 'This is perhaps the place to emphasize that, however much one may wish for a speedy return to a free economy, this cannot mean the removal at one stroke of the wartime restrictions. Nothing would discredit the system of free enterprise more than the acute, though probably short-lived, dislocation and instability such an attempt would produce.'[2] Not quite the spirit of Jeffrey Sachs, one would have thought! Here Hayek emphasizes the political and social cost of transition. But, as we shall see, there is an economic cost too, and all the greater because, unlike Western Europe in 1945, the 'East' still has to create many of the institutional and social-psychological preconditions which would be fairly easily re-created or mobilized in the West.

3 A theoretical detour: investment and neo-classical economics

The neo-classical paradigm is based on general equilibrium as an ideal, based upon perfect competition, perfect markets, perfect knowledge, in which a large number of producers of homogeneous products are price takers, can sell all they produce at *the* price, which either emerges spontaneously or is announced by the Walrasian Auctioneer. Of course, it is well known not only to the critics but also to the authors of such models that the real world is not like that. Axel Leijonhofhud divided economists into two categories: those who believe that, left to itself, the economy is self-balancing, and those who, on the contrary, envisage the possibility of cumulative disequilibrium. Then there are critiques from those known as 'Austrians', who stress the importance of the function of the entrepreneur under conditions of uncertainty, and who are surely closer to the problems of the real world, whether in Moscow or in Chicago itself. This is not the place to discuss the merits and de-merits of neoclassical models or of those who question their relevance, except in one respect: their irrelevance to investment.

The believers in the neoclassical paradigm will tend to the view that the closer we get to perfect competition, the more likely is the desired optimum. But this is clearly wrong if we are concerned with investment. And this not only because *time* is involved, and with it the inescapable uncertainty as to future prices of both output and inputs. (Neoclassical mainstream has problems with both time and uncertainty, as many critics have pointed out.) There is also the uncertainty as to how competitors might react to future prices, even if they are in some sense known. Real investment commits resources irreversibly. The assumptions on which perfect competition rests include that of perfect knowledge, i.e., your competitors know what you know. But one thing the models lack is information about what they will do. As G. B. Richardson pointed out over thirty years ago,[3] a profitable opportunity seen by all may prove available to none. If we know that a horse will win the race at odds of 10 to 1, the odds would not be 10 to 1.

Even in theory, equilibrium and profits from investing are uneasy bedfellows, in fact they cannot coexist. In equilibrium, profits tend to equal the rate of interest. Profits from investment arise out of existing or anticipated disequilibrium. Hence theoretically dubious is the concept of an 'equilibrium growth path': why should economic agents cause growth to occur by actions which, in equilibrium, would yield them no profit? Here the 'Austrians' are much closer to real life, and many years ago Ludwig Lachman wrote: 'There can be no such thing as dynamic macroeconomic equilibrium.'[4]

Investment occurs, to repeat, because of disequilibrium, and also, as Richardson points out, because of so-called market *imperfections:* imperfect knowledge (the competitors have not yet caught on), temporary monopoly or market dominance, long-term tie-up with banks, customers and suppliers, collusion with competitors, protection from foreign competition, co-ordination through government (as in Japan, South Korea, Taiwan, even France). All this would surely be understood by economists brought up in the Schumpeter tradition. One recalls, too, a recent book by Baumol[5] pointing to circumstances in which expensive investment in high-tech research can be undertaken jointly by several firms, spreading the cost and the risk, under conditions (frequently met with in real life, but disliked by neoclassical model-builders) of increasing returns to scale.

All the above considerations apply in real capitalist economies. To them one other point, of a more institutional kind, should be added. The process of investment requires a financial system that supplies the venture capital needed for long-term commitments. In both Germany and

Japan the banks and finance houses have traditionally invested in industry, and many sources, including a recent National Bureau of Economic Research (NBER) report, deplore the absence of such banks in the United States and Great Britain. So that when the 'eastern' countries speak of the need to create a modern and efficient capital market, they should be aware of the differences in this respect between capitalist countries.

The theoretical gap leads to gaps in thinking. Examples come to mind from recent British experience. Thus when electricity generation and supply were privatized and fragmented, the effect of this on investment was ignored. Yet there is plainly a major difference between having *one* (monopolist) institution responsible for estimating total future demand of this universally-used and totally homogeneous product, and a large number of enterprises, none of which carry this responsibility. It is true that the monopolist could (sometimes did) get its sums wrong, but it at least tried to do the sums. With many generators and distributors, with no knowledge of each others' intentions, and with electricity demand uneven through the year, one could have, even expect to have, either insufficient investment to provide for periods of peak demand, or overinvestment, as each tried to cash in on what each thought was a profitable opportunity. I took the view that the first of these possibilities was most likely, but was proved wrong. What we have had is over-investment, over-capacity.

This has been paralleled by overinvestment in office building, in London, Tokyo, New York, which has contributed to the recession and has led to a surfeit of empty offices and to bankruptcies of property companies and finance houses.

Or, to take a different example: the British government, guided by ideologists, has privatized and fragmented public transport. This has disrupted ties between the big public transport undertakings and the suppliers (of vehicles, railroad equipment, etc.), ties which exist in other countries of Western Europe, thereby contributing to a decline in British transport equipment production and to a large increase in imports. These consequences would simply not have occurred to the authors of the policies, as their kind of economics does not stress systemic inter-relationships. The effect of increasing uncertainty on the investment intentions of input-providers is not a question to which their training would draw their attention. (For one thing, such matters fall into the gap that separates macro from micro.)

It is also worth stressing, as theory seldom does, the link between investment (or lack of it) and unemployment. If it is the case that tens of millions are out of work (and do *not* 'prefer leisure'), it is surely naïve and unrealistic to imagine that the competitive lowering of wage rates would result in a full-employment equilibrium, if only because of the 'deflationary' effect on demand. Of course the converse does not hold either: a rise in money wages is no cure for unemployment. In practice, though substitutable at the margin, labour and capital are most often complementary: employment and investment are linked. That is why, both in the West and the East, there are good reasons for being troubled when a rise in unemployment and a fall in investment coincide, as they have done in 1990–92 in both Britain and Russia.

4 The investment problem in the 'East'

As already stressed, the ex-communist countries face a very large task of restructuring their economies, which calls for substantial investments. The state had in the past played the predominant role in planning and financing investment, and all too often this reflected not just the often arbitrary priorities of the leadership, but also the influence (or decibels) of sectional interests, represented in and through the current ruling party. A sizeable literature on investment criteria was largely ignored in practice, the more so because the irrational price system failed to indicate in any objective fashion either the urgency of need or the most economical way of meeting it.

It was therefore an understandable reaction for reformers to abandon investment planning, to believe the Western mainstream textbooks: investment (like most other things) will be determined and directed by market forces, which will also create spontaneously the needed capital-market institutions. Hence the ideas which would be best represented by Marek Dąbrowski: he is all for resisting 'interventionist pressures', he is against 'the demand for a kind of government investment policy', or budgeting sums allocated for restructuring, or 'state influence on the branch structure of the economy', or any 'priority in government (economic) policy', or 'interventionism as a substitute for the market mechanism'.[6] Similar views have been expressed by Václav Klaus, (at first) by Yegor Gaidar and, of course, by Margaret Thatcher in the United Kingdom. These views contain no industrial policy, no energy policy, no transport policy, and no investment strategy. All will come about by itself if and when macroeconomic stabilization is achieved (or in Mrs Thatcher's case, the ideal of zero inflation inspired by Milton Friedman).

Yet it is a feature of all 'eastern' countries, in varying degrees, that there is as yet only a rudimentary capital market, and little privately-owned capital. True, state enterprises have in some instances accumulated financial reserves, and could reinvest their profits. However, for reasons to be expounded, they have little incentive to do so, and are also subject to heavy taxation. In some countries more than in others there is also the uncertainty generated by inflationary expectations and political turmoil, so that would-be investors, domestic and foreign, are deterred. With the state increasingly withdrawing from investment financing, it is not surprising to find very steep declines in volume: by 49.3 per cent in Bulgaria, by 36 per cent in Czechoslovakia, by 50 per cent and more in Russia and Ukraine, and by 35 per cent in Romania, in a single year (1991 or 1992).[7]

Yet 'Restructuring actually understates the scope of the task in hand, because what is needed is nothing short of the orderly closing of the existing production structure and the creation of a whole new economy'.[8] We can see the scale of the task when observing the huge level of West German expenditure in East Germany (estimated at roughly $200 billion in three years), though only part of this sum represents investment expenditures. This is roughly ten times the expected sum of Western aid allocated to all the republics of the former Soviet Union, which have seventeen times the population of East Germany. Foreign capital is, needless to say, a valuable and desired source of investment financing. However, it can meet only a small part of total need. Internal sources of accumulation are vital, and yet one has the strong impression that this problem of investment has not figured high on the list of concerns of reformers and their Western advisers. Yet the matter is surely of vital importance. The voucher schemes, of which more in a moment, are not investment in real terms; they are a means of privatizing existing capital assets, not new capital designed to create or modernize productive capacity.

5 Relevant experience, Southeast Asia and Western Europe

Restructuring on a large scale, after the disasters of war, was successfully carried out in Western Europe in the ten or so years after 1945, and also in Japan and South Korea. This involved large-scale investments to reconstruct after war damage and to create a competitive (all too competitive!) and modern industry and infrastructure. Despite legend, this was not, repeat not, achieved by immediate laissez-faire measures, not by introducing full currency convertibility. The role of the state varied in different countries, and in fact still does. The NBER report on South Korea had much to say about 'an active interventionist government policy that was credible, coherent, and consistent. Investments to promote exports received top priority, and the economy was led through a fundamental industrial restructuring. The close link between government and business in Korea made this strategy work. The centrepiece was a comprehensive export-focused investment plan.'

The active role of Japan's Ministry of International Trade and Industry (MITI), including selective protectionism as well as investment co-ordination, is surely well known, not to say notorious. Taiwan shows similar features. This was not anything resembling Soviet-type centralized planning, for at least two reasons. Firstly, the plans were not compulsory (outside of the state sector itself, which did provide essential infrastructure); private business reacted to profitable opportunities, its investments were facilitated, not prescribed. Secondly, alongside whatever the state was planning or encouraging, private investors were actively investing, and in some instances (notably in Japan) made a major independent contribution, unhampered by plan bureaucracy. But this was emphatically not just the spontaneous free market or laissez-faire.

To restate what should be obvious, large-scale long-term investment in productive capacity is encouraged by a reduction in uncertainty and risk. I heard a South Korean economist tell a conference (it was in Hanoi) how the president held regular meetings with senior officials and top business, to discuss proposals for structurally significant investment and whether co-ordination or assistance was required.

Postwar Western Europe had a big backlog of investment, after many years of uncreative destruction. Different countries handled the problem in different ways. But laissez-faire was not seen as the answer. Priority was naturally given to reconstruction (e.g., of houses, transport facilities, energy). In Great Britain, for several years a Capital Issue Committee deliberately 'rationed' private-sector investments. Interest rates were kept artificially low, and to receive permission to invest it was necessary to show that it was to meet priority internal needs, or that it was a contribution to the export drive (the balance of payments was a major bottleneck item in those years, dollar shortage being particularly severe).

Internal priorities were closely linked with foreign assistance. Marshall aid provided resources which had to be used for specified purposes, approved by donor as well as recipient, even though it meant that exports of American consumer goods suffered as a result of the rationing of the available dollars. The aid was intended primarily for reconstruction, to enable these countries, enfeebled by years of war, to stand on their own feet. So the re-equipment of industry was more important than imports of American cars, for instance.

It is worth dwelling for a moment on this issue of priorities. It can be most vividly seen in a war economy. In theory no doubt the needs of war (guns, ammunition, planes) could compete for resources in the market with makers of cars, television sets, and tractors. In fact this is not allowed to happen: the needs of war were, so to speak, incommensurate. Or take a famine, howsoever caused: food for the starving becomes a priority task, even if there is more profit in importing Mercedes cars and Scotch whisky. Just as (one hopes) the sight of a child fallen into a canal causes one to act without first examining the financial reward which might be involved. (Economic orthodoxy in the 1840s prevented relief measures for the Irish famine in those years.)

So the extent to which one supersedes or modifies market forces depends in some degree on the presence or absence of emergency situations, as well as on the presence or absence of adequate market institutions, plus political uncertainty and inflationary expectations. To take one last example, suppose that power cuts are inevitable unless special measures are taken to supply the required fuel for electricity generations. It may well be that producing or importing many kinds of consumer goods would yield higher short-term profits. But if power is cut off, everything comes to a halt. One can readily envisage emergency situations in which reliance on the price mechanism alone would not have the desired result.

This brings one to the important and related issue of currency convertibility and liberalization of foreign trade. As a Russian report has noted: 'let us recall how many years after World War II it took West Germany, France, Japan, to move to convertibility. It took them not one or two years, but fifteen to twenty years, in the course of which they created a competitive economy.'[9] France and Italy finally freed capital movements as recently as 1990. Several countries (including Great Britain and France) limited the amounts which their citizens could use for vacations abroad, decades and more after the end of the war.

Several reasons can be advanced for delaying convertibility. One is closely linked with the point already made about priorities: thus in Great Britain the need to pay for imports of food, and raw materials for industry, seemed more vital than to allow the pent-up demand (pent-up as a result of war-time shortages) to use up scarce dollars on what were regarded as non-essentials. Similarly, domestic capital, and private-enterprise earnings of foreign currency were as far as possible prevented from freely moving or staying abroad. (Thus in the 1950s and 1960s it was illegal for British or French residents to keep accounts outside the sterling or franc areas.) A second factor of importance concerned exchange rates: this was a time when fixed exchange rates were the rule, though subject to occasional devaluations. To prevent or minimize the growth of currency black markets, and to avoid too great a devaluation, it was necessary to limit legitimate forms of convertibility, thereby reducing demand for dollars. By 'too great' a devaluation, is meant an exchange rate which, fully reflecting the immediate scarcities of both dollars and potentially importable goods, would lower the domestic currency exchange rate far below purchasing-power-parity, and, by increasing sharply the cost of essential imports, contribute to inflationary pressures. Of course there were some 'leaks', some evasions, but in fact there was only a very limited black market in dollars in Western Europe in those years. There can be no doubt that if currency convertibility had been introduced as early as (say) 1947–49, the rate for the dollar would have been far more unfavourable. There would also have been what might be called premature import competition. Dollar shortage provided temporary protection for infant (or convalescing) industries, some of which (especially in Japan and Germany) were later able to compete very effectively indeed, including the United States itself.

A feature of those years was the creation of a European payments union, to facilitate trade and clearing between the countries of Western Europe at a time of dollar shortage. In effect this gave a form of 'soft-currency preference'. Had the countries of Western Europe demanded settlement in dollars, this would have obstructed trade, in just the way that trade between former members of Comecon has plummeted since 1989. This has done evident harm to the economies of all these countries. No doubt past memories, plus the inadequacies of the so-called transferable rouble, help to explain what occurred. Again, the contrast of today's 'East' with the postwar 'West' is striking.

Ideology and the IMF's pressures have combined to produce a belief in the swiftest possible liberalization of both trade and payments. Thus for example Konstantin Kagolovsky spoke of a 'rate for the rouble that will be the same for all, licences and quotas will be liquidated. All foreign loans will be realized in the market by the market rate... Any administrative ways of supporting critically essential imports are shown to be totally pointless.'[10] Other and different views have already been quoted. Here is another, from a group of Polish economists: 'Import liberalization in Poland was introduced prematurely and on too wide a scale... We consider it necessary to protect the domestic market temporarily... Most in need of protection is the domestic market for consumer products.'[11] Moreover, at a conference in Washington in June 1992 sponsored by the IMF and the World Bank, the 'recessionary' consequences of 'premature free trade' were recognized.

The Russian report cited earlier also noted the effect on costs of the highly unfavourable exchange rate. Materials and components which need to be imported become extremely expensive at this rate, and 'it is impossible at such prices to sell final products on the home market. Meanwhile we are told that an open economy is preferable to a closed one. Sure it is. But to transit from state of affairs to another one needs time and clearly defined stages... Otherwise one can proceed through revolutionary rush from crisis to deeper crisis and then to chaos.'[12] The situation in some countries (e.g., Hungary, the Czech Republic) is different, but the above remarks seem quite apt if applied to Russia, Ukraine, and Bulgaria.

6 World prices?

Should world prices, measured at a free exchange rate, be applied as quickly as possible throughout the 'East'? Again, some countries (Hungary, for instance) had been edging toward world prices for many years before the collapse of communism, and so the needed adjustment was not too severe, the advantages clearly outweighing any disadvantages. But Russia is quite different, Ukraine also. At the end of December 1992 the exchange rate equalled 415 roubles to the dollar, or over 600 Ukrainian karbovantsi. At this exchange rate the average wage was below 20 dollars *a month*. Bread then cost about 100 times more than in 1989, about 20 roubles for a kilo loaf. It is surely a fantasy to regard 20 roubles (i.e., 5 cents) as 'too cheap'. A ride in the Moscow or St. Petersburg metro cost 6 roubles. At the free exchange rate, the (heavily subsidized) San Francisco 'muni' charges the equivalent of 330 roubles, i.e., much more than a day's wages. Since Sachs and similar advisers recommend that controls over wages be tightened, as part of the anti-inflationary package, it hardly needs proof that prices of necessities cannot rise to 'world' levels. (Imported consumer goods, however, do sell at high prices, as can be seen in the privately-operated stalls. But citizens with normal rouble incomes cannot afford to buy them.)

A wide difference between internal and world prices creates a number of problems, however. One relates to the effect on internal costs of imports of materials and components, and also of such items as grain and medical drugs. The Russian government inherited the practice of a special exchange rate, well below the free one, used for so-called 'centralized' imports, i.e., of those items deemed essential. This, while understandable, creates opportunities for corrupt deals. Yet it would be difficult to avoid some sort of subsidy, so long as personal incomes are so low. For example, imported medical drugs would be beyond the pocket of at least four-fifths of the population, while domestically-produced supplies have long been known to be seriously deficient.

More acute still is the problem in reverse: any good or service that is exportable yields a far higher sum than its sale for roubles in the internal market. In 1992 a taxi in Moscow would have taken you to the suburbs for 4 dollars (in London a rise for the same distance would cost four times as much), but this represents about twenty times the authorized rouble fare, so taxi drivers naturally sell their services to foreigners by preference. Far more important is the effect on the oil and gas industries. With a world price of oil at around $120 a ton, the equivalent in roubles would be over 50,000 roubles. This would also be the price charged to the Ukraine and other ex-Soviet republics as and when trade with them ceases to be on a preferential basis. The internal wholesale price of oil was far too low for far too long. But even during December 1992, though nominally 'freed', producers and wholesalers were subject to a steeply rising tax or levy in respect of any sales at a price that exceeds 8000 roubles. To multiply this six-fold would have catastrophic effects on agricultural and industrial costs, and indeed also on real incomes of citizens (what would then be the cost of a gallon of petrol, or of electricity for lighting or heating, relative to existing wage-levels?). In practice the regions and oil-producing enterprises are allowed to sell a portion of their output at genuinely free prices. There have been a variety of quotas, export licences and export taxes, but also corruption, since the money to be made transferring oil (and other exportable commodities) between categories is a standing temptation to the dishonest.

The *reductio ad absurdum* of the free exchange rate for the rouble may be seen in the fact that GNP in 1992, 15 trillion roubles, if converted into dollars at this rate, is actually less than Russia's exports in that year ($38 billion).

Everyone agrees that a single exchange rate, world prices, liberalized trade plus convertibility are desirable. But can such things be introduced in the present stage in Russia, given the distorted exchange rate and inflationary expectations? Already there is a substantial capital flight *from* Russia, far exceeding foreign aid and foreign investment, even though most of this flight is illegal.

A paper by the German banker, Axel Lebahn, after reminding his readers that convertibility was not achieved by West Germany until the 1960s, by France until the 1970s, stated: 'It is for me totally astonishing that, given the lack of trust among the people and the managers, who mostly think only of transferring a quick profit abroad, that anyone should propose convertibility within two months. I beg Western reform-advisers to take into account the specific conditions of Russia.'[13]

7 Privatization, investment finance and the budget deficit

A full discussion of the pros and cons of various forms of privatization would require another and very long paper. Different countries tackle the question in different ways. Several (first Czechoslovakia, now also Russia) provide investment vouchers to all citizens. In practice, privatization has proceeded more slowly than had been envisaged by the radical reformers: valuation problems, in some cases restitution to former owners, lack of private capital with which to purchase, fears of so-called 'nomenklatura privatization', or acquisition at low prices by 'the mafia', or by foreigners, and also in some cases bureaucratic delays, all played their part. Anyhow, at the time of writing a high proportion of productive enterprises remains in the public sector, while most private firms operate in the area of trade and distribution.

Vouchers do provide the means to purchase shares in privatized enterprises. However, they do not represent investment in any real sense, unless the proceeds of the sale of shares are invested. The vouchers are, after all, pieces of paper issued by the government, which, being saleable, increase money supply. True, some voucher-owners will 'invest' them in mutual funds now being created. However, as is pointed out by V. Kantorovich (son of the Nobel laureate) in a major article, given lack of experience, of knowledge, or of even the beginnings of a normal stock market, conditions will be most favourable for fraud and various machinations, of which he cites examples.

Both Kantorovich and the Czech economist Mertlík[14] point to what Mertlík called 'privatization agony'. The term relates to the ambiguous situation of management of state enterprises. In Kantorovich's words: 'state enterprises before privatization were, so to speak, suspended in mid-air, waiting, with no incentive for normal work.' There is also no incentive to pay bills or debts: in Russia, the Czech and Slovak Republics and Poland, unpaid debts have hugely increased. In the Czech Republic, most bank credits are used to finance privatization purchases, and hardly any credits are available for investment, according to Mertlík. And if the object of management is to acquire the enterprise during the privatization process (e.g., by buying out vouchers, or through closed or open auctions), the lower the valuation, the better. This actually provides a motive for inefficiency, as the valuation is inevitably affected by performance. Certainly there is no incentive for management to invest profits and, for instance in Poland, these are subject to almost confiscatory tax rates.

The mass distribution of vouchers as a means of privatization conflicts with the aim of encouraging a new class of entrepreneur-proprietors. Anatoli Chubais, trying to square the circle, publicly welcomed the purchase of vouchers from the poor by the rich: the poor might then be able to 'afford meat', i.e., would use the proceeds of the sale of vouchers for current consumption.[15] The point, well put by Caselli and Pastrello,[16] is: 'Too many people who invoke Schumpeterian entrepreneurship forget that Schumpeter clearly had Weberian entrepreneurs in mind. Even if such entrepreneurs do emerge during a process of "learning by doing", such a process necessarily takes a long time to accomplish, and meanwhile it is the "trade-orientated entrepreneur who emerges".' A similar point was made by László Csába in respect of Hungary: referring to what he called 'private entrepreneur of the irregular or "Mafia" economy', he duly noted that 'productive investment is the last thing they would think of'.[17]

Privatization is too easily seen as a cure for the inefficiency associated with state monopoly-enterprises. However, privatization does not of itself guarantee competence in management, and private monopoly can have the same effects as public monopoly. In fact, as British experience shows, public monopoly (at least before Thatcher) can be associated with a sense of duty to the public. It is worth noting one other consequence of privatization policies, most visible in Poland. The new private dealers avoid taxes, and most of the budget revenue in fact accrues from the public sector, which (in Poland in the early 1990s) 'still accounts for the largest part of national income and provides the budget with 84 per cent of its revenue'. Yet 'far from protecting the state sector, the economic programme of the government... applied various discriminatory and restrictive measures against it', including a heavy tax (the so-called *popiwek*) on excessive wage increases, which none the less had to be paid. 'Privatization' was unprepared, hasty and chaotic. It was carried out for ideological rather than rational reasons, 'and contributed to a fall in output and especially of investment'.[18]

8 Proposals to revive production and investment: foreign participation

The 'investment gap' has, of course, not passed unnoticed. The Hausner-Owsiak pamphlet quoted above speaks of the need for 'active state intervention, above all an industrial policy of the kind pursued by modern states with market economies... For example, the restructuring of the steel industry, heavy industry, environmental protection, support for research, etc.' The private sector 'has grown mainly in the sphere of services and trade, particularly the import of consumers' goods'. So the state has clear structural responsibilities, which cannot be left to market forces.[19] Another Polish pamphlet critical of laissez-faire policies speaks of 'identification of medium and long-term objectives of structural change and economic development, including an industrial policy'.[20] Similar Russian criticisms of the 'Gaidar' (or Sachs, or IMF) policies were numerous. I will only quote again the economic research institute of the Ministry of Economics: After deploring the lack of any long-term foreign-trade policy, the report goes on to advocate

> state sectoral (production) and regional programmes, worked out together by state institutions, domestic entrepreneurs, foreign partners and investors, international organizations... Today, when such programmes do not exist and the economy is drifting rudderless, foreign investors grant us loans unwillingly, imposing harsh conditions. This is quite understandable, since they do not know where their money will go and whether it will be properly used. The presence of clearly defined programmes, of carefully selected projects, drafted with the help of foreign experts, will change the situation. The programmes will act as magnets for our creditors...

Special priority would be given to develop exports. It is, the authors point out, absurd for a vast Russia to export only half of the exports of Taiwan or South Korea.[21]

One can foresee the objections: discrimination between sectors, a state role in financing investment, or subsidized interest rates, open up possibilities of abuse, distortions through political pressures by lobbyists, corruption. It is true, as Dabrowski pointed out, that to administer one needs 'a good civil service', and some 'eastern' countries do not have competent administrators. (I heard Ukrainian ministers speak of 'cadre hunger', and Russia too has yet to replace the political mechanism provided by party functionaries.) But the fact remains that an investment strategy is needed; one cannot expect the capital market to function when it does not yet exist, or entrepreneurs to borrow for investment at market rates of interest when these can be 50 per cent (Poland) or 150 per cent and more (Russia – and even this is very far below the rate of inflation!). And Western aid-givers, including the IMF, will surely be less than enthusiastic if their credits are disposed of by auction to the highest bidder, which would most likely be to importers of Mercedes, panty-hose and Nintendo, for instant profitable resale, while livestock is slaughtered for lack of food, and the (dollar-earning) oil industry continues its decline for lack of equipment. After all, credits are supposed to be repaid one day. Donors should expect them to be used for constructive purposes. There is a contradiction between this requirement and the IMF's own laissez-faire ideology, and of this the IMF itself is beginning to show awareness.

I can only echo Caselli and Pastrello: We cannot 'simply postulate that the shrinking state sector's place will be automatically taken by the private sector'. This is 'sidestepping the real problems: what to do with state enterprises, which are crumbling under the brunt of the recessionary environment. This is precisely the task of an explicitly-designed economic policy: such a policy has yet to be found.'[22] It had better be, and soon! One can also agree with a Russian research team: 'the underdevelopment of private financial institutions does not make possible the required investment activity', so that it is desirable to create a 'state investment bank', linked with 'a conscious policy of structural development'.[23]

I would stress that the above argument applies much more strongly to countries in the grip of acute crisis (e.g., Russia, Ukraine, Romania in the early 1990s), and much less to Hungary, the Czech Republic, and Poland.

9 Agriculture; a brief diversion

This, like privatization, requires a separate paper, and will receive only brief attention here, which should not belie its importance.

Question one is linked with privatization (or in some cases restoration to former owners). Should existing collective (co-operative) and state farms be dissolved? How many of the present members (employees) wish to take up independent farming? Should their views decide the issue? How can the existing farm management function if it has no confidence that the farms they manage will still exist in a year's time? What equipment (and other kinds of investment) would be needed by a new breed of small farmers? What size of farm would be economic? Are credits to be made available, and on what terms? Should land be bought and sold freely, also to non-agricultural interests and foreigners?

Question two: prices. In most of the 'East', terms of trade have turned very strongly against agriculture. Thus in Poland (where small holders predominate) peasant incomes have fallen sharply, and purchases by peasants of inputs (fertilizer, machines, etc.) too. In Russia and the Ukraine too the prices of farm inputs have risen about twice as fast as the prices of agricultural products. In Czechoslovakia 'average producer prices in industry in 1991, as against 1989, grew by three quarters [75 per cent] ..., only prices of agricultural products stagnated; their average level in 1991 was only 3.8 per cent higher than in 1989'.[24] Agricultural output is depressed by the fall in urban consumer purchasing power. And exports to the 'natural' markets of Western Europe are largely blocked by the West Europeans.

So, what policy to adopt? Should there be price support, which exists in most of the world? Subsidies? Low interest credits? Priority in fuel supplies where these are scarce? Can laissez-faire be the answer? And, most important, what policy to adopt for the surviving state and collective farms (and, in Poland, to private farms too small for an efficient agriculture)? (China's agriculture, mostly based on small fields and hand cultivation, by methods which can hardly have changed in a thousand years, does not provide a model for the Russian and Ukrainian prairies.)

10 'The Chinese model'; an alternative strategy?

Several Russian critics, including the influential Arkadi Volsky, have spoken of the Chinese model. The November (1992) issue of *Voprosy ekonomiki* contains two articles on the subject, one by an Englishman (J. Ross), and one by a Chinese (Shan Weiyan). What do they have in mind? Some think above all of political order, the continued dominant role of the Communist party in China, and of order as a precondition for marketization. All recognize that in China there have been big moves toward a market economy. However, these authors stress another and surely more important element in the Chinese road, which does give ground for serious thought. For unlike the countries of Eastern Europe, China's road has involved no fall in output, investment, or living standards. On the contrary, GNP in China in the last few years has risen by impressive percentages, as has consumption.

China has advanced not by privatizing large state enterprises, but by allowing or encouraging a wide variety of activities alongside them, apparently owing much to provincial initiatives: the enterprises are co-operative, collective, municipal, rural, private, some with foreign capital, some in special enterprise zones. Their growth has been most rapid. In many cases, to cite Martin Weitzman and Chenggang Xu, ownership is far from clear ('vaguely-defined co-operatives' is their label).[25] Weitzman questions the validity, at least for China, of the widely accepted dogma associated with the 'Property rights' school, that only private ownership (i.e., the appropriation of profit by the owner) is consistent with efficiency in resource utilization and the avoidance of shirking. His point is reinforced (in my view) when one adds the element of *scale*. Most Chinese enterprises in the non-state sector are small. Suppose twenty individuals (of any nationality!) jointly undertake any activity. It is surely by no means clear that it is always preferable for one to employ the other nineteen, or that they would shirk more if they worked in an enterprise jointly owned by them all. Or that ownership vested in a municipality or a rural council must be less effective than ownership by one man.

As for larger enterprises, employing (say) a thousand, while it is much more difficult to envisage smoothly-functioning co-operative ownership, it is equally unlikely that such an enterprise would have an identifiable *owner*. More likely (East and West) is a joint stock company with diffused, probably institutional, ownership, with a largely autonomous management.

Interestingly, several Russian critics of the privatization programme have argued for the desirability of a positive attitude to employee buyouts, and against replacing one anonymous owner (the state) by another (what the French call *société anonyme*, the impersonal corporation). Yet this is viewed with suspicion even by such moderate critics as János Kornai, and most of the reform proposals give cooperative or joint ownership a cold shoulder.

The essential feature of the Chinese reform experience for our present purposes, however, is its gradualism. It does not disrupt the work of existing state enterprises, retains a degree of control over them subjecting them to market pressures, including competition from the non-state sector, while the latter expands greatly, so that, by 1992, almost half of all labour outside agriculture was 'non-state' (but only a minority of 'non-state' was privately engaged or employed). To cite another conference paper: 'the non-state sector's share of industrial output increased from 22 per cent in 1978 to 47 per cent in 1991, and the private sector's share increased from zero in 1978 to over 12 per cent in the same period, both being achieved without destroying or radically changing the existing system.'[26]

Time will tell whether this is a slower road toward a 'capitalist' destination, or whether the aim is a mixed economy which would be characterized as 'market socialism', on lines envisaged in my book on *Feasible Socialism*[27] (which it so happens was translated into Chinese).

11 Conclusion

Most of the ex-communist world must rely on internally generated resources for the reconstruction and modernization of their economies. They require accumulation for investment, and also an investment strategy, involving some conscious choices of priorities, into which foreign capital can and should make a contribution. The idea that this can happen in some automatic way, once macroeconomic stabilization is achieved, is surely a fantasy. A process of privatization is under way and requires encouragement, but time is needed before market institutions and market culture are in place. They cannot just be decreed into existence. Meanwhile the role of the state is bound to be substantial, as it was also in the years of postwar reconstruction in Western Europe, Japan, and Korea. (In social services too, but this is not the subject of the present paper.) Existing state enterprises are operating under highly unfavourable conditions.

Free market dogma has become an obstacle, the more so as ex-Marxists find 'Chicago' a congenial alternative to their former beliefs. Devotees of this doctrine must face up to the theoretical and practical gap: no progress without investment (indeed, *regress* without investment). How are investment choices to be made, by whom, and how financed? If answer comes there none, all is not well. And what can be learned from China's success?

Notes

1. Winiecki, J. (1990), 'The Inevitability of a fall in output...', *Soviet Studies*, 43 (4), 669–84, and Winiecki, J. (1992), 'The Polish Transition Programme', *Soviet Studies*, 44 (5).
2. Hayek, Friedrich von (1944), *The Road to Serfdom,* University of Chicago Press, p. 209. I owe the quotation to B. Milvanovic.
3. Richardson, G.B. (1960), *Information and Investment*, Oxford University Press.
4. Lachman, Ludwig (1977), *Capital, Expectations and Market Process*, Kansas City, p. 117.
5. Baumol, W. (1993), *Entrepreneurship, Management, and the Structure of Payoffs*, Cambridge: MIT Press.
6. Dąbrowski, Marek (1992), *Reforming Communist Economies*, London.
7. See ECE (1992), *Economic Survey of Europe, 1991–92*, Geneva, and a variety of Russian and Ukrainian sources.
8. Blanchard, O., R. Dornbusch et al. (1991), *Reform in Eastern Europe*, MIT Press.
9. Report of the research institute attached to the Russian Ministry of Economics (1992), *Ekonomika i zhizn*, 49 (December), 5.
10. Kagolovsky, Konstantin (1982), *Izvestiya*, 6 May.
11. 'How To Get Out of the Present Economic Crisis in Poland' (1992), Polish Economic Society, Warsaw, 15, 31, 32.
12. Report of the research institute attached to the Russian Ministry of Economics (1992), *Ekonomika i zhizn*, 49 (December), 5.
13. Lebahn, Axel (1992), *Stand und Perspektive neuer deutsch-russischer Wirtschaftskooperation*, Berlin, p. 11. My translation, A.N.
14. Kantorovich, V. (1992) in *Nezavisimeya gazeta*, 20 April, and Mertlík, P. (1992), 'Macro-economic development and privatization in Czech-Slovakia', conference paper, Prague, September.
15. A. Chubais interview (1992), *Literaturnaya gazeta*, 18 November, p. 10.
16. Caselli, Gian Paolo and Gabriele Pastrello (1992), 'The Transition from Hell to Bliss: A Model', *Most*, 3, 51.
17. Csába, Lászlo (1991), *Acta Oeconomica*, 43 (3–4), 283.

18. Hausner, J. and S. Owsiak (1992), *Financial crisis of a state in transformation – the Polish case*, Ebert Foundation, Warsaw, October, pp. 39, 40.
19. Ibid., pp. 40, 42.
20. 'How To Get Out of the Present Economic Crisis...', op. cit., 33.
21. *Ekonomika i zhizn* (1992), 49, 5. See also Kuzminov, D. et al., 'Rrossiyskie reformy I mezhdunarodnyi opyt', *Voprosy ekonomiki* (1992), 11, where the authors recommend, inter alia, a 'Bank of economic recovery'.
22. Ibid., 51.
23. *Ekonomiki i zhizn* (1992), 40 (October).
24. Janacek, K. et al. (1992), 'Macro-economic and social analysis, Spring 1992', Institute of Economics, Prague, p. 9.
25. Weitzman, M. and Chenggang Xu (1994), 'Vaguely Defined Cooperatives', in Alec Nove and Ian D. Thatcher (eds), *Markets and Socialism*, Aldershot: Edward Elgar, pp. 538–51.
26. Qian, Yingyi and Chenggang Xu (1992), 'Why Chinese economic reforms differ: changing the existing system' (unpublished paper).
27. Nove, Alec (1991), *The Economics of Feasible Socialism Revisited*, London: Harper Collins Academic. For a bibliography of Nove's writings see Ian D. Thatcher (1995), 'Alec Nove: A Bibliographical Tribute', *Europe-Asia Studies*, 47(8), December.

4 Macroeconomic Collapse During Systemic Change

J. Barkley Rosser, Jr. and Marina Vcherashnaya Rosser[1]

1 Introduction

The process of transforming former command socialist economies into market capitalist ones in Central and Eastern Europe has engendered endless debate. On one side are those such as Brada and King (1992) and Brada (1993) who argue that neoclassical economics provides a ready explanation for how reforming societies should proceed, that 'big bang' policies of moving as rapidly as possible to free markets and privatization is the optimal strategy. Such arguments depend on a fundamental belief that the goal of a laissez-faire outcome is the ultimate desideratum and that any slacking on the way is sub-optimal.

This view recognizes that the big bang approach may cause high costs, social and economic, but argues that these are strictly short-run and that what is involved is a 'J-curve' effect with achievement of the 'final solution' arriving more quickly if the transforming society moves more quickly. Given that transformation entails socio-economic costs that can trigger a political backlash, as has emerged in many of the Central and Eastern European countries, this argument is simply reinforced. Rush, rush, rush before 'reactionary socialists' slow everything down. Advocates of this position claim Poland and the Czech Republic as supporting examples.[2]

Competing with this view is what has been labelled the 'evolutionary' view as typified by Murrell (1991, 1992). He argues that modern neoclassical theory itself raises serious doubts about the above scenario. Problems of asymmetric information, incentive incompatibilities, product differentiation and entry in previously monopolized markets, and other problems, all cry out for the need for an appropriate institutional framework to be in place before a systemic transformation can be carried out effectively. This view suggests the virtues of gradualism in the face of total institutional breakdown. China and its success with a gradualistic programme is cited in contrast with pervasive and severe macroeconomic collapse in Central and Eastern Europe.

In this chapter we show how excessively rapid big bang policies can bring about macroeconomic collapse. Our approach draws upon recent applications of interacting particle systems (IPS) theory to problems of co-ordination and information transfer within economies as initiated by Brock (1993). We combine this approach with the one taken by Aghion and Blanchard (1993) to model unemployment dynamics in Central and Eastern Europe. This allows us to model discontinuous shifts in the degree of signal co-ordination in an economy where sudden macroeconomic collapse might occur. Such breakdowns of signal co-ordination have a clear interpretation in terms of the evolutionary approach as reflecting the disintegration of institutional frameworks within which signal co-ordination previously transpired.

Section 2 of this chapter reviews the landscape of cases in terms of the debate over big bang versus gradualistic policy approaches. Section 3 presents the basic Aghion–Blanchard model of unemployment dynamics. Section 4 places it in the interacting particle systems context and shows the possibility of macroeconomic collapse. Section 5 discusses broader issues regarding the ultimate goals and outcomes of the different transformation processes in Central and Eastern Europe. Section 6 summarizes and concludes the chapter.

2 The transformation debate

Advocates of big bang–shock therapy regularly cite Poland and the Czech Republic as examples of the alleged success of their approach. Poland in particular was the most dramatic adopter of shock therapy in the form of the Balcerowicz Plan in 1990 with its sudden decontrol of prices, full convertibility of the złoty, and monetarist macroeconomic policy. The virtues of the Polish programme amount to a now rapid rate of GDP growth and a substantially lower rate of inflation relative to the hyperinflationary immediate pre-reform period.

The above are certainly true. However the downswing part of the 'J-curve' was indeed profound, the decline in output being at least as great as what happened in the Great Depression in the US.[3] The economy still has quite a way to go to return to where it was before the collapse. Despite all the talk of new prosperity, the political outcome tells the perception of the populace.

Both unemployment and inflation remain in double digits and appear to be stuck with little indication of dropping further. Inflation rates in the mid-30 per cent range are a substantial improvement over the much higher rates of 1989, but are still well above those of Western Europe or the US or Japan. Of course unemployment was near zero before so that the current situation of double digit unemployment rates is shocking for many Poles. That income distribution has become substantially more unequal along with cutbacks in the social safety net does not improve perceptions of the situation.

Yet another problem for advocates of shock therapy with respect to the Polish case is that Poland is not as good an example as has been claimed. In particular there has been the failure to privatize a significant chunk of the larger state-owned enterprises (SOEs), although most smaller SOEs have been privatized. Yet these large SOEs, many of which shifted to a workers' management type system during the Jaruzelski regime in the 1980s, have performed much better than predicted in expanding exports to Western Europe (Kamiński, Kwieciński and Michalek, 1993). They have not proven to be the 'dinosaurs' described by the advocates of instant privatization.

In this regard Poland resembles China much more than is generally recognized. Both have successfully growing economies undergoing transitions to market systems, although China has avoided the collapse that Poland experienced. But both have avoided mass privatization, preferring instead to allow privatization to emerge spontaneously in the form of new entrepreneurial firms arising within the institutional framework of the existing SOEs.[4]

Needless to say, defenders of the neoclassical big bang approach such as Brada (1993) deny the relevance of China for Central and Eastern Europe despite these similarities with Poland and the fact that Hungarian gradualistic market socialism was viewed as a model by the Chinese in their policy formulation for quite some time (Van Ness, 1989). With good reason Brada argues that relative to Central and Eastern Europe China differs in being much less developed, industrialized, and urbanized, along with being far more heavily populated and located in Asia with its different cultural and historical context. All of this is true. Nevertheless the contrast of countries with similar economic systems undergoing similar transformations and experiencing catastrophic collapses of Great Depression proportions while one (China) should be the world's fastest growing economy is deeply striking.

The other much cited case is that of the Czech Republic, which has had a much smaller decline than has Poland, with much lower unemployment and inflation and a higher per capita income, despite undergoing price decontrols and a dramatic privatization programme through vouchers. Also in contrast to almost all of the other Central and

Eastern European economies it continues to have an anti-communist reform government. Indeed its split with Slovakia reflected at least partly differences over economic policy with poorer Slovakia taking a more traditionalist and gradualist position. Finally the Czech Republic stands out as ahead of all the other Central and Eastern European economies except Slovenia in real per capita income.

Nevertheless there is more than meets the eye to the Czech case. Despite the loudly proclaimed pro-laissez-faire policy approach of its government some of the reasons why the Czech Republic has done as well as it has involve policy elements distinctly in contrast with what the government rhetorically supports. Thus although there has been mass voucher privatization, most of the vouchers are controlled by a small group of largely still state-owned banks (Portes, 1994). In turn these banks have propped up employment through soft budget constraint style subsidies (Ham, Svejnar and Terrell, 1994). These subsidies are gradually being withdrawn and unemployment is gradually rising, but this policy remains in sharp contrast with the image presented by the government.

It is not so surprising that the Czech Republic has been able to sustain such subsidies without too much damage so far. This partly reflects that in contrast to Poland and Hungary its communist government engaged in rigid command planning, leaving the economy with no inflation, unemployment, or budget deficits, and few foreign debts. This has made it easier for the Czechs to get away with a period of such subsidies than could Poland or Hungary, both having domestic inflation and heavy foreign debt burdens from before their communist governments were replaced.

Furthermore the extreme repressiveness of the Czech communist regime left a bad taste that has left the communists seriously lacking in popularity and credibility relative to the successor parties in Poland and Hungary. Especially in Hungary the communists were viewed as reformers, arguably more so than the first post-communist government. Thus it was not so hard for the populace to vote them back into power over inept reformers. In the Czech Republic the communists have an especially terrible reputation and the reformers have so far managed through careful policies to avoid the scale of collapse that has happened in its neighbours.

Yet another reason to doubt the efficacy of big bang approaches is provided by the experience of the now independent states that were formerly republics of the former Soviet Union. Although comparisons are complicated by those former republics which have moved the fastest, such as the Baltic states with stronger international currencies, a close look at the data suggests that with some exceptions those which have moved the most slowly have declined the least in output with some surprising reshufflings of rankings occurring as a result. One such reshuffling has been the apparent reversal of relative rankings of Russia and Belarus in per capita output terms, with more slowly moving Belarus now ahead of Russia (Rosser and Rosser, 1995, Chapter 11).

3 Transitional unemployment dynamics

The Aghion and Blanchard (1993) model[5] involves private sector jobs being formed as workers are made available by being laid off from the state sector. Higher marginal productivity in the private sector will lead to greater private sector job formation along with more workers being laid off in the state sector. However there are offsetting elements. The most important is that laid-off workers must be paid unemployment benefits from income taxes. Higher income taxes operate as a drag on private sector formation. These relationships are nonlinear in that there is an unemployment rate above which the negative impact of unemployment-driven taxes offsets the positive effects of state sector layoffs. If the rate of state sector layoffs exceeds what is sustainable at this maximum then the economy implodes to a high unemployment equilibrium without private sector job formation.

To see the basic idea behind the model, assume the total labour force equals 1, that labour working in the state sector equals E, private sector employment equals N, and the number of unemployed equals U. Initially $E = 1$ as the total labour force is employed in the state sector and an excess demand for labour eliminates unemployment. A shock to this system leads to $E < 1$ and $U > 0$ as an excess supply of labour emerges. Also assume that the given marginal product of state workers x is less than the given marginal product of private workers y and that taxes per worker z are the same in both sectors and pay for the unemployment benefits per unemployed worker b.

State sector firms are partly under the control of workers as in Poland who 'myopically' set wages to capture a portion of quasi-rents in the non-centrally planned environment. This implies a state sector wage equation:

$$w(E) = qx - z, \tag{4.1}$$

where w is private sector wages, $w(E)$ is state sector wages, and $q > 1$ reflects the capture of quasi-rents.

The rate of state sector layoffs and thus the rate of decline of E is given as s, presumed to be an exogenous policy variable.

The basic equation of private sector job formation is:

$$\frac{dN}{dt} = a(y - z - w), \tag{4.2}$$

where the value of a reflects the institutional framework including the state of the financial system, the legal system and definition of property rights, and the regulatory framework, as well as the more subtle matter of information flows and general signal co-ordination within the economy which will be discussed in more depth in the next section.

Let c be the constant difference between the 'value of being (privately) employed', $V(N)$, and the 'value of being unemployed', $V(U)$, determined by an efficiency wage outcome. Assuming that all private sector hires H come from the unemployed without turnover implies that private sector wages are:

$$w = b + c\left[r + \frac{H}{U}\right], \tag{4.3}$$

where r is the interest rate. $V(N)$ and $V(U)$ are determined by arbitrage equations:

$$V(N) = \frac{w + \dfrac{dV(N)}{dt}}{r} \tag{4.4}$$

$$V(U) = \frac{b + c\dfrac{H}{U} + \dfrac{dV(U)}{dt}}{r} \tag{4.5}$$

with total unemployment benefits, Ub, given by:

$$Ub = (1 - U)z \tag{4.6}$$

All of the above combine to imply a possible rewriting of the private sector job formation equation from its form as equation (4.2) to:

$$\frac{dN}{dt} = a\left[\frac{U}{U + ca}\right]\left[y - rc - \frac{1}{1 - U}b\right] = f(U) \tag{4.7}$$

which is depicted as the nonlinear function in Figure 4.1 with the rate of state sector layoffs s given as the horizontal line.

Figure 4.1

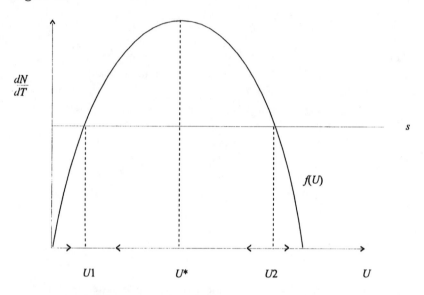

Equation (4.7) contains the conflict between the job-stimulating and job-suppressing aspects of unemployment with the first term showing the former and the second term showing the latter. The first term shows downward pressure on wages stimulating private sector job formation as unemployment rises. The second term shows the negative impact of unemployment benefits on such job formation. In Figure 4.1 U* depicts the level of unemployment beyond which the negative effects outweigh the positive effects.

Figure 4.1 shows a level of s that is not excessive and implies two equilibrium levels of unemployment, U1 and U2, the former, and lower, being stable and the latter, and higher, being unstable. This latter suggests that if the unemployment rate exceeds U2 then it will move to U3 at which dN/dt = 0, meaning that there is no private sector job formation at all. U2 is a critical level beyond which the economy discontinuously leaps to a 'bad' outcome.

Not only can the unemployment rate be too high, but so can the rate of state sector layoffs. Figure 4.2 shows what happens if there is a decline in the private sector job formation function, f(U), as will be modelled in the next section. However Figure 4.2 can also be interpreted as showing what happens if s is simply too high by comparing s to f(U)'. For the latter, s exceeds the maximum possible rate of private sector job formation occurring at U^*. In such a case the dynamic is for the unemployment rate to explode to $U2$, again with the outcome of a cessation of any expansion of the private sector as the economy goes into a high unemployment stagnant state.

Figure 4.2

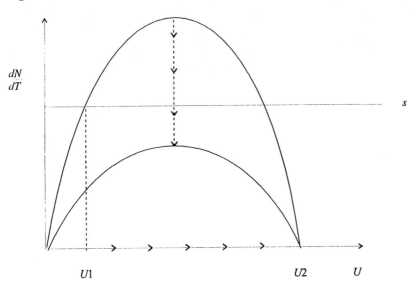

4 A model of signal co-ordination failure

We model intra-economy signal co-ordination using the IPS approach as developed by Brock (1993). This ultimately reflects the nature of the institutional framework including legal, financial, and regulatory factors. These combine to determine a system in which information flows and is able to be utilized for private sector job formation through entrepreneurial actions. Greater signal co-ordination allows for a more effective passage and utilization of such flows. The flows in turn reflect what are ultimately stochastic signals within the transitional economic environment.

Let there be F firms within the private sector of the economy, assumed to be a constant number.[6] These firms exist within a web of fully specified mutual relationships including buyer–seller relations and all production externality elements. Firm hires are determined by the relation between its marginal product of labour and taxes and wages, $y - z - w$, in conjunction with a discretely chosen attitude derived from a possible set, K. These attitudes take on individual firm values of $k(i)$ for firm i and can be positive (optimistic) or negative (pessimistic). A continuous function h applying to all firms and which can change over time determines the strength of $k(i)$. J is the average degree of interaction between firms, interpretable as the degree of signal co-ordination in terms of information flows. The average state of k's over all firms is m. B indicates 'intensity of choice', a rate of how much firms are either optimistic or pessimistic; $B = 0$ indicating random outcomes over the choice set.[7] There is a stochastic distribution of choices, $e(k(i))$ which is independently and identically distributed extreme value.

Assuming that direct net profitability to a firm of hiring a worker is $y - z - w$, not accounting for interfirm externalities, then the net addition of jobs to the economy per firm is:

$$\frac{\frac{dN}{dt}}{F} = (y - z - w) + Jmk(i) + hk(i) + \left(\frac{1}{B}\right)e(k(i)) \qquad (4.8)$$

Replacing the left-hand side of (4.8) with the right-hand side of (4.2) allows us to solve for a with:

$$a = 1 + F\frac{Jmk(i) + hk(i) + \left(\frac{1}{B}\right)e(k(i))}{y - z - w} \qquad (4.9)$$

This depends on the set of k's out of K that can be characterized across all firms by m, assuming an equal rate of interaction between firms.[8] If choices are restricted to $(+1, -1)$, then Brock (1993, pp. 22–3) shows that:

$$m = \tanh(BJm + Bh) \qquad (4.10)$$

where tanh is the hyperbolic tangent. BJ is a bifurcation parameter with a critical value of 1, there being a single solution with the same sign as h if $BJ < 1$, but two discrete solutions if $BJ > 1$, with $m(-) = -m(+)$. This bifurcation is depicted in Figure 4.3. Figure 4.2 depicts how a discontinuous decline in a could suddenly lower the private sector job formation function below the rate of state sector layoffs, thereby triggering a general macroeconomic collapse to $U2$.

Such a bad phase transition could arise from any movement from a higher segment to a lower segment and could reflect a variety of scenarios. One is a lowering of J as signal co-ordination under general optimism disappears with the dissolution of central planning without adequate market institutions to replace it. This could be a movement left and down from the upper right branch to the left branch and can be viewed as the canonical case of co-ordination failure.[9]

Figure 4.3

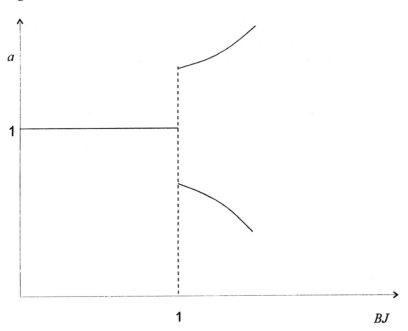

Yet another scenario involves no crossing of the bifurcation point, but assumes that the economy drops from the upper right branch to the lower right branch following a collapse of optimism with the breakup of the old institutional framework.

Finally what may be changing is the intensity of choice parameter *B* which presumably increases in the shift to a market economy. This implies a rightward shift across the bifurcation point with the possible outcome of waves of optimism and pessimism alternating. This scenario suggests that the outcome could be not just a collapse if the movement is to the lower right branch representing pessimism and collapse, but a movement is also possible to the upper right branch which would signal an acceleration of output within an intensely optimistic framework. This duality of possible discontinuous shifts may explain the extreme differences in outcomes between China (positive) and Central and Eastern Europe (negative).[10]

5 Whither policy in Central and Eastern Europe?

In the debate between the big bang and evolutionist positions there is a deeper issue that is rarely addressed directly. This has to do with the ultimate goal of the transformation processes happening in Central and Eastern Europe. Is the goal a Thatcherite laissez-faire outcome as still promulgated by the Czech regime, or is it something more intermediate, the much discussed but widely dismissed 'Third Way'?[11]

Certainly such advocates of the neoclassical big bang as Brada see such an outcome as the goal and say so openly. Free markets are efficient and the sooner Central and Eastern Europe get to them the better. Even if something less than full laissez-faire is viewed as optimal, pretending that full laissez-faire is optimal will lead to pushing as hard as possible and thus maximize the chance of getting to the optimal near-laissez-faire outcome. This has generally been the position of most advisers such as Jeffrey Sachs and the IMF, and is often viewed as taking an ideal form if the privatized entities involved are Western-based multinational corporations.

Although evolutionists such as Murrell disagree with the big bang policy approach in Central and Eastern Europe it is less than clear that they necessarily disagree with the ultimate goal. Thus in his 1991 paper Murrell lists numerous defects that can arise in laissez-faire markets. But he never suggests that the solution to these defects is government intervention in the market. What he argues instead is that these defects represent serious difficulties for economies in transition, most especially for those which engage in big bang policies. They will undo their institutional frameworks, and the absence of institutional frameworks will heighten the vulnerability of such economies to the various ills and defects arising from asymmetric information, principal–agent problems, and so forth. But the ultimate goal is still something approximating near-laissez-faire market capitalism. The only issue is how quickly and presumably surely to get there.[12]

An important question to raise is whether this presumptive ultimate goal is really appropriate for Central and Eastern Europe or whether something not nearly as far in that direction might really be superior. Instead of presenting a single such model, we present several possibilities that acknowledge elements already present in some of the Central and Eastern European economies and could be combined in formations as yet unseen and unformulated to develop a new system more genuinely reflecting the historical and social milieus of these societies. These possibilities are presented by considering several existing cases manifesting them.

One of these cases is Slovenia. Formerly part of Yugoslavia, Slovenia has the highest per capita income in Central and Eastern Europe. Although a gradual process of privatization is occurring, a solid majority of the capital stock remains in state hands (Rosser and Rosser, 1995, Chapter 14). In fact it remains not all that far from what it was when it was part of a unified Yugoslavia, a largely worker-managed market socialist economy. Unlike the former Yugoslavia, Slovenia has largely succeeded in achieving moderate levels of inflation and despite an output collapse associated with the breakup of Yugoslavia, its output is now growing.

Although the problems of the former Yugoslavia are beyond the scope of this chapter, it is important to note that a non-trivial portion of the literature on Yugoslavia suggests that the regional conflicts within. the former nation played a significant role in its macroeconomic difficulties during the 1980s (Prasnikar and Svejnar, 1991). That Slovenia is functioning reasonably well now suggests that its model may be more viable than is generally thought by outside observers. That the SOEs in Poland resistant to privatization have a substantial degree of worker management suggests that this is relevant to other Central and East European countries as well.

Of course it has been argued that Yugoslavia's (and Hungary's) problems arose from the soft budget constraint and that therefore there must ultimately be privatization.[13] Even if this is true, the ultimate outcome of this in some Central and East European countries may take the form of workers' ownership or cooperatives, as has been the case to a large extent in Russia. This is the trend in Slovenia as the natural evolution of the older system. Again the literature on cooperatives is voluminous.[14] The recent generalizations that seem to hold for them within market capitalist economies is that they can be more efficient because of reduced monitoring costs, can exhibit greater stability of employment because of greater wage flexibility, but suffer from credit availability problems, presumably something that could be remedied in an economy dominated by such enterprises.

Yet another alternative is that of China. While this alternative is not directly transferable to Central and Eastern Europe for various reasons, elements of the Chinese model may be transferable. In particular the most dynamic and distinctive segment of the Chinese economy has been its local market socialist sector, the town and village enterprises (TVEs), argued to be subject to hard budget constraints within vigorously competitive markets. These are descended from old commune and brigade enterprises in the Maoist period of local self-sufficiency in a largely rural economy and have evolved into forms seen nowhere else,[15] and thus may seem irrelevant to the urbanized and industrialized economies of Central and Eastern Europe.

Nevertheless in Russia and to a lesser extent in Central and Eastern Europe the disposition of some SOEs has taken the form of 'municipalization', turning them over to a local unit of government. There appear to be some circumstances where this may be a very feasible solution. In particular are situations where an enterprise is the main employer in a community and was the main provider of social services which have been closely linked with the enterprise. Rather than turning the provision of these services over to the community while privatizing the enterprise, there may be a smoother transition and continuation of the social safety net if there is municipalization and the creation of a de facto TVE.

Our final case is the former political centre of much of Central and Eastern Europe, namely Austria. Its system is now changing since joining the EU and privatization of former SOEs is going on. Nevertheless for decades Austria was a uniquely mixed economy with a substantial portion of its capital stock and major industries in state hands. Its macroeconomic policy has been dominated by a 'corporatist' approach to labour–management relations which restrained both wage and price increases, generating an admirable degree of stability.

The literature (Pryor, 1988; Pekkarinen, Pohjola and Rowthorn, 1992) recognizes a division between 'authoritarian corporatism' as in the classic fascist economies, the self-styled 'corporate states', and 'liberal corporatism' as exemplified by several of the Scandinavian economies.[16] Although closer to the liberal model, Austria is seen as somewhere in between, its corporatism being at least partly descended from the fascist model with 'chambers' for labour and capital and a larger role for government in bringing about the agreements.

The applicability of this model in Central and Eastern Europe seems to face several problems. The most serious is the same as that facing the big bang policies, the general weakness of institutional frameworks in these countries. To a large extent corporatism requires a strong institutional framework, including credible unions representing most workers and employers' organizations which can face them in economy-wide negotiations. Also the intervening governments must have credibility, a continuing problem in Central and Eastern Europe. Thus the corporatist solution does not look too promising in the short run. However, given their proximity to and historical connections with Austria, as well as the relatively high degrees of internal homogeneity in many of them,

Austrian or Scandinavian style corporatism, possibly combined with Austrian levels of state ownership, are not out of the question in the longer run as outcomes. Such corporatism can be seen as helping to overcome the co-ordination failure modelled in the previous section.

6 Conclusions

In this chapter, we reconsidered the problem of big bang versus evolutionist strategies in economic transformation in Central and Eastern Europe. In particular we modelled the problem of co-ordination failure within the transition context using the interacting particle systems approach which brings out the nature of interactions between agents within an economy. Such models suggest that there exist critical points beyond which discontinuous changes in the nature of internal interactions underlying co-ordination can happen bringing about a sudden collapse, or in some cases a sudden improvement, of such co-ordination with the attendant implications for aggregate output.

These results tend to support the evolutionist position in that it is the breakdown of institutional frameworks that can trigger such co-ordination failures with the resulting macroeconomic collapse. This could explain what we have actually seen in Central and Eastern Europe since 1989. The cases of Poland and the Czech Republic which have frequently been cited as supporting the big bang approach were seen as being more complicated and more equivocal than has usually been argued.

We took this beyond the question of evolutionism which can be consistent with support for an ultimate goal of a near-laissez-faire outcome by examining the issue of appropriate ultimate outcomes in Central and Eastern European economies. In so doing the cases of still largely worker-managed and market socialist Slovenia, China with its local market socialist TVEs, and Austria with its mixed economy corporatism were all examined for their possible relevance to the Central and East European countries. Elements of each of these models were seen to have some possible applicability in either the short or long run.

Notes

1. The authors wish to acknowledge materials or comments from William Brock, Dietrich Earnhart, Shirley Gedeon, and Mark Knell.
2. These examples are discussed in more detail later. We note, however, that Poland has already experienced the political backlash, despite its alleged economic success. Jeffrey Sachs, Poland's former IMF adviser, has expressed his lack of comprehension as to why this happened.

3. There has been great controversy regarding the scale of the decline. There is little doubt that it was not as great in real terms as the official data suggest. This is because on the one hand much of the new private sector activity remains unreported, at least partly because of a desire to avoid taxes. Also there is the argument of Winiecki (1991) that much of the decline was actually of undesired goods whose loss amounted to little, although this is of little comfort to those laid off as a result.

4. In this regard McKinnon (1992) argues that China represents the 'true Hayekian' outcome in that market capitalism has been allowed a gradual and spontaneous emergence and thus has a more solid foundation than if it had been artificially imposed from above and without.

5. We summarize only the simplest model of Aghion and Blanchard: one that assumes that firms are not forward-looking at all and that workers cannot influence the rate of state sector layoffs. However their extensions covering such cases do not fundamentally alter the nature of their conclusions or the basic framework that we present here.

6. We are able to do this by allowing some firms to have zero output. They may thus be merely 'potential' firms which have not yet actually come into existence.

7. B is 'temperature' in the original IPS literature (Kac, 1968).

8. The solution is substantially more complicated otherwise.

9. Such a co-ordination collapse is worsened if there is a simultaneous collapse of existing trade patterns as happened with the collapse of the CMEA and the breakup of the USSR (see Rosser, 1993, for the impact of the latter).

10. Yet another possibility is a transition into chaotic dynamics. That systemic transitions may involve transitions through chaotically dynamic states is explored in Rosser (1991, Chapter 17) and Rosser and Rosser (1994).

11. Some even discuss a 'Fourth Way' (Alexander and Skąpska, 1994).

12. Other examples of such an approach have led to proposals for temporary subsidies to firms during transition (Melitz and Waysand, 1994) and for temporary subsidies to credit markets as well (Calvo and Coricelli, 1992).

13. A variation of this is to suggest that the good performance of SOEs in Poland is due to their managers expecting eventual privatization and acting in anticipation of that. We note that the father of the soft budget constraint concept and recently an advocate of strong movement toward market capitalism, János Kornai, has lately (1994) exhibited greater concern over output declines in the CEECs and the need for growth.

14. See Bonin, Jones and Putterman (1993) for a review of this literature.

15. For discussion of their evolution see Ling and Zhongyi (1993) and of their performance see Jefferson and Rawski (1994).

16. Angresano (1992) suggests that despite its current problems Sweden can still serve as a role model for the Central and East European countries, particularly Hungary, although given its proximity and historical connections, Austria may be the more likely role model.

References

Aghion, Philippe and Olivier Jean Blanchard (1993), 'On the Speed of Transition in Central Europe', Working Paper no. 93–8, Department of Economics, MIT.

Alexander, Gregory S. and Grazyna Skąpska (eds) (1994), *A Fourth Way? Privatization, Property, and the Emergence of New Market Economies*, London: Routledge.

Angresano, James (1992), 'A Mixed Economy in Hungary? Lessons from the Swedish Experience', *Comparative Economic Studies*, 34, 41–57.

Bonin, John P., Derek C. Jones and Louis Putterman (1993), 'Theory and Empirics of Cooperative Firms: Will the Twain Ever Meet?', *Journal of Economic Literature*, 31, 1290–1320.

Brada, Josef C. (1993), 'The Transformation from Communism to Capitalism: How Far? How Fast?', *Post-Soviet Affairs*, 9, 87–110.

Brada, Josef C. and Arthur E. King (1992), 'Is There a J-Curve for the Economic Transition from Socialism to Capitalism?', *Economics of Planning*, 25, 37–53.

Brock, William A. (1993), 'Pathways to Randomness in the Economy: Emergent Nonlinearity and Chaos in Economics and Finance', *Estudios Economicos*, 8, 3–55.

Calvo, Guillermo and Fabrizio Coricelli (1992), 'Stagflationary Effects of Stabilization Programs in Reforming Socialist Countries: Enterprise-Side and Household-Side Factors', *World Bank Economic Review*, 6, 71–90.

Ham, John, Jan Svejnar and Katherine Terrell (1994), 'The Czech and Slovak Labor Markets During the Transition', mimeo, University of Pittsburgh.

Jefferson, Gary H. and Thomas G. Rawski (1994), 'Enterprise Reform in Chinese Industry', *Journal of Economic Perspectives*, 8, 47–70.

Kac, Mark (1968), 'Mathematical Mechanisms of Phase Transitions', in M. Chrétien, E. Gross, and S. Deser (eds), *Statistical Physics: Phase Transitions and Superfluidity, vol. 1*, Brandeis University Summer Institute in Theoretical Physics, pp. 241–305.

Kamiński, Bartlomeij, Andrzej Kwieciński and Jan J. Michalek (1993), 'Competitiveness of the Polish Economy in Transition', PPRG Discussion Paper no. 20, Warsaw University.

Kornai, János (1994), 'Transformational Recession: The Main Causes', *Journal of Comparative Economics*, 19, 39–63.

Ling, Zhu and Jiang Zhongyi (1993), 'From Brigade to Village Community: The Land Tenure System and Rural Development in China', *Cambridge Journal of Economics*, 17, 441–61.

McKinnon, Ronald (1992), 'On the Asiatic Model of Economic Reform and Self-Organization', *American Economic Review*, 82, 31–6.

Melitz, Jacques and Claire Waysand (1994), 'The Role of Government Aid to Firms During the Transition To a Market Economy: Russia 1992-1994', Document de Travail no. 9435, CREST-INSEE, Paris.

Murrell, Peter (1991), 'Can Neoclassical Economics Underpin the Reform of Centrally Planned Economies?', *Journal of Economic Perspectives*, 5, 59–76.

Murrell, Peter (1992), 'Evolutionary and Radical Approaches to Economic Reform', *Economics of Planning*, 25, 79–95.

Pekkarinen, Jukka, Matti Pohjola and Bob Rowthorn (eds) (1992), *Social Corporatism: A Superior Economic System?*, Oxford: Clarendon.

Portes, Richard (1994), 'Transformation Traps', *Economic Journal*, 104, 1178–89.

Prasnikar, Janez and Jan Svejnar (1991), 'Workers' Participation in Management vs. Social Ownership and Government Policies: Yugoslav Lessons for Transforming Socialist Economies', *Comparative Economic Studies*, 34, 27–46.

Pryor, Frederic L. (1988), 'Corporatism as an Economic System', *Journal of Comparative Economics*, 12, 317–44.

Rosser, J. Barkley, Jr. (1991), *From Catastrophe to Chaos: A General Theory of Economic Discontinuities*, Boston: Kluwer.

Rosser, Marina Vcherashnaya (1993), 'The External Dimension of Soviet Economic Reform', *Journal of Economic Issues*, 27, 813–24.

Rosser, J. Barkley, Jr. and Marina Vcherashnaya Rosser (1994), 'Long Wave Chaos and Systemic Economic Transformation', *World Futures*, 39, 197–207.

Rosser, J. Barkley, Jr. and Marina Vcherashnaya Rosser (1995), *Comparative Economics in a Transforming World Economy*, Burr Ridge: Richard D. Irwin.

Van Ness, Peter (ed.) (1989), *Market Reforms in Socialist Societies: Comparing China and Hungary*, Boulder: Lynne Riemer.

Winiecki, Jan (1991), 'The Inevitability of a Fall in Output in the Early Stages of Transition to the Market: Theoretical Underpinnings', *Soviet Studies*, 43, 669–76.

5   An Alternative Economic Policy for Central and Eastern Europe

Kazimierz Laski

1   Introduction

The purpose of this chapter is to evaluate some aspects of transformation policy prescriptions in the light of the 'stylized facts' derived from recent experience. We refer first of all to Poland, Hungary and the Czech and the Slovak Republics (previously Czechoslovakia) – in the following called the leading reform countries – as for these four countries the best statistical information is available. It is hoped that this evaluation may make possible the design of better policies which would minimize further adjustment costs, create the social basis required for the continuation of reforms and quicken the pace of economic recovery.

The chapter is organized in six parts. Some 'stylized facts' typical of economies in transition can already be detected; they are presented in section 2. Section 3 discusses the issue of deep recession – the most important stylized fact – and whether it has been necessary. The avoidable causes of recession are related by the author to the stabilization programme pursued. In section 4 the model underlying stabilization is described and juxtaposed to an approach based on the theory of effective demand. Apart from recession, another important stylized fact is persistent inflation. The relation between inflation and monetary and fiscal policies in Central and Eastern Europe is discussed in section 5. The last section is devoted to the important topic of the transition from stabilization to growth.

2   The stylized facts

The experience of the leading reform countries accumulated during the last few years allows some generalization concerning the achievements and failures of a typical stabilization programme.[1] These programmes proved to be relatively effective in three directions. First, the transition from a sellers' market to a buyers' market constrained by demand appears to have been largely achieved, as many of the traditional symptoms of shortage economy disappeared to a great extent. This is probably the most important achievement of the stabilization programme. Second, high open inflation, accompanying the collapse of central planning, has slowed down in Central and Eastern Europe even though the level of inflation remains high relative to Western Europe. Finally, the convertible currency trade improved in most cases, though it is uncertain how established this trend is.

The most important development since the collapse of central planning is the deep fall of the level of economic activity leading to a drastic decline of output and employment. The contraction comprises most sectors of the economy, with industry and construction (including residential building) hit severely. The level of consumption fell, though less than the general level of economic activity. The social groups that lost the most were the recipients of earned incomes (strongly reduced real wages; unemployment) and the peasants (mostly by increase of relative prices of industrial goods and services in relation to prices obtained by peasants). The welfare losses were accompanied by sharply increased income differentiation.

It should be stressed that the facts concerning the collapse of output are not undisputed. It is often argued that the relatively high dynamics of the private sector is not fully taken into account and that the share of the shadow economy in the gross domestic product (GDP) increases also. However, the role of these factors in explaining the collapse of output should not be overestimated. First, while illegal and non-registered activities have been booming during transformation, the importance of the traditional shadow economy, flourishing on the borders of and sponging on the 'shortage economy', diminished with the disappearance of that economy. Second, private activities increased mostly in trade (internal and external), building industry and truck transport but much less in industry, where the deepest declines occurred in general. Finally, the still relatively small share of the private sector in the economies of Central and Eastern Europe rules out any serious correction of the aggregate output decline resulting from this factor, at least at the beginning of the transformation process when the decline of the output was the strongest.[2]

It is also frequently argued that the decline of output concerns mostly 'unwanted output'. Portes (1992a, pp. 1–2) rightly criticizes the idea of 'unwanted output' as it refers to demand, and thus to price. Hence 'unwanted goods' in an extreme case must have such a low 'true' or 'world market' price that their production generates negative value added at world prices. However, the elimination of unwanted, value-subtracting output should increase rather than decrease output measured in comparable world market prices – which has not been the case.

In empirical terms, therefore, the macroeconomic consequences of stabilization policies have been somewhat mixed and confusing – much poorer than anticipated performance in terms of output recession, employment and welfare, but positive gains recorded, at least in the short run, in terms of reduced inflation and improved trade balance and, more importantly, in overcoming many problems of a shortage economy. From a policy perspective, a better understanding of these diverse facts will help to minimize the adjustment costs of continued stabilization and speed up the pace of structural adjustments and economic growth.

3 Transformational recession: unavoidable, but how deep?

The large output collapse experienced in Central and Eastern Europe during the implementation of the stabilization programmes is by far the most important stylized fact. Was this collapse, coined 'transformational recession' by Kornai (1993), provoked by external factors only or was it implied in the stabilization programmes and thus more or less avoidable?

Some recession caused by the transformation was certainly unavoidable. In a market economy – a demand-constrained system – the actual gross domestic product is determined by the level of investment and effective demand, given the production capacity, the price–wage relation and propensity to save out of wages and profits. As a rule effective demand stays behind potential supply (or potential GDP), resulting in some reserve production capacity and some unemployment. While some factors of production lie idle, others are used in a rather efficient way. The economy under these conditions is said to work under 'pressure', the market is characterized as a 'buyers' market'.

In a command economy – a supply-constrained system – factors of production including labour force are utilized intensively though rather inefficiently. Effective demand in this system could always be (and was) generated by a *fiat* of the Central Planning Board which also determined, at least in principle, the price–wage relation adjusting it to the expected uses of final output. In a command economy demand is as a rule ahead of potential supply, creating a permanent state of 'suction'. The market was a 'sellers' market', the economy was characterized by permanent shortages.

The transition from command to market economy requires the substitution of 'pressure of supply' for the former 'suction of demand', implying that effective demand is constrained at a level below potential supply, resulting in some reserve capacity and unemployment. They allow for flexibility of production (for adjusting the structure of supply to that of demand). Some decrease of actual GDP caused by cuts in total demand is thus unavoidable. In this sense some recession, implying immediate losses in production, employment and consumption, is part of every programme aimed at transforming a command economy into a market economy.

But the necessity of *some* recession does not mean that *every* recession is necessary and justified. Just because some recession is unavoidable anyway, all efforts should be made to keep the decline of production and the sacrifices provoked by it as small as possible. Most controversies concerning the transformation strategy are related exactly to the intensity of transformational recession.

The aggregate approach must be complemented by structural considerations. The factors partly responsible for transformational recession are put into three groups by Kornai (1993, pp. 18–29): (1) the mismatch between structure of demand and structure of supply and the poor quality of produced goods become a serious problem under conditions of market clearing prices; (2) the contraction of the state sector and large-size firms is not appropriately synchronized with the expansion of the private sector and small-size firms; and (3) administrative co-ordination failures create an organizational vacuum while market co-ordination does not yet bring the expected results. The latter factor is due mainly to the infrastructure (banking, fiscal and legal systems; managerial skills; mental attitudes) being in *statu nascendi.*

However, there is a difference between the structural problems in Central and Eastern Europe and the macroeconomic approach of Kornai. The passage from suction to pressure requires, first, the reduction of excess demand and, second, the reduction of effective demand below the level of potential output, hence aims directly at the decline of output and employment. But in the case of structural problems, measures reducing output in some branches or sectors of the economy could ideally be compensated by an expansion of other branches or sectors. Yet in practice this is very difficult or even impossible. The same applies to the mix between administrative and market co-ordination and to the non-adjustment of the structure of supply to that of demand. Hence while effective demand is intentionally reduced in relation to potential output, effective output and potential output itself decline unintentionally as a side effect of the transition process.

Laski et al. (1993) argues that the degree of contraction of effective and potential output depends on the policy pursued. Some production branches existing and even flourishing in the shortage economy would in any case meet difficulties in a market environment. Provided they had sufficient time and means to restructure, they might survive and eventually adjust their production profile and the quality of goods produced to the new requirements. Sudden trade liberalization and exposure to foreign competition may destroy parts of potential output.

To devise a policy aimed at balancing the process of contraction and expansion of branches, products and of different forms of co-ordination to avoid or minimize the potential output decline is admittedly very difficult. But policies of this kind were not even attempted. Instead they were limited primarily to stabilization measures consisting of restrictive monetary and fiscal policies. These policies, but not their *intensity*, were more or less adjusted to the transition from the suction of demand to the pressure of supply but ignored more or less completely structural problems. The latter were left to the action of the spontaneous market forces. The only exception was the privatization of big firms which anyway required quite a long time before achieving even a modest progress. Thus we claim that the collapse of output caused by structural factors cannot be considered being completely independent of the chosen policies.

It is frequently argued that the decline of aggregate output is mainly due to the loss of external markets caused by the collapse of the CMEA (the Council for Mutual Economic Assistance), especially of the Soviet market. This is undoubtedly an important question, although the collapse of the CMEA was not completely independent of the chosen transformation strategy either. Of course the CMEA was itself a byproduct of the shortage economies and could not survive the transformation process in its old form. However, no effort in this direction was even considered. The strategy included almost everywhere the transition in foreign trade to world market prices and to convertible currencies as rapidly as possible.

There are some methodological problems to solve when the quantitative role of the lost CMEA markets in total output decline is to be estimated. Various studies have shown that at most 20 to 30 per cent of the total decline of GDP can be attributed to the lost CMEA markets.[3]

There exists of course a big difference between a global and a partial approach. The lost CMEA markets, which may have played a larger or minor role in the aggregate output decline, turned out to be disastrous for certain branches of industry and especially in certain regions because the goods exported to new markets and those lost on the old ones were in the majority of cases not the same goods. It is, however, not consistent with aggregate analysis to take into account (as some do) losses in CMEA markets but disregard gains in other markets. Without the former the latter could not have materialized. Both are a result of trade liberalization.

The conclusion reached in Laski et al. (1993) is that the collapse of output is a fact, though some, but no substantial statistical corrections of its intensity may be justified. Further, internal and especially external factors, unrelated (or only partly related) to the chosen strategy of transformation, played an important role in the decline of GDP, but were not exclusively accountable. Hence, other factors responsible for this phenomenon should be looked for in the transformation process and in the chosen transformation strategy itself.

4 Conventional stabilization and effective demand

There is a certain irony in the current transition debate. The radical transformation of the command economy based on scarcity and sellers' markets into an economy largely characterized by buyers' markets and responsive to consumer choice implies two things, one frequently emphasized, but not the other. The commonly understood point relates to the microeconomic aspect of consumer sovereignty. However, in a buyers' market the level of output and employment tends to be increasingly demand-determined, i.e. aggregate demand becomes critically important in determining the level of output. As the demand constraints *strengthened*, conventional stabilization policy failed to anticipate the severity of the economic recession largely because its analytical scheme did not assign the appropriate role to the analysis of aggregate demand and the size of the market during the early phase of the transition process.

The stabilization programmes pursued in Central and Eastern Europe are similar to those practised in developing countries when their financial and monetary system, particularly balance of payments, gets into difficulty. They tended to be uniform and stereotyped as far as the hard-core macroeconomic policies are concerned. The intellectual basis of the so-called financial programming is the 'quantity theory of money'; it shows money demand as the product of price level, aggregate output level and velocity of circulation. Financial programming assumes that the velocity of circulation is roughly constant (or at least predictable) and that aggregate output is given exogenously from the supply side. In such conditions changes in the quantity of money must lead to corresponding changes in the price level. Hence credit restraint, limiting the growth of the quantity of money, becomes a central element of the stabilization programme as far as its basic goal is the suppression of inflation. In addition stabilization programmes usually contain the following elements: (1) the requirement of high interest rates, in addition to 'quantity rationing'; this is supposed to encourage (private) saving and to reduce demand for loans from the banking sector; (2) the requirement of reducing the 'fiscal deficit' through cuts in government subsidies and increases in prices of basic public utilities; (3) devaluation of the domestic currency, in the hope that this will directly improve the trade balance by making export cheaper to foreigners and import dearer to domestic residents; and (4) liberalization of the trade regime by moving from quantitative restrictions to price (tariff) restrictions as well as moving from a protectionist to a more liberal regime with lower tariffs.

Many programmes contain also two nominal 'anchors' to prevent the development of an inflationary spiral. The first anchor is usually represented by control of nominal wages, allowing only partial compensation for inflation and thus limiting the increase of labour costs. The second anchor is often the constancy (for some limited time) of the exchange rate, intended to break inflationary expectations and keep prices of imported goods more or less constant. Hence both anchors put some brake on cost-push inflation. By taking into account this important factor they are to some degree an extraneous element in the stabilization package based mostly on demand restriction.

While these are the typical elements of stabilization policy packages practised in Central and Eastern Europe, there have been some differences in their sequencing over time. The first step in the sequence, however, was always the introduction of a significant degree of price liberalization, preceding all other stabilization measures. This is so because in command economies prices did not as a rule balance demand for and supply of goods and services. At the same time the price structure in these economies was quite artificial and had to be adjusted to economic necessities, first of all to relative costs of production. These economies were in reality only half-monetarized shortage economies in which purchasing power was a necessary, but not sufficient precondition for acquiring a good. Therefore, the transformation of money into a real transaction medium and a store of value is an absolutely necessary step on the way from a command towards a market economy. A major element of the monetarization of the economy is price liberalization. In the context of Central and Eastern Europe, therefore, the policies of stabilization and of price liberalization became strongly interlocked. Consequently, stabilization and price liberalization should be treated together in evaluating actual experience even if, in the analytical construction of the model, they have a somewhat separate existence.

The basic logic of fighting inflation through credit restriction depends crucially on the assumptions that the level of output is exogenously given or at least predictable and the velocity of circulation of money is reasonably stable so that there is a predictable positive relation between the supply of 'money' and the price level, given the level of output. As a consequence the restriction on credit is seen primarily to affect prices and not the level of output. These assumptions do not appear to coincide with the stabilization policies implemented in Central and Eastern Europe.

The large declines in output observed in Central and Eastern Europe during the first three years of the monetarist stabilization programmes turned out to be significantly more severe than was predicted, i.e. the exogenously predicted fall in output was systematically and grossly under-estimated. In practical terms this means that the massive social and political costs of stabilization were miscalculated. In analytical terms, it implies the need to modify the framework of analysis so that the impact of restrictive credit policies and other related measures of stabilization can be more appropriately accounted for, especially in terms of their negative impact on the output level.

The principle of effective demand, pioneered by Keynes and Kalecki, is a more appropriate theory for determining the level of output. This theory characterizes equilibrium between aggregate demand and aggregate supply in terms of equality between (gross business) investment and savings (of private households and business). In an open-public economy investment includes the budget deficit (the difference between government expenditures for goods and services and government revenues, including social security payments and net of government transfers) and the export surplus (on account of goods and non-factor services) and savings net of taxation. Hence, the equilibrium between aggregate demand and aggregate supply in the general case requires an equality between savings and investment as the sum of private investment, the budget deficit, and the export surplus.

The interpretation of the equality between investment and savings in a demand-determined economy is crucial. Since expenditure determines income (and output) in a demand-determined economy, this equality shows that in every period, what can be saved is determined by investment. Savings, being determined in this way, in turn determine the volume of final output, as measured by the gross domestic product GDP through the savings ratio s, or the share of savings in final output. From this relationship, GDP is defined as:

$$GDP = \frac{1}{s}I,$$

where investment I is defined as the *sum* of gross private investment, the budget deficit and net exports and $1/s$ is the multiplier.[4] A change in GDP therefore appears as:

$$\Delta GDP = \frac{1}{s} \Delta I,$$

assuming s as constant, and if s is not constant GDP becomes:

$$\Delta GDP = GDP(gI - gs)$$

where gI and gs are the growth rates of total investment and the savings ratio respectively (i.e. g represents the operator for proportional change of a variable). As this equation does not apply when annual changes in I and s are large, the first equation implies that:

$$1 + gGDP = \frac{1 + gI}{1 + gs}$$

where $gGDP$ denotes the rate of growth of GDP. Rearranging, we obtain

$$\Delta GDP = GDP \frac{gI - gs}{1 + gs}$$

which applies when yearly changes of I and s are large.

The way in which investment determines savings and, in turn, via the savings ratio the volume of output is quite complicated. There are, however, two extreme cases – that of pure quantity adjustment and that of pure price adjustment. In the first case prices maintain a constant relation to costs, especially labour costs, thus the distribution of value added between wages and profits (and taxes) remains constant. This results in a more or less stable savings ratio even if we assume that the propensity to save out of profits (e.g. retained profits of enterprises) and out of wages differs significantly. In this case the volume of GDP increases more or less *pari passu* with I, while prices remain constant, if costs remain constant too. This is the case of pure quantity adjustment because prices, given costs, do not change. In the second case prices in relation to costs, especially labour costs, change. When prices increase in relation to costs the value added is shifted from wages to profits resulting in increased savings, while the volume of GDP remains constant in real terms. The expansion of I leads in the second case to inflation through pure price adjustment because, by assumption, quantities do not change.

The case that prevails in a given situation depends mostly on the level of capacity utilization and is closely related to factors determining prices. As far as the latter are concerned it is very important to differentiate between demand-determined and cost-determined prices. Prices of raw materials and energy and agricultural prices tend to be demand-determined. If demand increases (decreases) these prices tend to increase (decrease) too, while the quantities of goods remain given in the period under consideration. However, in an industrial economy most prices, namely prices of industrial goods and services, are not part of this group; instead, they are cost-determined. These prices tend to be relatively insensitive to demand in relation to costs, while their quantities increase or decrease in response to demand changes.[5] Cost-determined prices are also called mark-up prices because they are fixed at a level covering direct unit costs plus a mark-up. As long as capacity is underutilized, direct unit costs may tend to remain constant, but only if money wages and labour productivity are not strongly influenced by variations in the degree of capacity utilization. In that case quantity adjustment would prevail at low capacity utilization, and price adjustment would be the rule if utilization of capacity is high. Of course mixed cases cannot be excluded. In mixed cases both the savings ratio and the volume of real GDP would tend to change, the former through price adjustment and the latter through quantity adjustment.

The role of aggregate demand in determining the output level is important for understanding a crucial aspect of the recent stabilization experience in Central and Eastern Europe. As already noted, in all countries the decline of GDP was much stronger than predicted in the stabilization programmes. The unanticipated depth of the recession was, however, not subsequently explained: this failure represents the most important theoretical weakness of the stabilization programmes pursued. In particular, no effort has been made to evaluate, even approximately, the combined effects of the proposed curtailment of total demand on the level of output and employment. This has been the main reason for the wide gap between anticipated and actual recession. This conceptual shortcoming of conventional stabilization policy, arising from its failure to take into account the full impact of aggregate demand reduction on output, must be remedied for better designing of fiscal and monetary policies during transition.

Table 5.1 suggests that I declined very strongly in Central and Eastern Europe from 1988 to 1992. This decline was the primary, though not the only, cause of the collapse of output. By far the most important element of I is private business investment. Hence what happens to I depends as a rule on this investment. The restrictive monetary policy and high interest rates (as well as the unclear legal situation of state enterprises) could not but depress the level of investment during the stabilization period. As far as budget deficits are concerned the following pattern seems to have occurred. At the beginning deficits declined, in line with the goals of stabilization policies, or even disappeared completely; then, however, they started to increase and reached as a rule higher levels than prior to the start of the stabilization process. A more or less similar pattern can be observed in the net export balance. The balance of trade tends to improve at the beginning of stabilization policy, because of devaluation of the national currency and the limited internal market, and to deteriorate thereafter. The changes in investment can partly be compensated by opposite changes in the budget deficit and the balance of trade. But the size of the latter factors is limited so that for any longer period of time the decline in investment

Table 5.1 Savings ratios and components of savings for CSFR, Hungary and Poland, 1988–92

	Savings ratios s = S/GDP		S	I	GDP	Components of savings as % of GDP at constant prices		
	constant prices	current prices	previous year = 100 constant prices			BS	I$_B$	NX
CSFR								
1988	0.253	0.247	106.0	97.7	102.6	−0.3	22.4	2.6
1989	0.256	0.246	102.5	103.6	101.4	−0.8	22.9	1.9
1990	0.211	0.211	82.2	109.1	99.6	0.9	25.1	−3.1
1991	0.229	0.247	91.3	67.9	84.1	−1.1	20.3	1.6
1992	0.161	0.178	64.4	62.3	91.5	−1.8	13.8	0.6
Hungary								
1988	0.208	0.212	101.0	97.9	99.9	−0.7	17.5	2.7
1989	0.227	0.260	116.9	107.5	100.7	−2.8	17.4	2.5
1990	0.193	0.220	85.0	97.8	96.5	−0.03	17.2	2.0
1991	0.160	0.147	67.9	76.1	88.1	−2.3	16.6	−2.9
1992	0.144	0.150	96.8	46.4	95.7	−7.5	8.1	−1.2
1993	0.067	0.086	51.0	181.4	97.7	−5.5	14.9	−13.7
Poland								
1988	0.248	0.310	107.3	112.6	104.1	−0.2	21.7	2.8
1989	0.298	0.423	120.5	109.3	100.2	−3.5	23.7	2.6
1990	0.287	0.287	84.7	74.4	88.4	0.2	21.8	7.1
1991	0.240	0.199	77.8	84.9	93.0	−3.8	19.9	0.3
1992	0.255	0.210	109.0	85.1	102.6	−6.0	16.5	3.0
1993	0.214	0.178	87.1	116.9	103.8	−2.8	18.6	0.0

Notes: S is savings; I$_B$ is business investment; BS is the budget surplus; NX is net exports of goods and non-factor services. CSFR: constant prices of 1986; Hungary: constant prices of 1985; Poland: constant prices of 1990.
Source: WIIW estimates.

must result in a decline of savings. This decline is a necessary result of the conventional stabilization programmes, especially of the monetary and fiscal policies implied by them.

With a constant savings ratio the changes in GDP were proportional to changes in I. In the leading reform countries this was, however, not the case. In these countries we observed generally a reduction of the savings ratio (in constant as well as in current prices). It is possible that the observed reduction of the savings ratio was provoked primarily by the decline of the relative share of profits of state enterprises (with a propensity to save equal to unity) in the value added. Another factor could be the high propensity to consume out of profits in the new private sector. The tendency for savings ratios to decrease was an important factor in softening the decline in GDP caused by the strong reduction of savings in the course of the stabilization process.

The thrust of the argument in this chapter is that Keynesian 'multiplier analysis' would have predicted more accurately the depth of the recession – which turned out to be much more severe than anticipated – caused by conventional stabilization policies. At the same time, such a framework would have been better suited to distinguish between the autonomous (or exogenous) and the induced (or endogenous) components of aggregate demand, which is essential for the design of appropriate fiscal, monetary and trade policies during the transition. Thus, budget deficit and trade balance should be recognized as partly endogenous variables which adjust as a consequence of changes in the level of income and economic activity. This view is in contrast to stabilization programmes which tend to treat the government budget deficit as an exogenous policy variable and base much of the fiscal policy for stabilization on this assumption. Similarly, reduction in import was induced by recessionary output contraction. Since conventional stabilization programmes failed to anticipate the severity of the recession, they also failed to predict the consequent improvement in the trade balance in several countries during the first phase of stabilization through slackening of import demand due to recession. The improvement of the trade balance was attributed entirely to relative price changes through devaluation whereas it should have been realized that it was, at least partly, the consequence of declining aggregate income. This also points to the fragile nature of the improvement in the trade balance achieved which may begin to deteriorate again as soon as the economy starts to expand or the compression of import reaches its limits.

Conventional stabilization policy failed not only by not predicting correctly the consequences of reduced investment upon aggregate demand. It also failed by excessively reducing consumption, by far the major part of

GDP. It is true that in command economies effective demand of private households, given the price level, was as a rule higher than actual (and potential) supply of consumer goods. The resulting excess demand had to be removed and this goal was rightly an important part of the stabilization policy. However, the removal of excess demand does not necessarily mean a decline of real consumption if it is really limited to the excess part of demand only. This removal implies an adjustment of the monetary overhang (the stock part of excess demand), where it existed, and of the current monetary incomes, mostly money wages (the flow part of excess demand). It should be stressed that in countries with a significant monetary overhang high inflation often preceded stabilization measures and decimated really the stock part of excess demand. Thus, in many cases, the main problem was the adjustment of the flow part of excess demand, mostly wages.

Nominal wages and other nominal incomes were as a rule too high, given the level of consumer goods prices. Adjustment of nominal wages (as well as other nominal incomes) and prices under these conditions requires a rise in consumer goods prices in relation to nominal wages to such an extent that the real wage is being reduced to the level of the 'available' real wage. In these circumstances the wage earner suffers only a 'statistical' cut in his real income and is additionally compensated by the passage from a sellers' to a buyers' market.

Although the 'statistical' real wage must be cut in the framework of the stabilization policy, this does not apply to the 'available' real wage (and to other incomes, respectively). This conclusion was quite popular at the start of the stabilization policies, but after the start of the shock therapy, it disappeared from the discussion for reasons which are not clear, giving way to the argument that a drastic fall of real consumption out of wages (and other incomes) was an absolutely necessary measure in the successful battle against inflation.

The reduction of investment and the related fall of aggregate demand provokes a decline of GDP and employment. Under these conditions, even with given real wages, consumption (minus unemployment benefits) decreases *pari passu* with employment. If, in addition, real wages fall, then consumption decreases more strongly than employment and deepens the recession. It is not clear at all why some recession, even if it is accepted as an unavoidable step on the road from a command to a market economy, should combine reduction of employment with reduction of the real wage. If such a decline is intended, its effect upon aggregate demand should be taken into account when cuts in investment are planned.

5   Persistent inflation, monetary restriction and fiscal policy

While the conventional stabilization programmes failed to anticipate the depth of the recession in Central and Eastern Europe, their policy package turned out to be relatively more effective in fighting inflation. An immediate, though partial explanation of this phenomenon in the light of our preceding discussion would run along the following lines: the policy package aimed at curbing credit, budget deficit and related restrictive monetary and fiscal policies contracted demand. This demand contraction showed up partly in negative output adjustment resulting in recession and partly in price adjustment resulting in the slowing down of inflation. Moreover, the slowdown of inflation was helped further by a nominal wage anchor and by the international price discipline of the newly liberalized foreign trade regime, both of which kept a check on nominal price rises.

This simple explanation and the strategy of massive demand contraction for price stabilization is probably valid and unavoidable in a situation of hyperinflation (or acute inflation) with an overhang of liquidity with the public, as was the case in some of the Central and Eastern European countries in the initial phase of stabilization. However, it is equally important to realize that this policy of almost indiscriminate demand contraction may not only cause avoidable recession, but may actually turn out to be counterproductive in the changed circumstances of massive recession and relatively moderate inflation facing some of the Central and Eastern European countries.

The central analytical reason why massive demand contraction, if pursued for long, may turn out to be counterproductive is not difficult to appreciate. This strategy may end up not only by eliminating *excess* demand, but may begin adversely to affect the supply side of the economy in a way that makes the task of controlling inflation increasingly more difficult.

Since the actual level of aggregate output might be constrained either by the demand or the supply side, some measures of the conventional stabilization programme could affect both sides. For instance, restraint on domestic credit through quantity rationing as well as price rationing in the form of higher interest rates would adversely affect the demand-determined level of aggregate output by restraining budget deficit and also by discouraging private investment. It would at the same time reduce availability of working capital, especially for the smaller producing units in the economy; and for sectors with long gestation periods, e.g. housing and shipbuilding, affecting their supply-determined level of output. Thus, for different reasons, both the demand-determined and the supply-determined output levels are likely to decrease with greater degrees of credit control. This implies that changes in the level of output, either from the demand or from the supply side, are not independent of changes in the degree of credit restriction imposed.

Since the supply of money determines the price level in the monetarist approach to stabilization policy, continuing inflation, prevailing in the three leading reform countries, may induce the supporters of this policy to conclude that credit restriction did not go far enough. The monetarist approach requires that credit restriction should be continued, and even further tightened, *coûte que coûte*, till inflation is eliminated. Losses of net output caused by this policy may partly be irreversible if the capacities concerned are destroyed (e.g. existing supply of specialized intermediate inputs gets lost, workers with special skills change jobs, some factories are closed down etc.). In all these cases the restoration of effective demand later on could not easily restore the potential net output lost unnecessarily.

Nevertheless, there would be some intrinsic logic in the monetarist approach if all prices were demand-determined. But, as was already stressed, the prices of most goods in a modern society, excluding primary products like agricultural goods and raw materials, tend to be cost-determined and remain constant if unit direct costs remain constant. This is quite likely if firms produce below their capacity. Under this condition unit direct costs remain constant and are equal to marginal costs. Only when output approaches the capacity level, marginal costs increase (through the introduction of a second shift or the use of less efficient equipment, etc.) and, though more slowly, unit direct costs also increase. Hence, the assumption of constant unit direct costs is related to the existence of reserve capacity in industry, services etc. Only this reserve capacity makes it possible that increased demand causes mostly quantity and not price adjustment.

The fact that actual output as a rule stays behind potential supply, resulting in some reserve capacity and unemployment, is characteristic of the market economy and makes it demand-determined. This seems to be more and more the case at present in the leading reform countries also. Although aggregate demand is below potential supply in many cases, prices may not fall or even remain constant if unit direct costs are on the rise. In that case the persistent inflation in these countries is of a cost-push rather than of a demand-pull nature. Indeed the stabilization policy itself exerts a strong influence upon labour and non-labour costs. The most important factors influencing non-labour costs are the drastic increases in prices of energy, transport tariffs, rents and, especially, of the working capital (in the form of exorbitantly high interest rates), all fixed directly by the government. All these measures as well as the sharp increase in indirect taxation aim at improving the budgetary balance but at the same time fuel inflation by increasing non-labour costs. The continuing devaluation of national currencies plays a role, too, in increasing the costs of imported inputs.

The increase of non-labour variable cost is not the only reason for persisting inflation. Often labour costs are pushed up by the stabilization policy. If labour productivity were to remain constant, then the non-full indexation of nominal wages, implying decreasing real wages, would lead to a decline of unit real labour costs. However, it is typical of all countries undergoing stabilization that drastic cuts in output, especially in industry, are often not compensated by parallel cuts in employment, mostly for social reasons as unemployment is becoming a politically explosive issue. Thus the redundant labour inside enterprises increases further and labour productivity decreases. Under these conditions unit real labour costs increase if real wages remain constant or even decrease, but less so than labour productivity. Thus, there is an upward pressure on unit real labour costs whenever real wages do not fall as quickly as labour productivity.

Unit real labour costs are influenced by the stabilization policy in another way. As already mentioned, this policy implies sharp increases in prices of services, fixed by the government (rents, heating, electricity, transport tariffs). As their share in services is rather high the prices of services were often increased faster than the overall consumer price index. On the other hand, industrial producer prices very often rise more slowly than consumer prices. If, then, average money wages increase faster than industrial prices (i.e. real product wages increase) but more slowly than consumer prices (i.e. real consumption wages decrease), unit labour costs would increase even at given labour productivity.

Increase of labour costs (related and unrelated to labour productivity) in addition to increase of energy prices, transport tariffs and imported inputs prices, as well as very high interest rates, make the Central and Eastern European economies extremely prone to the new type of cost-push inflation which is different from that in industrially advanced countries. Provoked by the increase of costs in relation to prices, these economies also tend to observe a decline in the mark-up ratio and profitability in industry. This proves additionally that after a short initial period we are now confronted with a special type of cost-push rather than demand-pull inflation in the leading reform countries. But yet the stabilization policy continues addressing demand-pull inflation as the main danger.

A different policy of easing credit restraint might not only increase growth but also remove some elements of cost-push inflation. Indeed if effective demand increases, enterprises having free capacity and redundant labour force would react by increasing output rather than by increasing prices. With employment lagging behind the output expansion, labour productivity would increase in the short run and, given real wages, unit labour costs would tend to decline. A lower interest rate would play a similar role. At a given (or even slightly rising) mark-up ratio, and at expanding demand, cost-determined prices should therefore increase not faster than before but probably more slowly. True, food prices, which are demand-determined, would tend to behave differently, but in an open economy (as, for example, in the leading reform countries at present) they are under some pressure of international price discipline and could therefore not rise strongly either. By relaxing demand restriction, inflation would not accelerate but rather decelerate. The real problem with relaxing demand restriction is the foreign trade balance, as an increase in production requires expansion of imports, thus deteriorating the external position of the country. But this is a different problem, which should not be confused with the problem of controlling inflation in these economies.

In the leading reform countries persistent inflation is very often linked with deficit spending in these countries. But this relation is not supported by statistics. As was already mentioned, deficit spending increased in the course of the stabilization period, while inflation slowed down. It happens also that in some cases inflation is high while deficit spending is low, and that, in still others, inflation occurs although the state budget is balanced. The link between deficit spending and inflation is much more complicated than assumed in the stabilization programmes.

While almost all of the Central and Eastern European countries inherited an unviable fiscal structure from their earlier command system, this was mainly due to subsidies which increased sharply with rising costs while the administered prices were kept more or less constant. The problem became worse as in many countries the governments began losing control over nominal wage increases. The net result of these developments was that in the final stage, before the collapse of the command economy, budget deficits became unmanageably huge in many countries. In these cases it is understandable why the stabilization programme stipulated the need to reduce the budget deficit. This policy was quite successful in the short run, but in the medium term the budgetary situation deteriorated anew. The main reason for the increase in budgetary deficits were the collapse of output, decreasing profitability and inadequate tax collection from the private sector, playing an ever growing role in the economy.

The crucial question in this situation is whether it is correct to reduce government expenditures when government revenues, for whatever reason, decline sharply. Common sense as well as conventional stabilization policy suggests that expenditure reduction in the face of declining government revenue is the natural and correct response for restoring balance in public finance. But this view is based on faulty macroeconomic reasoning; nor is it supported by facts, as attempts at reducing the budget deficit by compressing government expenditures have so far produced even larger government budgets deficits.

The misplaced emphasis on trying to balance the budget *under all circumstances* stems from the inability of the monetarist approach to stabilization to cope with the problem of demand management in a sufficiently *flexible* manner. In times of recession due to deficient demand, a larger budget deficit, compensating for the decline in private investment, may help to stimulate the level of economic activity. Since the budget deficit is usually the most powerful policy instrument available to the government for stimulating demand in times of recession, it is simply unwise to surrender it under all circumstances, irrespective of the nature of the economic malaise, just because of some ill-founded, abstract principle of 'sound' public finance.

Ideally, from the point of view of demand management, budget deficits should be allowed for in times of demand deficiency. Conversely, budget surpluses should be achieved in times when the economy is overheated. However, since such fine-tuning of budgetary policies at the discretion of the government may not be feasible, particularly in Central and Eastern Europe, it is easier to follow a rule which, as in most advanced market economies, incorporates an automatic built-in-stabilizer mechanism. This essentially requires a system of public finance in which government expenditure is less sensitive than government revenue to variations in economic activity or GDP.

Unfortunately, this built-in-stabilizer property of the public finance system, instead of being continuously strengthened in Central and Eastern Europe, is being misunderstood under the stabilization programme. Instead of taking advantage of this automatic stabilization property, budgetary policies in these countries have often tried to eliminate deficits during recession by depressing government expenditure even further, which only worsens the recessionary situation. Indeed, it is easy to demonstrate logically that the attempt to balance the budget at the margin by cutting government expenditure by an amount equivalent to the revenue loss during recession, only deepens the recession by creating an even larger multiplier effect, which works in reverse to depress income further.

Compressing government expenditure in line with government revenue makes sense in circumstances where a decline in effective demand is envisaged, but not in all circumstances. It is really this which should be recognized as the principle of 'sound' public finance, and not the crude idea of blindly balancing the budget under all circumstances. Nevertheless, in most of Central and Eastern Europe deficit spending has been frequently opposed on many different grounds, for example, some believe that it 'crowds out' private investment, others hold that it fuels inflation through the creation of high-powered money by the Central Bank to cover government deficits, still others argue with the burden which the debt service would put on coming generations, and finally, for some it contradicts the ideology of the 'minimal State'.

It can be proved that appropriate demand management by the government may not only limit recession, but benefit also private business through increased profits – something which the ideological supporters of the free market often tend to overlook. Similarly, there is no evidence of an automatic transmission link from the quantity of money to the price level. Undoubtedly, tight money policy helps to control inflation by curbing excess demand. However, the root cause of the current inflation in the leading reform countries is not excess demand but rising costs. Thus, the fear of inflation through the creation of high-powered money seems largely misplaced in the present circumstances. As a matter of fact, the main mechanism for the 'crowding out' of private investment through government budget deficits operates mostly through a non-accommodative monetary policy. Simply put, higher deficit leads to higher demand and economic activity, which would tend to increase interest rates and discourage ('crowd out') private investment unless a correspondingly accommodative monetary policy is pursued. In these circumstances, a relatively easy money policy in unison with stimulation of demand through a moderate budget deficit would, in all probability, help to 'crowd in' rather than 'crowd out' private investment. The problem arising from a large budget deficit lies no longer in inflation but in the sustainability of the balance-of-payments position during such an expansionary policy in Central and Eastern Europe.

6 Stabilization and economic expansion

Economic policy-making during transition has to proceed on the twin understanding regarding both the *scope* of reform and its *basis*. It needs to be recognized that the scope of the reform is defined broadly by three distinct but interlinked elements, namely, systemic or institutional changes, liberalization of prices and trade needed in the market economy and finally a set of commensurate macroeconomic policy measures. A common fallacy here is the confusion between the *aims* of reform or what we called the policy objectives and the *means* of reform or what we called the policy instruments. The fallacy arises from assuming that the aims of reform or the policy objectives, e.g. a liberalized trade regime or extensive private ownership of property, can be achieved simply by treating them as instruments of policy that are to be applied in the early stages of reform. This confusion between policy objectives and instruments could result in an unviable or self-defeating reform programme, e.g. sweeping trade liberalization or privatization may fail to be sustainable, precisely because they were introduced too early without the necessary prerequisites being satisfied. In judging the *scope* of reform it is therefore essential to identify the prerequisites which constitute the *basis* of the reform.

During the difficult process of transition, a minimum degree of social and political consensus should be seen as the essential *basis* of the reform. Without this, the process of transition through reforms is unlikely to be sustainable. Our main objection to conventional stabilization policies and the massive recession they almost deliberately deepened, arises from this very fact. Instead of attempting to create consensus among the main economic actors, the reform policies envisaged by the conventional stabilization programmes tended systematically to undermine the initial optimism and consensus which existed in Central and Eastern Europe right after the collapse of the command system. In its design and application, conventional stabilization has failed largely because its economic consequences were socially divisive and not directed at building social consensus during the hard times of transition.

Fortunately, from an economic point of view, consensus-building is not only essential, but also quite naturally attainable through a set of economic policies that are conducive to economic growth in Central and Eastern Europe. The first step in this direction is to recognize the central role of aggregate demand management in recessionary circumstances. In the first place, conventional stabilization erred because it did not adequately take into account in its theoretical framework the influence exerted by the reduction in aggregate demand on the level of economic activity. As a result, it systematically underestimated the recessionary impact of stabilization on output and employment and its divisive impact on society.

However, once the importance of aggregate demand management is recognized in the present circumstances of Central and Eastern Europe, two policy implications follow more or less directly. *First*, aggregate demand expansion could have a considerably faster speed of adjustment compared to supply expansion. Therefore, the positive impact of the policies we recommend should be visible within a short time span which is of crucial practical importance in a democracy. This is because the enterprises and other micro-units or the agents in the economy respond relatively slowly to changed incentives. At the same time, restructuring and other similar measures are time-consuming. In contrast, at least one of the important elements governing aggregate demand, namely expansionary fiscal policy through government budget deficit, can be adjusted relatively fast, once we reject intellectually the mistaken idea that the government should try to reduce its budget deficit under *all* circumstances. Indeed, the very attempt to reduce the budget deficit in a deep recession becomes self-defeating by deepening the recession even further. Moreover, by accepting the mistaken notion that a balanced budget is the basis of 'sound' fiscal policy under *all* circumstances, governments in Central and Eastern Europe are surrendering their most crucial policy instrument for stimulating economic growth.

This is also related to a *second* policy implication of demand management in Central and Eastern Europe. There is no disagreement that, for various reasons, government budget deficits should not be used indiscriminately over a long time for stimulating demand. It would be decidedly preferable from the policy point of view over the longer run to stimulate other major components of aggregate demand, namely, business investment and trade surplus. Nevertheless, these components of aggregate demand are far less under the immediate direct control of the government (compared to budget deficit) and can be influenced only indirectly and relatively slowly. For this reason, there is a logic to an initial devaluation to improve the trade balance, and a substantial degree of liberalization of prices. The reason is that given the legacy of the command economy, some initial steps in the direction of more realistic exchange rates and prices were essential, not only for introducing competition, but also for improving the trade and investment climate in these economies. It is also from the same policy perspective that we point to the need to improve the profitability of private investment in long-term capital formation by following a monetary policy which reduces the exorbitantly high nominal interest rates. However, the central point is to realize that, as the economic climate for business investment and export promotion (i.e. the other main components of aggregate demand) can improve only slowly, and indirectly, an initial stimulation of demand through government budget deficit would play a complementary role in improving the longer-run economic climate for growth.

It deserves emphasis that business investment plays a crucial role in transition and growth, while government fiscal and monetary policies can play only a supportive role. In this respect, our perspective is not so different from that of conventional stabilization. But on the critical issue of *how* to improve the profitability of and stimulate private investment, conventional stabilization policies have clearly failed so far. This is amply evidenced by the fact that the presumed automatic transition from stabilization to economic growth is proceeding much more slowly than expected. The main reason for the "diminished expectations" is the inadequacy of the theoretical framework of conventional stabilization, in so far as it fails to see the influence of aggregate demand management on the profitability of private investment.

Different measures of conventional stabilization are aimed at increasing the profit margin per unit of sale. However, total profits depend not only on that margin *per unit* of sale, but also on the *volume* of sales. In other words, the rate of profit, i.e. profit per unit of invested capital (in accountants' book value), depends both on the profit margin and on the degree of capacity utilization (which may be assumed equal to the volume of sales, assuming no change in inventories).

The rate of profit realized may go down if the improvement in the margin of profit per unit of output is quantitatively outweighed by a decline in the degree of capacity utilization. The problem with the conventional stabilization package, intending mostly to increase the profit margin per unit of sale, may now become obvious. It may increase the profit margin, but decrease capacity utilization and the volume of sales disproportionately more through demand restriction, so that the rate of profit realized, as well as that expected, may decline in the process. The result would be a worsening, not an improvement in the climate for private investment due to stabilization, as indeed is being evidenced in several of the Central and Eastern European economies.

The way out of this dilemma in the short run is to rely on expansionary fiscal and monetary policies, especially government budget deficit, greater availability of credits and lower nominal interest rates as the borrowing cost of finance for business. By expanding demand, these policies will raise the degree of capacity utilization and simultaneously increase the expected rate of profit to encourage private investment. In Central and Eastern Europe there is no justification for the belief that government budget deficit would 'crowd out' private investment; instead, in all probability, it would 'crowd in' more private investment by playing a complementary role.

The mutually reinforcing or symbiotic relation between government policy and private investment needed during transition also draws attention to the central *social* advantage of suitably targeting expansionary demand management policies in deep recession. By expanding private profitability through higher capacity utilization brought about by larger government expenditure on essential welfare measures and socio-economic infrastructure, a strong economic basis for social consensus during transition may be created. The point may be illustrated by the telling example of residential building.

The situation with respect to housing construction has deteriorated at an alarming rate in Central and Eastern Europe. Expansionary government fiscal and monetary policies targeted partly at improving the desperate housing situation would create some economic hope and thus a basis for consensus among the population at large. Even more importantly, it would indirectly improve the climate for private investment by raising total profit through higher sales.

Housing construction is an important example of expansionary demand management in Central and Eastern Europe, but not the only one. The same role can be played by investment in infrastructure, by financing of different measures foreseen in the industrial policy framework or by direct support of the developing private sector, especially small firms. It has been one of the tragic errors of economic policy in these countries to sacrifice these sensible options for consensus building in the mistaken belief that even in a deep recession the budget must be balanced and contractionary policies continued. As a result, some policy makers have taken recourse to ideological measures for building consensus, such as privatization through distribution of vouchers. However, even though this may be appealing to the public for a short while, it can hardly be sustained over a longer period. In all probability it has been counterproductive even in the short run by worsening the climate for private investment and by creating ambiguities in property rights and in the structure of control at the enterprise level.

In normal conditions, there are two major barriers to expansionary government policies for creating such social consensus which are also frequently emphasized in the policy debates in Central and Eastern Europe. These two barriers are inflation and trade deficit. While under normal conditions inflation is propelled largely by excess demand the current inflationary process in most of these countries is not rooted primarily in excess demand, but is rather of a cost-push nature. The way out of this inflation is not further demand compression, but raising short-term labour productivity through higher capacity utilization, which in turn requires expansionary policies. Paradoxically the immediate inflationary barrier in Central and Eastern Europe can be overcome not by further demand contraction but rather by demand expansion. It should, however, be accompanied by an income policy adjusting money wage claims to increasing labour productivity.

The real barrier to expansionary demand policies in Central and Eastern Europe might be created by an unsustainable position regarding the trade deficit. Recognition of this barrier calls for a more controlled pace of trade liberalization, especially concerning import, in the near future and also for specifically designed industrial policies for export promotion in the longer run. The pressure on the balance of payments could also be eased partly by undertaking primarily expansionary investment programmes which are not directly import-intensive (like housing construction mentioned earlier). A judiciously controlled pace of import liberalization combined with a government capital expenditure pattern which has relatively low import content, could provide the needed direction for combining expansionary policies with a tolerable balance-of-payments position. The situation could be eased tremendously through a substantially higher inflow of foreign capital and granting alleviations in debt servicing. Such international cooperation and assistance could no doubt be of help in the path of transition. But even without sufficient international support, which Central and Eastern Europe is hoping for, the alternative path to transition we are proposing has a considerably higher chance of success.[6] The fundamental reason for this is our emphasis on the need for social cooperation as the basis for any politically sustainable strategy. In our view, economic policies must be designed to build social consensus during the most difficult years of transition. Without this essential basis for economic policy, the fragile democratic system may not survive a drawn-out economic crisis in some of these countries.

Notes

This paper draws heavily on Laski et al. (1993). Background research for the working paper was carried out by a study group under the direction of Kazimierz Laski, and included Amit Bhaduri, Friedrich Levcik, Dragoslav Avramović, János Fath, Michael Landesmann, and Dariusz K. Rosati, as well as the staff of WIIW. The final paper was compiled by Amit Bhaduri, Kazimierz Laski and Friedrich Levcik.

1. We concentrate here on stabilization problems, hence disregard the important though limited progress in the privatization issue and the rather modest achievements in the field of economic restructuring.

2. It is quite amazing that some students of the transformation process who vehemently disputed data concerning the decline of output, suddenly lost their critical attitude when in the first part of 1992 statistics started to show a slowing down of the decline in the leading reform countries.
3. For details see Vintrová (1993, pp. 28–34), Chmiel (1991) and Kádár (1992, p. 7).
4. In the national income accounting framework, equilibrium in the national economy appears as:

$$GDP = C + I + G + NX = W + R$$

where income is composed of wages W and profits R, both before taxation, and expenditures are composed of private consumption C, gross business investment I_B, government expenditures for goods and services G, and trade balance on account of goods and non-factor services NX. Subtracting taxes T (including social security payments and net of government transfers) and consumption from both sides of the equation we obtain:

$$I_B + (G - T) + E = [(W + R) - T] - C$$

or:

$$I_B + NX = S + BS$$

where the right-hand side represents savings (net of taxation) and $BS = T - G$. Since the budget deficit BD equals $-BS$, total investment I in the national economy can be written as:

$$I = I_B + BD + NS = S$$

The interpretation of the last equation in a demand-determined economy with buyers' markets is crucial. Since expenditure determines income (and output) in the demand-determined situation, this equation shows that in every period, what is saved is determined by private investment plus budget deficit plus the export surplus.
5. This is quite convincingly illustrated by data concerning price and quantity changes in industry and agriculture. In 1991, in the three leading reform countries (and already in 1990, in Poland), when the effects of restricted real demand were already fully felt, agricultural procurement prices declined sharply in relation to industrial producer prices, while agricultural output dropped much more slowly than industrial output. Hence, industry reacted to decreasing real demand mostly by volume changes, agriculture mostly by price changes.
6. However, a substantially softer frame of conditionality (like dropping the insistence on lowering the budget deficit under conditions of economic recession) for credits to be granted by international institutions or the G-24 would be indispensable.

References

Ackley, Gardner (1978), *Macroeconomics: Theory and Policy*, Collier Macmillan International Editions.

Altmann, Franz Lothar, Hermann Clement and Aleksandar M. Vacić (1991), Introduction to 'Reforms in Foreign Economic Relations of Eastern Europe and the Soviet Union', ECE, *Economic Studies*, 2, United Nations, New York.

Bhaduri, Amit (1992), 'Conventional Stabilization and the East European Transition', in Sándor Richter (ed.), *The Transition From Command to Market Economies in East-Central Europe*, Boulder: Westview Press, pp. 13–32.

Bhaduri, A. and S. Marglin (1990), 'Unemployment and the Real Wage: the Economic Basis of Contesting Political Ideologies', *Cambridge Journal of Economics*, December.

Blanchard, Olivier, Rudiger Dornbusch, Paul Krugman, Richard Layard and Lawrence Summers (1991), *Reform in Eastern Europe*, Cambridge, Mass.: The MIT Press.

112 *Kazimierz Laski*

Bolkowiak, Izabella (1992), 'Przyczyny załamania systemu dochodów państwa' (The causes of the collapse of the system of state revenues), *Życie gospodarcze* (Weekly), no. 22 (2718), Warsaw, 31 May.

Bruno, Michael (1992), 'Stabilization and Reform in Eastern Europe: A Preliminary Evaluation', *IMF Working Paper* WP/92/30, International Monetary Fund, May.

Brus, Wlodzimierz and Kazimierz Laski (1989), *From Marx to the Market. Socialism in Search of an Economic System*, Oxford: Clarendon Press.

Bugaj, Ryszard (1990), 'Rząd kocha makro', *Gazeta wyborcza,* 15 June.

Calvo, G.A. and F. Coricelli (1991), 'Stabilizing a Previously-Centrally-Planned Economy: Poland 1990', *Economic Policy: A Europect Forum*, Prague, 17–19 October 1991, mimeo, vol. I, pp. 208–25.

Cavallo, Domingo (1977), *Stagflationist Effects of Monetarist Stabilization Policies* (unpublished Ph. D. dissertation), Harvard University, Cambridge, Mass.

'Central European' (1992), *RFE/RL Research Report*, March.

'Central European' (1992), *RFE/RL Research Report*, April.

'China really is on the move' (1992), *Fortune International*, 20 (5 October), 27.

Chmiel, Józef (1991), 'Sytuacja ekonomiczna Polski w 1991 roku i sugestie co do przyszlej polityki gospodarczej', in *Prowizoryczny szacunek produktu krajowego brutto w 1991 roku*, Zakład badań statystyczno-ekonomicznych Głównego Urzędu Statystycznego i Polskiej Akademii Nauk, Studia i Materiały, Zeszyt 40, Warsaw.

Dąbrowski, M. (1991), 'Gorączka inflacyjna' (Inflationary fever), *Rzeczpospolita*, 4 February.

Datta-Chaudhuri, M.K. (1981), 'Industrialization and Foreign Trade: the Development Experience of South Korea and the Philippines', in Eddy Lee (ed.), *Export-Led Industrialization and Development*, International Labour Organization.

Dornbusch, R., F. Leslie and C.H. Helmers (1988), *The Open Economy: Tools for Policy Makers in Developing Countries*, Oxford: Oxford University Press.

Dornbush, R. (1990), 'From Stabilization to Growth', *NBER Working Paper 3302*, National Bureau of Economic Research, Cambridge, Mass.

Drewnowski, Jan (1990), 'Paradoksy polskiej gospodarki', *Trybuna* (Political Quarterly), no. 65/121, London.

'Eastern Europe hesitates' (1992), *The Economist*, 16 May.

Flassbeck, Heiner (1992), 'Verfehlte Geldpolitik', *DIW-Wochenbericht*, 59 (31–32), Berlin, 30 July.

Glikman, Paweł (1990), 'Recesja i rozwój', *Życie gospodarcze*, no. 21 (2013), 27 May.

Główny Urząd Statystyczny (1990a), Komunikat o sytuacji społeczno-gospodarczej kraju w 1989 r., Statystyka Polski, no. 2 (9), Dodatek Rzeczpospolitej, 1 February.

Główny Urząd Statystyczny (1990b), *Biuletyn statystyczny*, no. 1, Warsaw.

Główny Urząd Statystyczny (1991), *Informacja o sytuacji społeczno-gospodarczej kraju. Rok 1990.*, 25 January.

Gomułka, Stanisław (1990), 'Stabilizacja i wzrost: Polska 1989-2000', paper presented at a conference organized by the Institute of Finance in Poland, 30–31 May (mimeographed).

Havlik, Peter (1991), 'East–West GDP Comparisons: Problems, Methods and Results', *WIIW Research Reports*, no. 174, The Vienna Institute for Comparative Economic Studies, Vienna, September.

Hume, Ian (1992), Statement of the Chief of the World Bank Mission to Poland, as quoted in *Gazeta wyborcza*, no. 158 (930), 7 July.

Hunya, Gábor (1991), 'Speed and Level of Privatization of Big Enterprises in Central and Eastern Europe – General Concepts and Hungarian Practice', *WIIW Research Reports*, no. 176, The Vienna Institute for Comparative Economic Studies, Vienna, October.

Kádár, Béla (1992), 'Vissatekintees es elörepillantás', *Külgazdaság*, no. 3.

Kalecki, Michał (1935), 'The Essence of the Business Upswing', in Jerzy Osiatyński (ed.), *Collected Works of Michal Kalecki*, Volume I, Capitalism, Oxford: Clarendon Press 1991.

Kalecki, Michał (1937), 'A Theory of Commodity, Income, and Capital Taxation', in Jerzy Osiatyński (ed.), *Collected Works of Michal Kalecki*, Volume I, Capitalism, Oxford: Clarendon Press 1991.

Kalecki, Michał (1971), *Selected Essays on the Dynamics of the Capitalist Economy*, Cambridge: Cambridge University Press.

Khan, Mohsin S. and Malcolm D. Knight (1985), 'Fund-Supported Adjustment Programs and Economic Growth', *IMF Occasional Paper*, no. 41.

Kluson, V. (1992), 'Alternative Methods of Privatization', *Prague Economic Papers*, 92/1.

Kołodko, Grzegorz W. (1991), *Transition from Socialism and Stabilization Policies. The Polish Experience*, paper presented at the 32nd Annual Convention of the International Studies Association, 'New Dimensions in Internal Relations', Vancouver, 19–23 March 1991, mimeographed.

Kołodko, Grzegorz W. and Michał Rutkowski (1991), 'The Problem of Transition from a Socialist to a Free Market Economy: The Case of Poland', *The Journal of Social, Political and Economic Studies*, vol. 16, no. 2, Summer.

Kornai, János (1980), *Economics of Shortage*, Amsterdam: North-Holland Publishing Company.

Kornai, János (1993), 'Transformational Recession. A General Phenomenon Examined through the Example of Hungary's Development', *Economie Appliquée*, no. 2.

Lane, Timothy D. (1992), 'Die Umgestaltung der polnischen Wirtschaft', *Finanzierung & Entwicklung*. Vierteljahresschrift des Internationalen Währungsfonds und der Weltbank in Zusammenarbeit mit dem HWWA Institut für Wirtschaftsforschung-Hamburg, vol. 29, no. 2, June.

Laski, Kazimierz (1990), 'O niebezpieczeństwach związanych z planem stabilizacji gospodarki narodowej', *Gospodarka narodowa*, no. 2/3, Warsaw.

Laski, Kazimierz et al. (1993), 'Transition from the Command to the Market System: what went wrong and what to do now?', *WIIW Working Papers*, no. 1, The Vienna Institute for Comparative Economic Studies, Vienna.

Levcik, Friedrich (1991), 'The Place of Convertibility in the Transformation Process', in John Williamson (ed.), *Currency Convertibility in Eastern Europe*, Institute for International Economics, Washington, D.C.

Lipiński, Jan (1990), 'Przypuszczalne skutki pobudzenia wzrostu popytu. Aneks no. 2', in *Drogi wyjścia z polskiego kryzysu gospodarczego*, PTE Warszawa, December.

Lipiński, Jan (1991), 'Warunki wyjścia z recesji' (Conditions of coming out of the recession), *Gospodarka narodowa*, no. 11–12, Warsaw.

McCracken, Paul W. (1990), 'Thoughts on Marketizing State-managed Economies', *Economic Impact*, no. 71, 1990/2.

Molta, M. (1992), 'Sunk costs and trade liberalisation', *Economic Journal*, May.

Nuti, D.M. (1990), *Internal and International Aspects of Monetary Disequilibrium in Poland*, paper presented at the Working Group on Aid Programs for Hungary and Poland, meeting of 6 February 1990 at EC–DG–II, Brussels, mimeographed.

'Ökonomische Problematik der Notenbankfinanzierung' (1985), *Finanzmärkte*, Beirat für Wirtschafts- und Sozialfragen, Vienna.

Oppenheimer, Peter (1991), 'Economic Reforms and Transitional Policies: Summary of Discussion', in M. Kaser and A.M. Vacić (eds), *Reforms in Foreign Economic Relations of Eastern Europe and the Soviet Union. Economic Studies*, no. 2, United Nations Economic Commission for Europe, New York.

Paradysz, Stanisław (1991), 'Analiza struktury produkcji przemyslowej w latach 1989 i 1990. Aneks Nr. 1', in *Drogi wyjścia z polskiego kryzysu gospodarczego*, Ekspertyza dla Komitetu Badań Naukowych, Polskie Towarzystwo Ekonomiczne, Warsaw, December.

Pasinetti, Luigi (1988), 'Technical Progress and International Trade', *Empirica. Austrian Economic Papers*, vol. 15, no. 1.

Pohl, Reinhard (1992), 'Geld- und Kreditexpansion gegenwärtig kein Inflationssignal', *DIW-Wochenbericht*, vol. 59, no. 36, Berlin, 3 September.

Polak, J.J. (1957), 'Monetary Analysis of Income Formation and Payments Problems', *IMF Staff Papers*, pp. 1–50.

Portes, Richard (1992a), 'The contraction of Eastern Europe's Economies' (Comments on M. Blejer and A. Gelb, IMF-World Bank Conference, 4–5 June 1992), mimeographed.

Portes, Richard (1992b), 'Is There a Better Way?', *International Economic Insights*, vol. III, no. 3.

'Privatization: A Special Report' (1992), *RFE/RL Research Report*, vol. 1, no. 17, April.

Raport Instytutu Finansow (1992), no. 30, Warsaw, October.

Rosati, Dariusz K. (1992), paper presented at the conference on 'The Current State of and Future Prospects for Political and Economic Transformation in East-Central European Countries', Vienna, 3–4 December, mimeo.

Rostowski, J. (1991), 'A Comment', in H. Siebert (ed.), *The Transformation of Socialist Economies*, Institut für Weltwirtschaft, Kiel.

Rubel, Maria and Grzegorz Wójtowicz (1990), 'Bilans płatniczy 1989', *Życie gospodarcze*, no. 14, 9 April.

Sachs, Jeffrey (1990a), 'Interview. Charting Poland's Economic Rebirth', *Challenge*, January–February.

Sachs, Jeffrey (1990b), 'A Tremor, Not Necessarily a Quake, for Poland', *International Herald Tribune*, 30 November.

State Bank of Czechoslovakia (1992), *CSFR Balance of Payments 1991*, Annual Report 1991.

Tanzi, Vito (1992), 'Financial Markets and Public Finance in the Transformation Process', *IMF Working Papers* WP/92/29, International Monetary Fund, April.

Taylor, L. (1988), *Varieties of Stabilization Experience*, Oxford: Clarendon Press.

Taylor, L. (1991), *Income Distribution, Inflation and Growth*, Cambridge, Mass.: MIT Press.

Tinbergen, J. (1952), *The Design of Economic Policy*, Amsterdam: North-Holland Publishing Company.

United Nations Economic Commission for Europe (1992), *Economic Survey of Europe in 1991–1992*, United Nations, New York.

Vintrová, Růžena (1993), 'Macroeconomic Analysis of the Transformation in the CSFR', *WIIW Research Reports*, no. 188, The Vienna Institute for Comparative Economic Studies, Vienna, January.

Valentinyi, Akos (1992), 'Monetary policy and stabilization in Hungary', *Soviet Studies*, vol. 44, no. 6.

Wiles, Peter (1991), 'Die kapitalistische Siegessicherheit in Osteuropa', *Europäische Rundschau*, no. 3.

Wyczałkowski, Marian (1991), quoted in '... Rada ekonomiczna', in *Życie gospodarcze*, no. 47, 24 November.

6 Patterns of Economic Transition and Structural Adjustments[1]

Amit Bhaduri

1 The framework

The current state of the debate on macroeconomic 'stabilization' and 'structural adjustment' has an exceptionally unclear theoretical basis. It is often implicitly assumed, if not explicitly stated, that the various policies of economic liberalization would tend to strengthen private initiative in relation to the public sector in order to spearhead the process of transition to a more efficient, market-oriented economy. This paper presents a general analytical scheme for identifying the circumstances under which this could be feasible.

While both the public and the private sector coexist in any economy, the nature of their economic interaction can be varied depending on the particular structure of the economy. The method of enquiry followed in this paper consists of capturing formally the possible patterns of interaction and analysing their dynamic implications from the point of view of economic transition.

Economic interaction entails that each sector's revenues as well as costs are influenced by the economic activities of the other sector. Let subscripts 1 and 2 stand for the public and the private sector respectively. Assuming for simplicity that the level of economic activity of a sector is proxied by the level of output of that sector, the equations defining the profits of the two sectors are:

$$\pi_i = R_i(Y_1, Y_2) - C_i(Y_1, Y_2), i = 1, 2 \tag{6.1}$$

where p_i = profit, R_i = revenue, C_i = cost, and Y_i = output, of sector i.

Total differentiation of (6.1) yields the increment in profit in each sector as:

$$d\pi_1 = m_{11}dY_1 + m_{12}dY_2$$

$$d\pi_2 = m_{21}dY_1 + m_{22}dY_2 \tag{6.2}$$

116

where

$$m_{ij} = \left(\frac{\partial R_i}{\partial Y_j} - \frac{\partial C_i}{\partial Y_j} \right), \quad i, j = 1, 2$$

Thus, the diagonal elements m_{ii} represent the difference between marginal revenue and marginal cost in a sector i, when the other sector j has an unchanged level of economy activity. The off-diagonal elements m_{ij} ($i \neq j$) capture the nature of economic interaction between the two sectors, e.g.

$$m_{12} \equiv \left(\frac{\partial R_1}{\partial Y_2} - \frac{\partial C_1}{\partial Y_2} \right)$$

shows how the marginal revenue and the marginal cost of (public) sector 1 are affected when, despite its own output level remaining unchanged, its marginal revenue and cost are affected due to changes in the level of output of (private) sector 2. A symmetrical interpretation holds also for m_{21}.

Economic interactions captured by the non-zero off-diagonal terms ($m_{ij} \neq 0$, $i \neq j$) are possible through different routes. Broadly speaking, purely demand-side interactions, e.g. through substitutability or complementarity between the goods produced by the two sectors, affect the marginal revenues through price or quantity competition affecting the price elasticity of demand. More importantly, demand and marginal revenues are also influenced by the 'size of the market', so that the level of economic activity of each sector contributes to aggregate demand. Pure supply-side interactions influence costs. However, most important liberalization policies do not operate exclusively either on the demand- or on the supply-side. Let a few examples suffice to illustrate the point. A contractionary domestic credit policy – a typical component of 'financial programming' in IMF-style stabilization policy – reduces demand to depress marginal revenue, but may also increase marginal cost through higher cost of borrowing finance for working capital (see Bhaduri, 1992; Calvo and Coricelli, 1992). A restrictive fiscal policy resulting in lower government budget deficit, not only depresses marginal revenue through the lowering of aggregate demand, but may also lower marginal costs, especially if it also results in a lower interest rate.[2] Devaluation of the domestic currency is known to increase domestic revenue per unit of export as well as domestic costs of the imported inputs. Finally, price liberalization may depress marginal revenue through international price competition, but also domestic costs through the assured availability of cheaper or better-quality imported inputs and reduction in inventory holdings (Kornai, 1993; Winiecki, 1992). In short, macroeconomic policies operate typically both on the demand- and on the supply-side, and thus affect both marginal revenue and marginal cost of a sector, directly (i.e. through the diagonal elements m_{ii}) as well as indirectly (i.e. through the off-diagonal elements m_{ij}, $i \neq j$). Consequently, evaluation of macroeconomic policies within the present framework is feasible only to the extent we can predict how the coefficients m_{ij} change in response to such policies.

2 Transitional dynamics

Economic transition would generally require structural adjustments in the pattern of production of an economy, especially through the creation of new capacities in particular lines of production.[3] If the private sector is to play a leading role in this process, private investments must respond to the stimuli offered by the various policies of economic liberalization. In a market environment, at least as a first approximation this could be interpreted as the response of the composition of public to private investment to the differences in the profit expectations of the two sectors.[4]

Since we presume that structural adjustments proceed through additional capacity creation in different branches of production, incremental output in a sector results from investments carried out in that sector. Assuming constant incremental output capital ratios, equation (6.2) is transformed into

$$d\pi_1 = a_{11}X_1 + a_{12}X_2$$

$$d\pi_2 = a_{21}X_1 + a_{22}X_2$$

(6.3)

where $a_{ij} = m_{ij} b_j$, and the incremental output capital ratio of a sector, $b_j = (dY_j/X_j)$, and $X_j =$ investment in sector j ($j = 1, 2$).

From equation (6.3), the rates of return on investments in the two sectors are defined in terms of their investment composition, i.e.

$$r_1 = a_{11} + \frac{a_{12}}{x}$$

$$r_2 = a_{21}x + a_{22}$$

(6.4)

where the rate of return on investment in a sector, $r_j = (d\pi_j/X_j)$ and $x = (X_1/X_2)$. If the pattern of investment responds to differences in the rates of return on investment, then[5]

$$\frac{\dot{X}_1}{X_1} - \frac{\dot{X}_2}{X_2} = \frac{\dot{x}}{x} = k(r_1 - r_2), k > 0, x > 0 \tag{6.5}$$

We set $k = 1$ without any loss of generality in the present context for notational simplicity, to obtain from (6.4) and (6.5)

$$\dot{x} = -a_{21}x^2 + (a_{11} - a_{22})x + a_{12}, x > 0 \tag{6.6}$$

The dynamics depicted by (6.6) are easy to examine if we assume that (marginal) revenue and cost conditions remain roughly constant during the process of transition. Because this means that additional outputs resulting solely from new investments are not subject to economies of scale leaving all the coefficients a_{ij} constants.[6] Thus, changes over time in the investment composition of the two sectors are guided by a simple quadratic equation on the right-hand side of (6.6).

Nevertheless, even this simple case provides some interesting economic insights that can be more easily described by drawing analogies from evolutionary biology.[7]

Somewhat like two interacting biological species, when the public and the private sector are in a mutually supportive role of symbiosis, the profit of each sector would tend to increase due to a higher level of economic activity of the other. For instance, this may happen on the supply side through the creation of external economies which reduce marginal costs

$$(\text{i.e. } \frac{\partial C_i}{\partial Y_j} < 0, \ i \ne j)$$

or on the demand side, because marginal revenue is increased through an expansion of the market of one sector due to higher activity in the other

$$(\text{i.e. } \frac{\partial R_i}{\partial Y_j} > 0, \ i \ne j)$$

As a result, in such cases of *mutual symbiosis* all the off-diagonal terms would have positive signs. It is easy to check from (6.6) that, with both a_{12} and a_{21} positive, there is only one positive root at $x = x^*$ which defines a stable composition of public to private investment.[8] Because to the left of x^*, x increases, while to its right x decreases.[9]

Figure 6.1

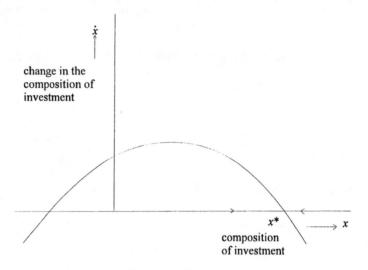

Figure 6.1 illustrates this case of mutual symbiosis between the public and private sectors. It also shows that, in a cooperative economic arrangement of mutualism, economic transition is necessarily incomplete, as both sectors coexist and settle to a steady composition of investment at $x = x^* > 0$.

In the polar opposite case, the two sectors are in fierce *competition* because an increased level of economic activity in either sector reduces the level of profit of the other sector. With the off-diagonal elements a_{12} and a_{21} both negative, the only positive root at $x = x^*$ is unstable in the entire range $x > 0$, as shown in Figure 6.2. This implies that relentless competition leads to the 'competitive extinction' of one sector by the other, resulting in complete economic transition. This occurs in favour of (the private) sector 2 if initial investment composition $x_0 < x^*$, but in favour of (the public) sector 1 if $x_0 > x^*$.[10]

Between the polar extremes of unambiguous economic cooperation and conflict between the public and the private sector leading from incomplete (Figure 6.1) to complete (Figure 6.2) economic transition, more ambiguous cases may arise. For instance, when the profits of (the public) sector 1 are increased as a result of higher economic activity in (the private) sector 2, e.g. through the generation of higher demand for the former's output, coefficient a_{12} is positive. However, higher output of (the public) sector 1 may reduce at the same time private profits, e.g. through discriminatory allocation of credit in favour of the public sector to make a_{21} negative. Similarly, one could think of examples of economic interaction in the obverse case with $a_{12} < 0$ and $a_{21} > 0$.

Figure 6.2

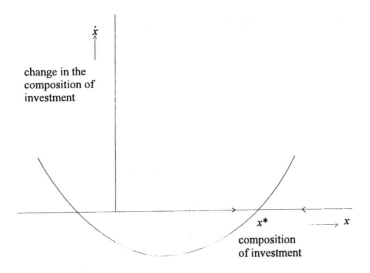

In all such cases of mixed or ambiguous interaction where the two sectors are partly in a co-operative and partly in a conflictive economic relation, the off-diagonal elements (a_{12} and a_{21}) have mixed signs.[11] It is easy to check from equation (6.6) that this may result in multiple equilibria, i.e. two positive, real roots, x^* and x^{**}, of which one is stable but the other unstable. For instance, with $a_{21} > 0$ but $a_{12} < 0$, we would have Figure 6.1a, while Figure 6.2a holds in the obverse case, $a_{21} < 0$ but $a_{12} > 0$. Moreover, real (positive or negative) roots may not even exist, as is shown by the corresponding broken curves in the two diagrams. Note in particular that, if both the sectors have roughly the same rate of return on investment without interaction, i.e. $a_{11} = a_{22}$, then in *all* cases characterized by mixed signs for the off-diagonal elements, roots are conjugate complex and real solutions do not exist. However, since x continuously increases or decreases in all these cases, *complete* economic transition could result.

Figures 6.1a and 6.2a[12]

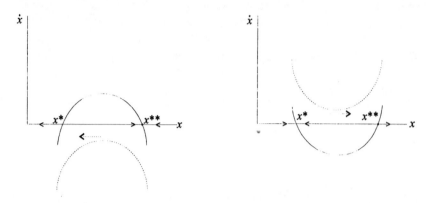

3 Economic implications

Before the preceding somewhat abstract characterization of the different patterns of transitional interaction between the public and the private sector can be applied to specific problems, some economic implications of equation (6.3), which provided the basis for the transitional dynamics, need to be highlighted.

Equation (6.3) implies a distinction between the commercial and the social profitability of a sector. While the commercial rates of return (r_j) were obtained in equation (6.4), the social return on investment in either sector can be obtained by summing up the corresponding column elements of (6.3).[13] Social profit generated per unit of investment in (the public) sector 1 and (the private) sector 2 respectively are,

$$n_1 = (a_{11} + a_{21})$$

$$n_2 = (a_{22} + a_{12})$$

(6.7)

The difference between the generation of social profit in equation (6.7) and its commercial appropriation in equation (6.4) per unit of investment in a sector characterizes the nature of its economic interaction with the other sector. More explicitly, from (6.7) and (6.4),

$$f_1 = (n_1 - r_1) = \frac{a_{21} X_1 - a_{12} X_2}{X_1}$$

and

(6.8)

$$f_2 = (n_2 - r_2) = \frac{a_{12}X_2 - a_{21}X_1}{X_2}$$

The right-hand side of (6.8) shows the *net* positive or negative contribution made to the other sector per unit of investment in a sector. Moreover, this difference between the generation and the appropriation of profit by a sector does not depend only on the investment decision made by that sector, but also on the investment by the other sector. Thus the appropriability of the benefits of investment depends on the particular regime of property rights, which may be biased in favour of either sector (see section 4).

Our framework was deliberately simplified by restricting the dynamic analysis to only positive values of x (e.g. equation 6.5). Since *gross* investment including depreciation is necessarily non-negative, this restriction could be justified when X_j is gross investment in sector j.[14] But it obscures the role that depreciation might play through disinvestment resulting in declining productive capacity in some sectors during the process of structural adjustment. Since the concept of the incremental output capital ratio is meant to relate causally incremental (capacity) output to *net* investment, we have

$$v_j = \frac{dY_j}{I_j}$$

with

$$X_j = I_j + D_j; j = 1, 2$$

where v_j =   the (engineering) ratio of incremental output
                        to net investment, assumed constant
         I_j =   net investment
         D_j =   depreciation, and
         X_j =   gross investment.

Since $b_j = (dY_j/X_j)$ in equation (6.3), we have

$$b_j = (I - u_j)v_j; j = 1, 2 \tag{6.9}$$

where $u_j = D_j/X_j$.

Therefore, so long as $I > u_j$ implying positive net investment, the signs of the corresponding coefficients a_{ij} in (6.3) are unchanged, and the dynamics of economic transition presented in the last section do not change qualitatively. However for $u_j > I$, net investment in sector j becomes negative and the signs of corresponding a_{ij}'s are reversed. This reversal of the relationship between the two sectors due to declining productive capacity in a particular sector becomes useful for analysing problems like a shrinking military sector and sudden loss of the traditional export markets (section 5).

4 Specific applications

Our framework is used to analyse some specific problems that have arisen during the process of economic transition, especially in some former centrally planned economies trying to transform themselves into market-oriented systems.[15]

a) Infrastructural investments by the public sector

The ideology of a 'minimalist state' suggests that the economic role of the public sector needs to be limited only to infrastructural investments in economic and social overheads like health and education. At most, its role should extend temporarily to some areas requiring very large investments, e.g. energy or communication, when private investment is found wanting. In our framework, this would allow (the private) sector 2 to appropriate part of the externalities created by infrastructural investments by (the public) sector 1, since both reduction in costs and expansion in the demand for private sector's output could take place, i.e. from (6.2)

$$m_{21} \equiv \left(\frac{\partial R_2}{\partial X_1} - \frac{\partial C_2}{\partial X_1} \right) > 0$$

Also from (6.3) and (6.9)

$$a_{21} = m_{21}b_1 = m_{21}(I - u_1)v_1 > 0$$

so long as net public investment in infrastructure remains positive.

If (the public) sector 1 benefits also from investment by (the private) sector 2 then $a_{12} > 0$. This would be the case of mutual symbiosis of Figure 6.1, indicating *incomplete* transition in the sense that positive investments by both sectors continue over time in the ratio of $x = x^*$. However, if the public sector is disadvantaged by private investment, i.e. $a_{12} < 0$, then it leads to Figure 6.1a: either incomplete transition results at $x = x^{**}$; alternatively, in the case of conjugate complex roots of the broken curve in Figure 6.1a, the economy heads for a complete transition with x decreasing, and private investment dominating over time. Interestingly, the larger is the benefit rendered by public infrastructural investment to private profit, the more likely appears this latter tendency towards a complete transition. Formally, the discriminant T in the quadratic equation (6.6) tends to become negative when $a_{12} < 0$ but a_{21} assumes large, positive values because

$$T = \left[(a_{11} - a_{22})^2 + 4a_{12}a_{21} \right]^{\frac{1}{2}} \tag{6.10}$$

However, such a process of complete transition would be economically difficult to sustain. Equation (6.4) shows why: with $a_{21} > 0$ and $a_{12} < 0$, the rates of return on investment decrease in *both* the sectors as x decreases in Figure 6.1a. Consequently, the *relative* domination of private over public investment has to take place in an economy with indefinitely declining profit expectations all around, hardly a suitable investment climate for structural adjustments. The moral is clear: the private sector cannot continue to bite the public hand (i.e. $a_{12} < 0$) which feeds it so generously (i.e. $a_{21} > 0$ and 'large') and yet succeed in making the complete transition to the 'free enterprise' system!

b) Biased property rights and privatization
Equations (6.7) and (6.8) in section 3 captured how a wedge could be driven between the generation of profit and its commercial appropriation by a sector due to economic interactions between the sectors. Nevertheless, accounting identity for the economy as a whole requires that total profit generated equals total profit appropriated. Or, in terms of increments in economy-wide profits, $d\pi = d\pi_1 + d\pi_2 = n_1X_1 + n_2X_2 = = r_1X_1 + r_2X_2$, which implies from (6.8),

$$X_1f_1 + X_2f_2 = 0, \; X_j > 0 \; (j = 1, 2) \tag{6.11}$$

i.e. the net appropriation of profits by one sector equals the net contribution to profits by the other sector.

In this framework property rights may be considered *biased* in favour of a sector i if $f_i < 0$ allowing sector i to be a *net* appropriator of profits. Market-oriented reforms are usually based on the supposition that, not only would (the private) sector 2 have a higher commercial rate of return than (the public) sector 1, but this tendency may even need strengthening through a bias in property rights in favour of the private sector. Measures such as privatization often have this implicit objective.[16]

Therefore, a configuration supposed to be working in favour of market-oriented reforms may be characterized by

$$r_2 > r_1 \text{ and } f_2 < 0, \text{ i.e. } r_2 > n_2 \tag{6.12}$$

implying from (6.11),

$$f_1 > 0, \text{ i.e. } n_1 > r_1$$

Note the above set of inequalities are *sufficiently* satisfied if

$$n_1 > n_2 \tag{6.13}$$

i.e. (the public) sector 1 has a higher social rate of return, despite being less profitable commercially.

Since the total rate of return can be written as a sectoral weighted average of either commercial or social profit, i.e.

$$\frac{d\pi}{X} = r = (r_1 x + r_2)(1 + x)^{-1} \tag{6.14}$$

where $x(1 + x)^{-1}$ and $(1 + x)^{-1}$ are the shares of sector 1 and 2 respectively in total investment, we have

$$\frac{dr}{dx} = (n_1 - n_2)(1 + x)^{-2} \tag{6.15}$$

Equations (6.5) and (6.12) to (6.15) depict a process of transition, propelled by market-oriented reforms, in which the commercial rate of return on private investment is higher (equation 6.12), driving in turn the composition of investment in favour of the private sector (equation 6.5). Accordingly, x falls over time which, from (6.13) and (6.15), implies a falling overall rate of return r in the economy. Moreover, under the classical assumption that domestic saving is a constant fraction only of profit, this implies a declining rate of growth in total saving and investment in a self-financing economy. With no change in net capital inflow from abroad, incremental investment is financed from incremental profit,[17]

$$dX = s.d\pi, 1 > s > 0$$

which yields

$$\frac{dX}{X} = g = sr \tag{6.16}$$

Consequently a falling rate of return through (6.15) also implies a declining growth in total investment due to (6.16).

However the above scenario may be considered over-simplistic. It may be argued that the propensity to save out of private profit is usually higher than that out of public profit, especially when the growth of the private 'black' economy escapes the tax net. Under these circumstances, it would appear that a higher commercial rate of return enjoyed by the private sector also helps in generating more savings in the economy. In order to analyse this situation, equations (6.14) and (6.16) are reformulated as

$$g = (s_1 r_1 x + s_2 r_2)(1+x)^{-1} \tag{6.17}$$

where $r_2 > r_1$ and $1 > s_2 > s_1 > 0$, i.e. (the private) sector 2 has both a higher commercial rate of return and a higher propensity to save out of profit. Using (6.4) and (6.17), we obtain

$$\frac{dg}{dx} = [s_1(a_{11} - a_{12}) - s_2(a_{22} - a_{21})](1+x)^{-2} \tag{6.18}$$

Since in view of (6.8) a bias in favour of private property rights involving $f_1 > 0$ and $f_2 < 0$ reduces to

$$a_{21} x > a_{12} \tag{6.19}$$

the persistence of this bias throughout the process of transition implies that inequality (6.19) would hold for all positive values of x, a condition *sufficiently* satisfied if

$$a_{21} > 0 \ \ and \ \ a_{12} < 0 \tag{6.20}$$

where configuration (6.20) corresponds to the dynamics depicted in Figure 6.1a.

Relations (6.18) and (6.20) together imply that,

$$\frac{dg}{dx} > 0 \ \ if \ \ \frac{s_1}{s_2} > \frac{a_{22} - a_{21}}{a_{11} - a_{12}}$$

Since (s_1/s_2) is a positive fraction less than unity by assumption, the satisfaction of the above inequality *necessarily* requires[18] $(a_{11} - a_{12}) > (a_{22} - a_{21})$ or, $n_1 > n_2$, as in condition (6.13). Therefore, as the higher commercial rate of return on private investment assumed in (6.12) keeps driving the composition of investment in its favour through the decreasing value of x in equation (6.5), the growth of total investment declines, if (6.13) holds in a regime biased persistently in favour of the property rights of the private sector. To re-emphasize, this possibility exists even if the private sector has a higher propensity to save and enjoys a higher commercial rate of return on its investment (equation 6.17). This apparently paradoxical result follows from the *persistent bias* in property rights in favour of a sector allowing it to be *always* a net appropriator of profits (e.g. conditions 6.19 and 6.20). Such a strategy during transition runs the danger of being counter-productive in so far as higher commercial profitability due to biased property rights (e.g. condition 6.12) may at times hide the fact that a sector is socially less profitable (e.g. condition 6.13).

c) Disinvestment: demilitarization and asset-stripping
Production may be disrupted seriously from different types of 'shocks' during the process of transition. It could result from a sudden loss of external markets (e.g. CMEA) or discontinuing largely 'useless' production of armaments or extremely poor-quality products which find superior, and at times even cheaper substitutes in a more liberalized regime of imports and prices.[19] More interestingly, it could also result from uncertain property rights in many public enterprises during the process of transition which separates *de jure* public rights from *de facto* rights of inside groups like managers, workers' representatives or, in some cases, local authorities (Olson, 1992; Schmieding, 1993). The *de facto* use-rights to property would then escape the control of *de jure* ownership-rights of the state in these public enterprises.

While any such 'large' disruption resulting from whatever source cannot be captured satisfactorily in terms of the 'small' cumulative changes of our model, it suggests a more systematic way of confronting these problems. Serious disruptions usually mean decline in the productive capacity in particular branches of production. In our framework, this is analysed by assuming that gross investment, although positive, stays significantly below replacement and depreciation requirements in those particular branches, and by some constant fraction.[20] In particular, this corresponds roughly to the case of asset-stripping, where the inside groups in some public enterprises try to 'consume' the assets through various devices like fictitious sale of assets or diversion of enterprise funds to private uses.

Consider the case where all such disinvestments are concentrated entirely in (the public) sector 1. This means that the signs of the coefficients along the first column in equation (6.3) (i.e. a_{11} and a_{21}) are reversed since $u_j > 1$ in equation (6.9). If prior to the disruptive shock both these coefficients were positive, they turn negative after the shock. As a result, from equation (6.4), the rates of return in both the sectors decline at any given value of x. Generally, this would create no additional problem for transition towards the private enterprise system, so long as private return r_2 exceeds public return r_1, after the shock.[21] However, this need not be always the case. For instance, if $a_{12} > 0$ prior to the shock, the decline in r_2 may be even greater than that in r_1 for all $x > 0$ (with the initial positive value of a_{21} turning negative through disinvestment in sector 1) after the shock. This possibility is diagrammatically exhibited in Figure 6.3 by plotting r_1 and r_2 from equation (6.4), both before and after the shock.[22] In such a case depicted in Figure 6.3, the shock would tend to change the composition of (gross) investment in favour of the public sector over time through equation (6.3), steering the economy in an unintended opposite direction.

Figure 6.3

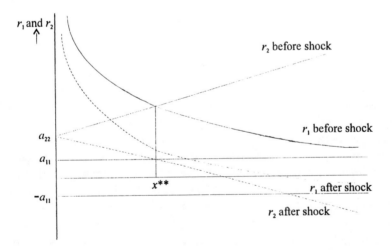

The moral of the story deserves emphasis: if the public and the private sector initially happen to be in an arrangement of mutual symbiosis prior to the shock (note both a_{12} and a_{21} are assumed positive prior to the shock in Figure 6.3), a strong disruptive shock to the public sector leading to its disinvestment may turn out to be even more disastrous for the profitability in the private sector.

5 Summary and observations

Economic liberalization is premised usually on the assumption that the private sector would spearhead the process of required structural adjustments. However, since in no economy the private sector operates in isolation, it is necessary to specify the patterns of interaction between the private and the public sector under which this may be feasible. This chapter attempts to provide an analytical framework to examine this problem.

The framework captures formally various possibilities. Somewhat in analogy with the biological evolution of two interacting species, the economic interplay between the public and the private sector could span the whole range, from mutual symbiosis of cooperation to relentless competition. Not surprisingly, coexistence of the two sectors is possible only with some degree of cooperation between them. Otherwise, under relentless competition, one sector would completely dominate the other. Thus, economic transition towards the private enterprise system would be 'incomplete' or 'complete' depending largely on the pattern and extent of economic interaction between the public and the private sector (section 2).

The pattern of economic interaction between the sectors also differentiates the 'social' from the 'commercial' return on investment in a sector. The social profit generated by a sector differs from the profit appropriated by that sector, depending on the particular regime of property rights (section 3). This idea has important consequences when applied to some specific problems that arise during the process of transition, like a programme of public investments in economic and social infrastructure, persistent 'bias' in property rights in favour of a sector or massive disruptions in investment by a sector. Counter-examples were deliberately chosen in these problem-areas to highlight a general proposition: policies that *appear* to favour the private sector may fail to do so in reality, if the pattern of economic interaction between the sectors is not taken into account (section 4).

These ideas became analytically tractable in the context of a simplified model. Two simplifying assumptions deserve special emphasis. First, the patterns of interaction between the sectors were examined in terms of their investments, but not output changes. While this translation is easy to make from equations (6.2) to (6.3) by means of incremental output–capital ratios it implies that additional output results only from the creation of new capacities, but not from changes in degree of utilization of existing capacities. This assumption may be justified in the present context in so far as structural adjustments deal with changes in the structure of productive capacities in the economy. However, it must be emphasized that this simplification amounts to concentrating solely on the longer-run problem of structural adjustments, ignoring the short-run problem of changes in output through capacity utilization.

The second simplifying assumption is linked to the first. The analytical simplicity of the model depends critically on assuming the constancy of the coefficients of economic interaction between the sectors (i.e. a_{ij} in equations (6.3) to (6.6)) which, in turn, require marginal costs and revenues to be roughly constant. This assumption may be more palatable when changes in the *scale* of operation through investment, rather than changes in the degree of utilization of existing capacities are considered. However, in principle, increasing or decreasing returns to scale as well as other factors (e.g. technical progress) leading to variable coefficients of economic interaction (a_{ij}) could be considered at the cost of greater mathematical complexity. It would introduce sharper non-linearities in the analysis (beyond the simple quadratic equation (6.6)). And the reason why we do not wish to examine such non-linearities is not simply its mathematical complexity: one needs to have good economic reasons for introducing non-linearities in the relevant form. It also deserves emphasis here that only the model with constant interaction coefficients (a_{ij}) becomes easily generalizable to the case of many sectors.

Notes

1. Research support from The Vienna Institute for Comparative Economic Studies (WIIW) and its research director, Kazimierz Laski, are gratefully acknowledged without involving them either in my views or errors that may remain. I am also indebted to Egon Matzner and the late Josef Steindl for many discussions on the issue of property rights during the process of transition.
2. A contractionary fiscal policy coupled with an unchanged monetary policy would lead to lower interest rates in standard IS-LM analysis, e.g Branson (1989).
3. We concentrate on the problem of creation of new capacities rather than the utilization of existing capacites during transition – an issue commented upon at some length in section 5. For a discussion focusing on the problem of capacity utilization and aggregate demand (in the context of East European transition) see Laski et al. (1993).
4. While the private sector may be assumed to consist of both domestic and foreign firms, problems of balance of payments associated with foreign investment are not considered in this chapter.
5. For simplicity, it is assumed that expected return is governed by realized return on investment in the simplest manner (e.g. static expectations).
6. See section 5 for a discussion on this point. Also note from equations (6.2) and (6.3) that the diagonal coefficient (a_{ii}) can be interpreted simply as constant profit margin per unit of sale, under the assumption of cost-determined prices. See Kalecki (1971) for a classic statement of the theory of cost-determined prices.
7. Various attempts at modelling formally different aspects of evolutionary biology and 'stability' of ecosystems have become common. See, in particular, Nicolis and Prigogine (1977), Rescigno and Richardson (1967), May (1976) as well as the classic work of Lotka (1956).

8. The roots are necessarily real, and of opposite signs.
9. We restrict the analysis to $x > 0$ and do not discuss the singularity at $x = 0$. Economically, this is plausible if investment is gross and not net – a point discussed in greater detail in section 3.
10. See previous endnote.
11. The constancy of the coefficients (a_{ij}) do not permit reversal of interaction e.g. from conflict to cooperation at different levels of x. This requires introducing 'significant non-linearities' (see section 5) without which the model has little mathematical richness, e.g. compared to the celebrated predator and prey dynamics due to Volterra and Lotka, see Hirsch and Smale (1974).
12. In Figure 6.1a the (private) sector 2 has beneficial symbiosis with (public) sector 1, i.e. $a_{21} > 0$. But the latter has a competitive relation with the former, i.e. $a_{12} < 0$. Only the larger root x^{**} is stable. With no real root (broken curve), x continuously decreases, i.e. the relative size of the private sector increases. In Figure 6.2a the (private) sector 2 has a competitive relation with (public) sector 1, i.e. $a_{21} < 0$. But the latter has beneficial symbiosis with the former, i.e. $a_{12} > 0$. Only the smaller root x^* is stable. With no real root (broken curve), x continuously increases, i.e. the relative size of the public sector increases.
13. The definition of social profit is independent of the sectors which appropriate it. Commercial profit, on the other hand, depends precisely on the ability to appropriate interaction.
14. See also endnote 9.
15. Although this has been the focus of our enquiry, the analysis presented in the chapter could also find some applications to problems of structural adjustments in developing countries, especially under economic liberalization programmes encouraged by the Bretton Woods institution.
16. Privatization does not necessarily imply a regime of *biased* property rights in favour of the private sector. However, in so far as commercial incentives to the private sector are strengthened through altering property rights, this entails increasing its power of appropriating profits, although it might still not make it a *net* appropriator.
17. In an open economy, investment equals savings plus current account deficit, with no changes in international reserves. By a self-financing economy, we mean a constant current account deficit being financed by a constant inflow of capital, so that additional investment has to be financed by additional profits yielding equation (6.16).
18. If $a_{11} > 0$ which means $r_1 > 0$ for at least a range of positive values of x.
19. The conventional approach is to distinguish between a 'demand' and a 'supply' shock, depending on the nature of shift in either curve, e.g. Borensztein, Dimitri and Ostry (1993).
20. There is no economic reason why the fraction u_j should be treated as constant. This is the price we pay for simplicity.
21. Some of the problems of transition with declining rates of return have been discussed in the preceding paragraphs of section 4.
22. In an early attempt to capture economic interaction in a different context, I had used similar diagrammatic analysis, e.g. Bhaduri (1981).

References

Bhaduri, A. (1981), 'Class relations and the pattern of accumulation in an agrarian economy', *Cambridge Journal of Economics*, vol. 5, no. 4, December, 233–46.

Bhaduri, A. (1992), 'Conventional stabilization and the East European transition', in S. Richter (ed.), *The Transition from Command to Market Economies in East-Central Europe*, Boulder: Westview Press, pp. 13–32.

Borensztein, E., G.D. Dimitri and J.D. Ostry (1993), 'An empirical analysis of the output declines in three eastern European countries', *IMF Staff Papers*, vol. 40, no. 1, March, 1–31.

Branson, W.H. (1989), *Macroeconomics: Theory and Policy*, 3rd edition, New York: Harper, ch. 5.

Calvo, G.A. and F. Coricelli (1992), 'Output collapse in Eastern Europe: the role of credit', paper presented at the conference on 'The macroeconomic situation in Eastern Europe', organized by the World Bank and IMF, 4–5 June.

Hirsch, M.W. and S. Smale. (1974), *Differential Equations, Dynamical Systems and Linear Algebra*, New York: Academic Press, ch. 12.

Kalecki, M. (1971), 'Costs and prices' in *Selected Essays on the Dynamics of the Capitalist Economy*, Cambridge: Cambridge University Press.

Kornai, J. (1993), 'Transformational recession', *Economie Appliquée*, vol. 46, no. 2, 181–227.

Lotka, A.J. (1956), *Elements of Mathematical Biology*, New York: Dover.

May, R.M. (1976), 'Models for two interacting populations', in R.M. May (ed.), *Theoretical Ecology: Principles and Applications*, Oxford: Blackwell Scientific Publications.

Nicolis, G. and I. Prigogine (1977), *Self-organization in Non-equilibrium Systems*, New York: John Wiley, ch. 18.

Olson, M. (1992), 'Why is economic performance even worse when communism is abolished?', University of Maryland, mimeo.

Rescigno, A. and I. Richardson (1967), 'The struggle for life; two species', *Bulletin of Mathematical Biophysics*, vol. 29, 377–88.

Schmieding, H. (1993), 'From plan to market: on the nature of the transformation crisis', *Weltwirtschaftliches Archiv*, Review of World Economics, vol. 129, no. 2, 216–53.

Laski, K. et al. (1993), 'Transition from the Command to the Market System: what went wrong and what to do now?', *WIIW Working Papers*, no. 1, The Vienna Institute for Comparative Economic Studies, Vienna, March.

Winiecki, J. (1992), 'The transition of post-Soviet-type economies: expected and unexpected developments', *Banca Nazionale del Lavoro Quarterly Review*, no. 181, June, 171–90.

7 Balance-of-Payments Constrained Growth in Central and Eastern Europe

Michael Landesmann and Josef Pöschl

1 Introduction

A crucial question to ask is whether the Central and East European countries (CEECs) have embarked upon a catching-up process. Needless to say, this question is vital for any realistic prospects of integrating Central and Eastern Europe into the European Union (EU) over the next ten to fifteen years.

This issue is also relevant for forecasting likely trade patterns between CEECs and other European economies and, more generally, the place of CEECs in the international division of labour. Several authors, including Abramovitz (1986, 1994), Verspagen (1991), Fagerberg, Verspagen and von Tunzelmann (1994), Ben-David (1994), have developed general models to deal with the possibilities of both. None of these models have been applied to current developments in CEECs. Landesmann (1995) focuses on the patterns of industrial and trade specialization in Central and Eastern Europe and asks whether there is evidence of a 'catching-up' process.

This chapter takes a more macroeconomic view of CEEC growth prospects and examines potential growth paths given the stringent constraints that the balance of payments (BOP) imposes on small open economies in the process of catching up. The question of BOP-constrained growth has been extensively studied in other contexts but – as far as we are aware – not yet in the context of the current transition and of longer-run growth scenarios of Central and Eastern Europe. In our analysis we apply and extend the balance-of-payments growth model developed by Thirlwall (1979) and McCombie and Thirlwall (1994).

In the context of current East–West European integration, BOP constraints will be an important factor in closing the income and technological gap between the CEECs and the EU. BOP constraints have been persistent features of catching-up processes in the past. Japan and

Korea faced them until the late 1970s and mid-1980s respectively, as did many of the Latin American countries in the 1970s and 1980s, Finland in the 1960s and 1970s, etc. BOP constraints will be even more important as small, open economies (such as most CEECs) attempt to minimize the use of trade policy instruments to meet the guidelines for early integration with the EU.

To demonstrate the BOP constraint on medium- to long-term growth patterns it is necessary to take into account the factors that affect this constraint. Of these factors, we identify two groups: factors that affect trade flows of goods and services and those that affect the other accounts of the BOP (the invisible, income and capital accounts).

Traditionally, two sets of structural parameters determine long-term export and import flows of goods and services: income elasticities (i.e. the reaction of import and export flows to income growth domestically and in export markets respectively) and price elasticities (the reaction of these trade flows to relative price movements). Catching up includes changes in the compositions of exports and imports over time and these changes affect income- and price-elasticities. Countries that start off with a substantial 'technology gap' (interpreted in a wide sense, including insufficient marketing, design, distributive capabilities) have to compensate for substantial 'asymmetries' in both income and price elasticities on the export and import side respectively. The reason for this is that they initially have to compete in the lower-income and more price-elastic end of the product spectrum. Over time, as catching up proceeds, this asymmetry gets reduced.

A second influence on trade flows is 'real competitiveness'. In this context the crucial variable is the evolution of the real exchange rate, or the nominal exchange rate discounted by the relative movements in the prices of imports and of import-competing commodities on the one hand, and of exports and of competing products on export markets on the other hand. We analyse factors that determine the evolution of the different components of 'real competitiveness', for instance the developments of relative wage rates and of productivity growth, and nominal exchange rates (given their strongly 'undervalued' position at the beginning of the current transition in CEECs). We also take account of 'quality catching up' which affects price competitiveness (per unit of standardized quality).

As to the second group of factors determining net inflows on the balance of payments, we analyse trade in invisibles, income accounts, capital accounts, and changes in reserve holdings.

The evidence suggests that there is a lot of country differentiation in how different CEECs compensate trade deficits in goods trade by means of surpluses in the other accounts. For instance, the Czech Republic, Slovenia and Hungary already have substantial positive net balances in invisibles trade due to income from tourism; Poland and the Czech Republic have substantial income from personal transfers (i.e. nationals working abroad). Different patterns of foreign direct investment (FDI) and portfolio investment are quite well known and, similarly, there are substantial inter-country differences in debt servicing which counts as a capital outflow. We carefully analyse all the above components of the non-goods trade accounts, income and capital accounts and project possible outcomes based on the current positions and likely future developments of the different CEECs.

The paper outlines three scenarios for longer-term balance-of-payments constrained growth paths of CEEC economies. These three scenarios are distinguished by the extent to which *different degrees of East–West European integration* might affect the external constraints on economic growth in Eastern Europe:

A base scenario (*Association Scenario*) is an extrapolation of the current state in East–West European integration and particularly of CEEC–EU relationships up to the year 2008. A second scenario (*Integration Scenario*) envisages 'near full membership'[1] of CEEC economies whereby a first group of countries (the Czech and Slovak Republics, Hungary and Poland) are assumed to become full EU members by the year 2003 and a second group (Bulgaria and Romania) by the year 2005. Finally, a pessimistic scenario (*Creeping Disintegration*) explores the implications of deteriorating CEEC–EU economic relations (a gradual re-emergence of protectionist barriers, less FDI and deteriorating access to international financial markets). The discussion of the three scenarios provides a basis to assess quantitatively both positive and negative implications of more or less rapid processes of CEEC–EU integration, although the net effect from more rapid integration is estimated to be positive.

The paper is concluded by a discussion of a number of economic policy implications of the preceding analysis.

2 The extended Thirlwall model and some modifications
2.1 Long-run steady-state growth
The Thirlwall model starts with the basic balance-of-payments identity:

$$P_d X + F = P_f ME \tag{7.1}$$

where X and M are the quantities of exports and imports respectively, F is the value of nominal (net) capital inflows measured in domestic currency, P_d is the price of exports in home currency, P_f is the price of imports in foreign currency, and E is the exchange currency (units of domestic currency for 1 unit of foreign currency).

Taking rates of change of the variables in equation (7.1) we obtain a condition for overall balance-of-payments equilibrium growth such that the rate of growth of the value of imports must equal a weighted average of the rate of growth of the value of exports and the rate of growth of the value of net capital imports:

$$\theta(p_d + x) + (1-\theta)f = p_f + m + e \tag{7.1'}$$

Lower-case letters represent rates of growth of the variables defined in (7.1) and θ and $(1-\theta)$ represent the shares of exports and net capital flows in total domestic receipts from abroad, i.e. $\theta = P_d X/(P_d X + F')$ and $(1-\theta) = F/(P_d X + F')$.

Next we define export and import functions as:

$$M = a \left(\frac{P_f E}{P_d} \right)^{\psi} Y^{\pi} \tag{7.2}$$

$$X = b \left(\frac{P_d}{P_f E} \right)^{\eta} Z^{\varepsilon} \tag{7.3}$$

where a and b are constants; ψ is the price elasticity of demand for imports ($\psi < 0$); η is the price elasticity of demand for exports ($\eta > 0$); π is the income elasticity of demand for imports; ε is the income elasticity of demand for exports; Y is domestic (real) income and Z is the level of (real) income in export markets.

Taking again rates of change of the variables, we obtain

$$m = \psi(p_f + e - p_d) + \pi y \tag{7.2'}$$

$$x = \eta(p_d - e - p_f) + \varepsilon z \tag{7.3'}$$

Substituting equations (7.2') and (7.3') into (7.1') and rearranging, we obtain:

$$y^* = \frac{(\theta\eta + \psi)(p_d - e - p_f) + (p_d - e - p_f) + \theta\varepsilon z + (1-\theta)(f - p_d)}{\pi} \tag{7.4}$$

The variable on the left-hand side, y^*, represents the BOP-constrained real income growth rate. The first term on the right-hand side gives the volume effects (on the trade balance) of relative price changes; the second term gives the terms of trade effect; the third term gives the effect of exogenous changes in real income growth in export markets; and the last term gives the effect of the rate of growth of net capital inflows on domestic real income growth.

The impact of the effects of various parameter constellations in a play model is seen in Table 7.1. In this table two basic types of scenarios are used to describe the BOP-constrained growth paths. In scenarios A current accounts are balanced and hence no support is given to domestic growth through capital imports ($\theta = 1$; $f = 0$). In scenarios B current accounts are in deficit which in itself affects the BOP-constrained growth rate and net capital imports alleviate this constraint. Both types of scenarios assume the growth rate of external demand (z) is 3 per cent per annum; and the inflation differential between domestic inflation p_d and foreign inflation p_f is 15 per cent and 4 per cent p.a. respectively.

In most scenarios (except A4, A5) a basic asymmetry in price elasticities (of exports and imports respectively) is maintained. The rationale for such an asymmetry is that CEECs export lower-processed, lower-quality commodities to the West than they import and these can be assumed to be more price-sensitive. We can thus confidently expect that the price elasticity of CEECs' exports to the world (mostly the industrialized West), η, to be greater than that of CEECs' imports (again mostly from the West), ψ. As CEEC economies upgrade their product structure, we could expect this asymmetry to narrow but we can safely assume that the gap will persist to some extent over the entire horizon of this exercise. One could make a similar argument about asymmetries in income elasticities, but we discuss this issue in more detail later on.

The following qualitative results emerge from Table 7.1:

(1) The move from a balanced to an unbalanced current account (compare the base scenarios A1 and B1) does have a severe deflationary impact on the BOP-constrained growth rate y^* if it is not sufficiently compensated by higher net capital imports (see scenarios B2, B3).

(2) The asymmetry in price elasticities accentuates the impact of real devaluations in a positive direction and real appreciations in a negative direction (compare scenarios A2 and A3 with A4 and A5).

(3) Scenarios B4 to B7 show respectively the impact of real depreciations and appreciations in the scenario of an unbalanced current account (scenarios B4 and B5), and of asymmetries in income (rather

than price) elasticities for exports and imports respectively (scenarios B6 and B7).

Table 7.1 The extended Thirlwall model (equation 7.4)

			Price elasticity		Income elasticity		Rates of change (%) of						
Exports	Imports	Coverage ratio	of exports	of imports	of exports	of imports	domestic prices	nominal exchange rate	foreign prices	real exchange rate	net capital inflows	demand in export markets	BOP-constrained GDP
X	M	θ	η	ψ	ε	π	p_d	e	p_f		f	z	y^*
Scenario A: Balanced Current Accounts													
A	50	50	1	0.8	0.6	1.2	1.2	15%	11%	4%	0%	0%	3%	3.00%
Real Depreciation or Appreciation with asymmetric price elasticities													
A	50	50	1	0.8	0.6	1.2	1.2	15%	15%	4%	-4%	0%	3%	4.33%
A	50	50	1	0.8	0.6	1.2	1.2	15%	7%	4%	4%	0%	3%	1.67%
Real Depreciation or Appreciation with symmetric price elasticities													
A	50	50	1	0.6	0.6	1.2	1.2	15%	15%	4%	-4%	0%	3%	3.67%
A	50	50	1	0.6	0.6	1.2	1.2	15%	7%	4%	4%	0%	3%	2.33%
Scenario B: Unbalanced Current Accounts													
B1	45	50	0.9	0.8	0.6	1.2	1.2	15%	11%	4%	0%	17%	3%	2.87%
Higher capital import growth													
B2	45	50	0.9	0.8	0.6	1.2	1.2	15%	11%	4%	0%	22%	3%	3.28%
B3	45	50	0.9	0.8	0.6	1.2	1.2	15%	11%	4%	0%	27%	3%	3.70%
Real Depreciation or Appreciation													
B4	45	50	0.9	0.8	0.6	1.2	1.2	15%	15%	4%	-4%	17%	3%	3.93%
B5	45	50	0.9	0.8	0.6	1.2	1.2	15%	7%	4%	4%	9%	3%	1.13%
Asymmetries in income elasticities													
B6	45	50	0.9	0.8	0.6	1.4	1.2	15%	11%	4%	0%	17%	3%	3.32%
B7	45	50	0.9	0.8	0.6	1.2	1.4	15%	11%	4%	0%	17%	3%	2.46%
Quality catch-up: q = 2%													
B8	45	50	0.9	0.8	0.6	1.2	1.2	13%	11%	4%	-2%	17%	3%	3.57%

Notes: The real exchange rate is $p_d - e - p_f$. Scenario B8 includes 'quality-adjusted' domestic price inflation $(p_d - q)$ and movements in the real exchange rate $(p_d - q) - e - p_f$.

Given that scenario B with an unbalanced current account is the historically more realistic case for catching-up economies and that one can expect a sustained asymmetry in price elasticities in trade of CEECs with the West, we can see from the scenarios that it is difficult to achieve a higher real income growth than the outside world (which is necessary for 'catching up') if the growth rates of net capital imports are high. One powerful instrument is the real depreciation of the currency; however, there are problems to use this instrument on a sustained basis as will be discussed in the next section.

One additional factor to consider is that a process of catching up involves *inter alia* a catching up in the quality of domestically produced commodities (either sold on domestic or on export markets). A simple way to introduce this factor is to redefine p_d as the 'quality-adjusted' growth rate in the price of exported or domestically sold commodities.[2] Scenario B8 shows that such a specification of quality catching up has the same effect as a real depreciation and thus provides effectively a counterweight to differential inflation rates of domestic and foreign producers.

2.2   Dynamic (year-by-year) solution of the model

A straightforward technical extension of the Thirlwall model is to solve it year by year so that some of the parameters become endogenous. The most immediate structural parameter that should be endogenized is the degree of imbalance on the current account, expressed by the ratio θ, since the development of the levels of exports and imports is endogenous in our model. The second extension we make is the endogenization (at least partially) of net capital flows. The latter is a complex issue and is discussed in more detail in section 3.3.

The partial endogenization of net capital inflows in this dynamic version of the model begins by disaggregating Net Capital Inflows (F):

$F =$ Foreign direct investment (FDI-net) + Portfolio Investment (net) +
    + Issuing of new (net) debt – Interest payments (rD) and repayment
    of old debt (βD),   (7.5)

where r is the rate of interest.

Furthermore, the level of net debt evolves as:

$$D_{t+1} = D_t - \beta D_t + \alpha'(M - X) \qquad (7.6)$$

where D_t is the level of net debt in period t;[3] β is the repayment ratio of

Table 7.2: The extended Thirlwall model with endogenous coverage ratio and semi-endogenous net capital imports (year-by-year solution)

	η	ψ	ε exports	ε imports	π exports	π imports	p_d domestic prices	e nominal exchange rate	p_f foreign prices	$p_d - e - p_f$ real exchange rate	$p_d - q$ quality-corrected export prices	$(p_d-q)-e-p_f$ real exchange rate (quality corrected)	z in export markets	y^* BOP-constrained GDP growth	y^q quality-adjusted BOP-constrained growth	q quality catch-up rate	x exports (real)	m imports (real)	D debt (level)	$rD+\beta D$ debt service (DS)	F net capital imports	fe net capital imports	θ import coverage ratio (X/M)	DS/EX debt service-export ratio	Y/Z GDP GAP	α coverage ratio of trade imbalance through capital imports
1993	0.8	0.6	1.8	1.8	2.0	2.0	15.0%	13.0%	4.0%	-2.0%	14.0%	-3.0%	3.0%	2.8%	3.0%	1%	7.0%	4.3%	45.0	4.5	9.0	15.0%	90%	10%	50%	-180%
1994	0.8	0.6	1.8	1.8	2.0	2.0	12.0%	10.0%	4.0%	-2.0%	11.0%	-3.0%	3.0%	3.7%	3.9%	1%	7.0%	6.2%	47.8	4.8	11.8	31.5%	90%	9%	50%	-200%
1995	0.8	0.6	2.0	2.0	1.8	1.8	10.0%	8.0%	4.0%	-2.0%	8.0%	-4.0%	3.0%	4.2%	4.7%	2%	7.6%	6.4%	51.3	5.1	14.8	24.9%	89%	8%	51%	-182%
1996	0.8	0.6	2.0	2.0	1.6	1.6	8.0%	4.0%	4.0%	0.0%	5.0%	-3.0%	3.0%	4.3%	5.1%	3%	6.0%	6.8%	56.8	5.7	17.9	21.0%	88%	7%	53%	-171%
1997	0.8	0.7	1.6	1.6	1.4	1.4	8.0%	4.0%	4.0%	0.0%	4.0%	-4.0%	3.0%	3.6%	5.1%	4%	4.8%	5.1%	64.4	6.4	20.5	14.8%	87%	7%	55%	-159%
1998	0.8	0.7	1.4	1.4	1.4	1.4	8.0%	4.0%	4.0%	0.0%	3.0%	-5.0%	3.0%	3.0%	4.9%	5%	4.2%	4.3%	74.1	7.4	23.1	12.6%	87%	7%	57%	-154%
1999	0.8	0.7	1.2	1.2	1.4	1.4	8.0%	4.0%	4.0%	0.0%	3.0%	-5.0%	3.0%	2.6%	4.5%	5%	3.6%	3.6%	85.4	8.5	25.8	11.6%	87%	7%	59%	-150%
2000	0.8	0.7	1.2	1.2	1.4	1.4	8.0%	4.0%	4.0%	0.0%	3.0%	-5.0%	3.0%	2.5%	4.4%	5%	3.6%	3.5%	98.4	9.8	28.6	10.8%	87%	8%	60%	-147%
2001	0.8	0.7	1.2	1.2	1.4	1.4	8.0%	4.0%	4.0%	0.0%	4.0%	-4.0%	3.0%	2.5%	4.0%	4%	3.6%	3.5%	112.9	11.3	31.7	10.9%	87%	8%	61%	-145%
2002	0.8	0.7	1.2	1.2	1.4	1.4	8.0%	4.0%	4.0%	0.0%	5.0%	-3.0%	3.0%	2.5%	3.6%	3%	3.6%	3.5%	129.1	12.9	35.2	11.0%	87%	8%	62%	-143%
2003	0.8	0.8	1.3	1.3	1.4	1.4	8.0%	4.0%	4.0%	0.0%	5.0%	-3.0%	3.0%	2.7%	4.1%	3%	3.9%	3.8%	147.2	14.7	39.1	11.1%	87%	8%	63%	-142%
2004	0.8	0.8	1.3	1.3	1.4	1.4	8.0%	4.0%	4.0%	0.0%	6.0%	-2.0%	3.0%	2.8%	3.7%	2%	3.9%	3.9%	167.5	16.8	43.7	11.6%	87%	8%	64%	-140%
2005	0.8	0.8	1.3	1.3	1.4	1.4	8.0%	4.0%	4.0%	0.0%	6.0%	-2.0%	3.0%	2.8%	3.7%	2%	3.9%	3.9%	190.3	19.0	48.8	11.7%	87%	8%	65%	-139%
2006	0.8	0.8	1.3	1.3	1.4	1.4	8.0%	4.0%	4.0%	0.0%	6.0%	-2.0%	3.0%	2.8%	3.7%	2%	3.9%	3.9%	216.0	21.6	54.5	11.7%	86%	9%	65%	-137%
2007	0.8	0.8	1.4	1.4	1.4	1.4	8.0%	4.0%	4.0%	0.0%	7.0%	-1.0%	3.0%	3.0%	3.4%	1%	4.2%	4.1%	245.0	24.5	60.9	11.7%	86%	9%	66%	-135%
2008	0.8	0.8	1.4	1.4	1.4	1.4	8.0%	4.0%	4.0%	0.0%	7.0%	-1.0%	3.0%	3.0%	3.4%	1%	4.2%	4.2%	277.9	27.8	68.3	12.2%	86%	9%	67%	-134%

Note: Capital imports (F) are defined as $F = -(r + \beta)D + sX$, where s is the ratio of the positive components in the capital accounts (see equation 7.6) to total exports; s was assumed to be 0.3 throughout; the interest rate r was assumed to be 5%, the debt repayment ratio β 0.1, and the quality catch-up rate q variable throughout the simulation. α, the coverage ratio of the trade imbalance through net capital imports, is defined as $\alpha = F/(M - X)$.

the principal as a fraction of the old debt; $(M - X)$ is the imbalance in the current account (for both visibles and invisibles); and α' is the degree to which gross capital inflows cover the imbalance in current accounts.

Table 7.2 presents a stylized view of a year-by-year solution for the growth path of a catching-up economy (with quality catching up) and substantial growth rates in (semi-endogenous) capital inflows which leads to a reduction of the real income gap over a 15-year period by about 30 per cent (last column). In the dynamic solution of the (stylized) model in Table 7.2 we have explicitly presented the evolution of the stock of debt (D), of debt service $(rD + \beta D)$, and of net capital inflows (F) for which a simple rule has been applied to deal with the positive components in formula (7.6) above.[3]

Table 7.2 also includes the debt service-to-export ratio $((r+\beta)D/X)$. This performance ratio describes the degree to which net capital inflows – including all the positive components of equation (7.6) – cover the current account deficit (the ratio α) and the evolution of a 'GDP gap' (Y/Z) assuming an initial value of 50 per cent. The model takes as exogenous the elasticity parameters, the domestic and foreign inflation rates, the movements in the nominal exchange rate, the overall demand growth in export markets (z) and then calculates endogenously the time paths of X_t, M_t, D_t, Y_t, D_t and F_t given their initial values in period 0. The successful closure of the GDP gap from 50 per cent to 82 per cent in this simulation is particularly due to high (semi-endogenous) net flows of capital imports and a high 'quality catch-up' rate q. The (non-quality adjusted) real exchange rate is kept constant except for the 2 per cent real devaluations in 1993 to 1995.

3 Applying the BOP-constrained growth model to CEECs in transition

We now bring actual data into the picture to make some conjectures (scenarios) about the potential BOP-constrained growth paths of CEECs up to the year 2008. Before we do that, however, we would like to draw a stylized picture of how we can adapt the model to represent the qualitatively different phases through which CEECs have moved since 1989 and will continue to move depending upon their ability to catch up with the West. In outlining these phases, we will however take no notice of the domestic aspects of the so-called transformational recession (Kornai, 1992) since the focus of our analysis are the longer-term structural constraints linked with the balance of payments.

3.1 Phases in CEEC trade integration and catching-up with the West

It might be useful to distinguish three phases in the growth trajectory of CEECs over the period from 1989 to 2008.

The first phase (from 1989/90 to 1997/98) was one in which CEECs experienced the effects of a dramatic process of trade liberalization with the West. This process could be conceived as one in which rationing constraints were lifted both for Western exports to the East as well as for CEEC exports to the West. Such a period is characterized by exceptionally high growth rates in both exports and imports as the rationing constraints are lifted and trade becomes determined by positions on the demand curves. Furthermore, we expect a (more or less) gradual shift of the demand curves as the demand side learns about the characteristics of those producers from whom they had been rationed.[4] As our model assumes elasticity parameters from demand curves it cannot deal appropriately with a situation in which there is a move from a rationed situation to one in which rationing has disappeared. The effect of such a move is not immediate, as the very minimal presence in the past of CEEC exporters on Western markets and vice versa did not allow a proper evaluation of the supply characteristics of these producers. The 'proper' income elasticities which express such an evaluation will therefore evolve rather slowly. Even without any actual change in the suppliers characteristics and any capacity constraints, we would thus assume that there will not be an immediate jump to a 'natural' market share position that would be in line with a full appreciation of the different suppliers characteristics. We would expect export growth rates to be rather high over this period of adjustment until 'natural market share positions' are reached given suppliers characteristics. This process will be built into our model by assuming rather high income elasticities for this period in which both Western exporters to CEEC markets and CEEC exporters to Western markets move towards their 'natural' market share positions (such positions have been estimated by a number of models, such as gravity models; see e.g. Collins and Rodrik, 1991, Hamilton and Winters, 1991, Baldwin, 1994).

We would expect, for a number of reasons, that Western exporters would move more quickly to 'natural' market share positions, as they will be better equipped to develop their marketing and distribution links in CEEC markets and since actual contact with suppliers is necessary for the demand side to be able to express their evaluations of suppliers characteristics properly. Hence over the first phase, we would assume rather unusually high income elasticities for both exports and imports, but we would expect those for imports to be even higher than those for exports.[5] This takes into account the likely asymmetries in the speeds of the respective movements towards the longer-run demand curves after the rationing constraints are lifted. After a while, CEEC producers build up their distributive channels and can get evaluated on their objective suppliers' characteristics. Thus their export income elasticities remain high until they reach their 'natural' market positions. Once 'natural market share' positions are reached, i.e. the historical impact of the previous rationing situation has worn off, then the long-run underlying demand elasticities are actually coming through. This is when we move to phase two below.

A stylized picture of the assumed paths of the income elasticity parameters is presented in Figure 7.1.

Figure 7.1   Stylized paths of income elasticities for exports (ε) and imports (π) for CEECs

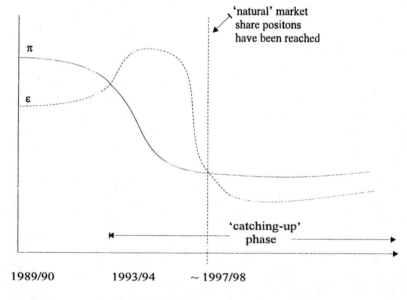

There are a number of reasons why strong devaluations would be a rational policy to pursue particularly in the early part of phase one. Firstly, because of the initial difference in the speed of catching up towards 'natural' market positions of Western vis-á-vis CEEC producers; a real devaluation will give consumers an incentive quickly to learn about the characteristics of cheap new suppliers. Secondly, due to the longer-run difference in the compositions of commodities sold by CEEC vs. Western suppliers, there is a gap in price elasticities as discussed in section 2. Given the high price elasticity vis-á-vis CEEC producers' sales both on domestic and foreign markets there are strengthened volume responses to both (real) depreciations and (real) appreciations. Thirdly, in the early part of the first phase there is not yet much 'quality catching up', since sales come from existing capacities and organizational

Figure 7.2 'Quality catch-up'

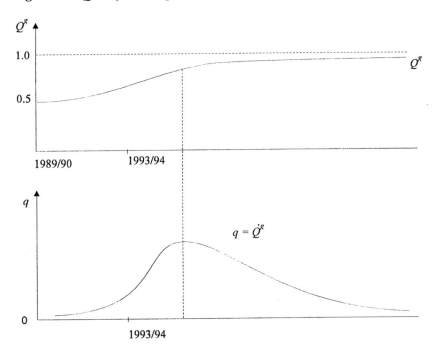

$$Q^g = \frac{Q^{cc}}{Q^{we}} \quad \text{'quality gap' between CEEC products and West European products;}$$

$$q = \frac{dQ^g}{dt} = \dot{Q}^g$$

structures did not have much time to change yet. Once quality catching up sets in, this can take the place – as shown in Table 7.1 above – of traditional real depreciations of the currency. Another reason is that in the early phase, capital inflows might still be hesitant plus there might be burdens of past debt, so that real devaluations might be one of the few instruments to alleviate the BOP constraint. There are still other reasons, such as the possibility that in the early phase the 'real wage resistance' to a serious undervaluation of the currency might still be weak given the disrepute of historical labour organizations and the broad popular acceptance of some measures of incomes policy in this period.

The second phase (roughly from 1998 to 2008) is one in which we assume that underlying 'natural' income elasticity parameters fully take over from the transitionally very high ones. There is the impact of a gradual (possibly 'hump-shaped') 'quality catching-up' process. Furthermore, as we assume catching up, there will be a gradual erosion of the gaps in (longer-term) income and price elasticities which CEEC and Western producers face respectively (see Figure 7.2).

In this phase we expect contradictory forces to impinge on relative cost- and price-competitiveness (see the more detailed discussion in section 3.4). On the one hand, we expect productivity growth to be rather high, as the economies embark on a high growth path (emerging from a period of very low capacity utilization) and they are beginning gradually to reap the rewards of technology transfer. However, there will also be attempts to increase the very low wage levels of CEEC workers and there will be pressures to revalue the strongly undervalued currencies (compared to the purchasing power parity (PPP) rate) as this affects the international purchasing power of domestic consumers (for imports and in foreign travel). These pressures for a revaluation of the currency are strengthened by the hesitancy of policy-makers to allow the nominal exchange rate to adjust fully to neutralize relative inflationary pressures. Rather, in the current context of Central and Eastern Europe, policy-makers use the nominal exchange rate as an anti-inflation device.

The third phase (post 2008) is fictive as it assumes a new steady state, i.e. new steady-state (BOP-constrained) growth paths of different CEECs which reflect whether and to which degree the different economies have 'caught up' with the West (as reflected by the remaining gaps in income and price elasticities) and to which degree they receive the benefit of continuous access to high capital inflows required to counteract structural BOP constraints in the longer run. The picture we draw considers the improbability of convergence of all CEECs to one steady-state growth path but that different CEECs will have – in most likelihood – different chances to escape or continue to be affected by the structural reasons for BOP-constrained growth.

3.2   Estimates for price and income elasticities for CEECs

The methodology we adopt is that of utilizing international estimates of income- and price-elasticities in trade for different commodity groups

Table 7.3 Initial income and price elasticities

	SITC 2+3	SITC 0+1+4	SITC 5+6+7+8+9	compositional discount factor	ε SITC 2+3	SITC 0+1+4	SITC 5+6+7+8+9	total	η SITC 2+3	SITC 0+1+4	SITC 5+6+7+8+9	total	SITC 2+3	SITC 0+1+4	SITC 5+6+7+8+9	π SITC 2+3	SITC 0+1+4	SITC 5+6+7+8+9	total	φ SITC 2+3	SITC 0+1+4	SITC 5+6+7+8+9	total
Bulgaria	15.0	25.0	60.0	0.7	0.9	0.8	2.2	1.26	-0.6	-0.8	-1.2	-1.00	8.0	47.0	44.0	1.0	0.8	1.7	1.50	-0.6	-0.8	-1.2	-0.94
Czech Republic	11.9	8.4	79.7	1.0	0.9	0.8	2.2	1.93	-0.6	-0.8	-1.2	-1.09	17.0	8.0	75.0	1.0	0.8	1.7	2.02	-0.6	-0.8	-1.2	-1.06
Hungary	9.1	22.4	68.5	1.0	0.9	0.8	2.2	1.77	-0.6	-0.8	-1.2	-1.05	18.0	6.0	76.0	1.0	0.8	1.7	2.04	-0.6	-0.8	-1.2	-1.07
Poland	18.1	12.5	69.4	1.0	0.9	0.8	2.2	1.71	-0.6	-0.8	-1.2	-1.04	21.0	12.0	67.0	1.0	0.8	1.7	1.90	-0.6	-0.8	-1.2	-1.02
Romania	13.0	7.0	80.0	0.6	0.9	0.8	2.2	1.23	-0.6	-0.8	-1.2	-1.09	36.0	16.0	48.0	1.0	0.8	1.7	1.63	-0.6	-0.8	-1.2	-0.91
Slovakia	8.7	6.1	85.1	0.8	0.9	0.8	2.2	1.62	-0.6	-0.8	-1.2	-1.12	25.0	9.0	66.0	1.0	0.8	1.7	1.89	-0.6	-0.8	-1.2	-1.01
Slovenia	4.9	5.5	89.6	1.0	0.9	0.8	2.2	2.06	-0.6	-0.8	-1.2	-1.15	17.0	7.0	76.0	1.0	0.8	1.7	2.03	-0.6	-0.8	-1.2	-1.07

and then combine these with the commodity compositions of the different CEECs' exports to arrive at country-specific estimates of aggregate price- and income-elasticities. There is also some allowance made that, owing to the 'quality gap' of CEEC economies within each commodity group, income-elasticities tend to be lower and price-elasticities higher than would be the case for more advanced economies.

Table 7.3 gives a breakdown of the export and import structure of each of the CEECs' exports by broad commodity groups. The shares of the different commodity groups in the countries' exports were used as weights to arrive at aggregate estimates for the countries' income- and price-elasticities. International estimates of income- and price-elasticities (see Houthakker and Magee, 1969, and Stern et al., 1976) show that agricultural products and food processing tend to be more price-elastic than manufactured produce and raw materials. Similarly, manufactured products and more processed (higher value added) products are more income-elastic and less price-elastic than raw materials, semi-processed commodities and agricultural produce. We made a rough selection of price- and income-elasticities for these commodity groups (see Table 7.3) and these together with the weights adopted (derived from the CEECs' export structure) plus 'quality discounts' are used to compile aggregate income- and price-elasticities for each of the CEECs' exports.

On the import side, we have again used some international evidence that income-elasticities are somewhat lower in low real income economies than in high income countries. Furthermore, although one might argue that low income level consumers are also more price-sensitive than those on higher incomes, we none the less maintain our hypothesis that the price-elasticities for exports from CEECs are initially higher than for CEEC imports (see the argument in section 2). The reason is that, in the circumstances of Central and Eastern Europe, consumers are also rather keen to catch up on the higher quality and greater diversity of Western products and are thus less price-sensitive than they would otherwise be given their income position.

3.3   Details on invisible trade balances and capital accounts

In order to study in detail the contributions of the non-trade acccounts to the balance of payments, we undertook a rather extensive compilation of information about the BOP structure (on current and capital accounts) of CEEC economies since 1989. This information guided us in our views concerning the current and future evolution of net capital imports (F). Before returning to equation (7.6) which shows the components of net capital flows, we would like to undertake a decomposition of the overall trade balance on current accounts into visible and invisible trade. Figure 7.3 shows the evolution of the net invisible trades and of certain items of net capital imports (FDI and portfolio investment) over the period 1990 to 1994 (all items are expressed as per cent of total commodity exports). Trade in invisibles consists basically of the three items of service trade (transport, travel and other services trades) and of transfers. Trade flows of invisibles could be a major factor in either alleviating or reinforcing pressures on the balance of payments. We can see from Figure 7.3 that, for example, the Czech Republic had major surpluses in the travel (tourism) component in its invisible trade, while Poland receives major net flows through transfers. In the context of our model we projected the evolution of the net surpluses (deficits) of the different components of invisible trade directly, each time in relation to the volume of goods exports.

Hence we decompose

$$X - M = (X^G - M^G) + (X' - M') \tag{7.7}$$

where $(X^G - M^G)$ and $(X' - M')$ refer respectively to the net surpluses on the visible and invisible components of the current accounts respectively. Our projections of the evolution of net balances for different items in the invisibles accounts were done by using historical information on invisible trade flows and relying on WIIW forecasts about the likely evolution of the ratios:

$$s^i(t) = \frac{X^i(t) - M^i(t)}{X^G(t)} \tag{7.8}$$

where $X^i(t) - M^i(t)$ refers to the net trade balance of a particular item i (i = transport, travel, other service trades) in the invisible accounts in year t. Thus while the net trade balance for goods trade is explicitly modelled by means of trade equations with explicit income and price-elasticities for export and import flows, net surpluses for invisibles are projected in the form of the above ratios in relation to the exports of goods.

Similarly we proceed with the various positive items in the capital accounts (see equation (7.6) above); using again the different countries' historical record and consulting experts on the likely evolution of the ratios:

$$s^{FDI}(t) = \frac{FDI(t)}{X^G(t)}, \, s^{PF}(t) = \frac{Portf.Inv.(t)}{X^G(t)} \text{ and } s^c(t) = \frac{Net \, Credit(t)}{\Sigma_i s^i X^G(t)}$$

Figure 7.3 Net surplus/deficits in invisibles and capital accounts (in per cent of goods exports)

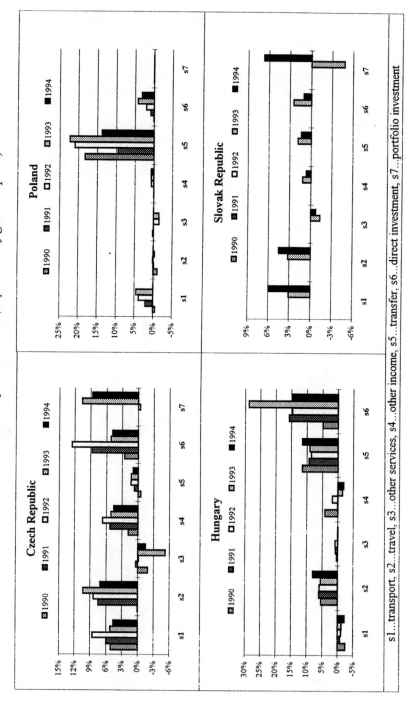

s1...transport, s2...travel, s3...other services, s4...other income, s5...transfer, s6...direct investment, s7...portfolio investment

Figure 7.3 (continued)   Net surplus/deficits in invisibles and capital accounts (in per cent of goods exports)

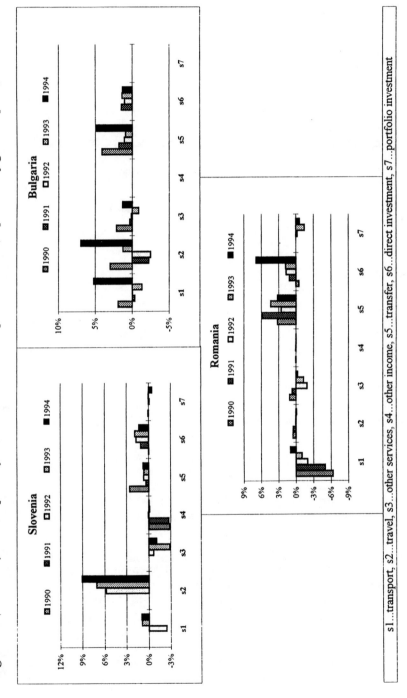

s1...transport, s2...travel, s3...other services, s4...other income, s5...transfer, s6...direct investment, s7...portfolio investment

where *FDI*, *Portf.Inv.* and *Net Credit* refer respectively to the Foreign Direct Investment (net), the Portfolio Investment (net) and Net New Credit items in the capital accounts.

In this way we can rewrite our BOP identity in the form (ΔR refers to change in official reserves):

$$(X^G(t) - M^G(t)) + \Sigma_i s^i(t) X^G(t) = -F(t) + \Delta R(t) \qquad (7.9)$$

where net capital inflows are

$$F(t) = (s^{FDI}(t) + s^{PF}(t) + s^C(t)) X^G(t) - (r + \beta) D_t$$

Drawing the terms together (and dropping the time subscripts) we have

$$(X^G - M^G) = -(\Sigma_i s^i + s^{FDI} + s^{PF} + s^C) X^G + (r + \beta) D_r + \Delta R \qquad (7.10)$$

or simplifying,

$$S^G = -S^I + F + \Delta R$$

where S^G is the net trade surplus in goods, S^I is the net trade surplus in invisibles, F is net capital imports, and ΔR is the change in official reserves.

We will find it useful to present in our simulations as a ratio the degree to which surpluses on invisibles trade plus net capital imports cover potential trade deficits in goods trade.

$$\alpha = \frac{S^I + F}{-S^G} \qquad (7.11)$$

Estimates regarding the evolution of the fractions $s^i(t)$, $s^{FDI}(t)$, $s^{PF}(t)$, $s^C(t)$ for the different CEEC economies are available in Landesmann and Pöschl (1995).

3.4   Evolution of cost- and price competitiveness

Our approach to projecting the evolution of (real) competitiveness, i.e. the term $(p^d - q) - e - p^f$ (see equation (7.4)) is the following:

First, we approximate relative prices through relative unit labour costs, i.e.

$$\frac{P^d}{P^f} = \frac{ULC^d}{ULC^f E} = \frac{W^d (\mathrm{Prod}^d)^{-1}}{W^f (\mathrm{Prod}^f)^{-1} E} \qquad (7.12)$$

where *ULC*, *WR* and *Prod* refer, respectively, to unit labour costs, wage rates and levels of labour productivity in the two countries (d...domestic, f...foreign) and *E*, as before, to the nominal exchange rate.

In growth rates we have

$$(w^d - w^f) - e - (prod^d - prod^f) \qquad (7.13)$$

and, adding the developments in relative per-unit quality, we obtain for the development of domestic real competitiveness (*rc*)

$$rc^{-1} = (w^d - w^f) - e - (prod^d - prod^f) - (q^d - q^f) \qquad (7.13')$$

We do one more thing and that is to express the wage rate in terms of the purchasing power parity (PPP) rate and adding the development of the ratio between the nominal and the PPP rate as an additional term (that ratio E/E^{PPP} is often called the ERDI, the exchange rate deviation index). We obtain a formula for the development of real competitiveness in terms of three 'gaps', the wage gap, the productivity gap and the quality gap, and the development of the ERDI.

$$rc^{-1} = (w_{PPP}{}^d - w_{PPP}{}^f) - (e - e_{PPP}) - (prod^d - prod^f) - (q^d - q^f) \quad (7.13'')$$

$$\underbrace{\hspace{2cm}}_{\text{wage gap}} \quad \underbrace{\hspace{1.5cm}}_{\text{ERDI}} \quad \underbrace{\hspace{2cm}}_{\text{productivity gap}} \quad \underbrace{\hspace{1.5cm}}_{\text{quality gap}}$$

Table 7.4 presents the developments of the ERDI, the wage rates, productivity levels, and unit labour costs (all in PPPs) for the different CEECs over the period 1990 to 1994. We also present these indicators in relation to those of Austria which can be interpreted as 'gaps'.

As for the forecasts we assume the following dynamic evolution of these various gaps:

Take, as an example, the 'quality gap' $Q = Q^{EE}/Q^{EU}$ where the Q^{EE} and Q^{EU} stand respectively for the quality level of Eastern and Western European products. Then the dynamic evolution of the quality gap is assumed to follow a logistic pattern of the type (see Figure 7.2):

$$q = \frac{dQ}{dt} = g_1 + g_2 g_3 \left(\frac{1 - Q^{EE}}{Q^{FIN}} \right) \qquad (7.14)$$

where Q^{FIN} could be a certain percentage of the Western European quality level which could be realistically achieved in the final (third-stage) steady state.

*Table 7.4   Estimated wage rates, unit labour costs (ULC), and ERDI
1990–94 (annual averages)*

	1990	1991	1992	1993	1994[a]
Czech Republic					
Exchange rate, Kč/$	17.95	29.48	28.29	29.15	28.78
Average annual wages, $	2170.70	1542.74	1979.64	2404.12	2810.28
Wage rates[b]	33.34	25.79	26.57	28.65	29.73
Unit labour costs[b]	17.61	14.26	17.52	21.54	23.89
Average annual wages[c]	6292.43	5184.22	5564.59	6188.53	6583.14
ERDI	2.90	3.36	2.81	2.57	2.34
Hungary					
Exchange rate, Ft/$	63.20	74.81	79.00	92.04	105.12
Average annual wages, $	2553.04	2876.73	3386.43	3543.42	3904.11
Wage rates[b]	28.67	27.73	27.93	27.31	28.19
Unit labour costs[b]	27.08	33.96	37.32	39.94	41.50
Average annual wages[c]	5410.87	5574.99	5850.01	5898.14	6240.56
ERDI	2.12	1.94	1.73	1.66	1.60
Poland					
Exchange rate, Zl/$	9500.00	10583.00	13631.00	18146.00	22727.00
Average annual net wages, $	1300.55	1991.46	2146.81	2157.57	2286.27
Wage rates[b]	20.68	22.16	21.92	22.39	23.05
Unit labour costs[b]	20.13	32.70	30.85	29.98	29.55
Average annual wages[c]	3903.20	4454.46	4590.52	4836.39	5103.38
ERDI	3.00	2.24	2.14	2.24	2.23
Slovenia					
Exchange rate, tolar/$	11.32	27.57	81.29	113.24	128.81
Average annual net wages, $	5996.82	4492.71	4548.60	4962.13	5403.31
Wage rates[b]	29.92	27.57	26.70	28.70	29.90
Unit labour costs[b]	52.68	42.15	40.27	43.35	43.55
Average annual wages[c]	5647.59	5541.78	5591.62	6198.45	6618.67
ERDI	0.94	1.23	1.23	1.25	1.22
Slovak Republic					
Exchange rate, Sk/$	17.95	29.48	28.26	30.79	32.04
Average annual wages, $	2150.64	1525.64	1918.90	2087.04	2397.00
Wage rates[b]	33.03	28.08	29.90	30.63	32.80
Unit labour costs[b]	19.70	15.88	19.30	22.04	23.61
Average annual wages[c]	6234.29	5644.43	6260.90	6617.05	7262.54
ERDI	2.90	3.70	3.26	3.17	3.03
Austria					
Exchange rate, S/$	11.37	11.68	10.99	11.63	11.40
Average annual wages, $	23208.00	24062.00	27003.00	26600.00	27950.00
Average annual wages, $ PPP	18875.54	20103.00	20942.26	21600.31	22139.70
Unit labour costs, PPP-adjusted	1.39	1.42	1.58	1.58	1.62
GDP per capita, $ (PPP)	16673.82	17653.79	18242.27	18502.98	19385.93

Notes: [a]Projection. [b]Wage rates and ULC are relative to Austria (= 100) in US$ PPP.
[c]Average annual wages refer to annual wages per employee in US$ PPP.
Source: WIIW calculations.

The equation above shows the evolution of the quality gap as a function of two additive terms: the rate g_1 with which quality improves internationally in advanced economies, and the second term which shows the contribution to quality growth which the existence of a quality gap could make. As the quality gap disappears, i.e. Q^{EE}/Q^{FIN} approaches zero, the contribution of the second term becomes smaller and smaller until it disappears completely. With $g_2 = 1.0$ the second term represents the evolution of the potential for quality catching up and g_2 represents the utilization rate of this potential. When $g_2 < 1.0$, then the potential for catching up is not fully utilized. In future analysis, the g_2 rate could become a function of the evolution of corporate domestic reforms, of the impact which foreign collaborations can have on quality upgrading etc. Parameter g_3 represents the speed by which the economy moves along the logistic.

Equivalent equations (as (7.14)) regulate the dynamics of the closure of the wage gap and the productivity gap between the different CEECs and Western Europe. The evolution of the ERDI is assumed to follow a similar pattern, as the high degree of 'undervaluation' of domestic currencies will – in the longer run – disappear as CEEC economies proceed on the path of overall catching up and institutional reform.[7] Of course, in the parameterization of all these equations we can allow for country-specific assumptions concerning the levels of productivity, wage rate, quality and ERDI which will be reached in the third phase (see section 3.1) as well as assumptions concerning the pattern and speed of catching up as described by parameters g_2 and g_3.

4 Country growth profiles

The model as presented in the previous sections allows us to introduce a number of those characteristics which are relevant in distinguishing different CEECs' growth prospects in the medium and longer run. We will simply enumerate these characteristics in the following and refer back to them when discussing the individual projections for the different CEEC economies.

(i) Differentiation of income and price-elasticities: Here we can distinguish two different compositional factors which lead to different country estimates of aggregate income- and price-elasticities: (1) differences in the broad sectoral compositions (in SITC groups 2+3, 0+1+4, and 5–9) of a country's exports (and imports; but the latter will be assumed uniform across all CEECs); and (2) differences in the different countries' 'compositional discount factors' within SITC group 5–9 (i.e. manufacturing) which account for differentiation across countries in the composition of their exports towards higher or lower income-elastic products.

(ii) Developments in 'real competitiveness' (*rc*): Here the projections of all the different determinants in the evolution of 'real competitiveness' are important (see section 3.4), i.e. the initial levels and the envisaged paths of development of the following variables: ERDI; wage gaps and productivity gaps; quality gaps.

All these variables follow a logistic pattern, but the initial and final levels on those logistic curves and the speed of movement along the logistic depends upon the implementation of country-specific ideas concerning patterns of catching up.

(iii) Differences in the structure and evolution of invisible accounts and longer-term capital movements: Here we take as a basis the historical track record in terms of country-specific structures of the invisible accounts (net balances in transport, travel and other services, as well as in transfers) and project these into the future with assumptions concerning the evolution of comparative advantages in these items.

As regards FDI flows and portfolio investment, we again make conjectures concerning the future development of these items in the different economies, given their historical records since 1989 and prospects for further privatization programmes and other developments in the corporate sector.

Another distinguishing characteristic refers to the levels of initial foreign debt and future flows connected with servicing this debt. There is also a possibility of introducing country differentiation concerning the conditions of servicing this debt (maturity structure, interest rates) and of taking up new loans.

Finally, the levels of reserves are different across economies and the degrees to which countries can rely on this buffer.

There are two general factors which influence most of the factors discussed under (i)–(iii) above and hence affect our views of country-specific developments: (1) the geographical location of the particular CEEC; and (2) the degree and expected dates of further integration with the EU.

Point (1) affects particularly our views concerning the extent and speed of 'supply-side catching up'; it also affects our views concerning future FDI and portfolio investment flows as well as our assumptions concerning the 'natural market positions' in EU markets (see section 3.1 above).

Point (2) concerns us in the next section.

5 High CEEC–EU integration and creeping disintegration scenarios

In this section we want to discuss in detail the channels through which prospects of high CEEC–EU integration (up to full membership) would affect our catching-up projections of CEEC economies.

In our projections we introduce high integration through the following channels: (i) faster productivity and quality catching-up; (ii) faster wage catch-up; (iii) faster upgrading of commodity structure (move to more intra-industry trade) leading to a faster disappearance of asymmetries in income- and price-elasticities; (iv) impact on invisible and income accounts: more trade of transport services (balance impact neutral); more tourism in both directions (for countries with viable tourist industries greater scope for surpluses, for the others bigger deficits); more deficits in other services (here lies one of EU's comparative advantages); more personal transfers (since access to EU labour markets will ease); (v) impact on capital movements: more FDI and portfolio investment; easier access to credits and better conditions for debt servicing; (vi) greater pressure towards reducing the 'undervaluation' of the national currencies: speed-up of institutional changes and of market functioning will increase convergence of price structures; more pressure to achieve a higher level of international purchasing power because of greater tourist flows and more imports; more pressure to achieve monetary stability and use of the nominal exchange rate as an anchor with the view of coming closer to the Maastricht criteria; (vii) greater openness of EU markets (impact on z is the most immediate variable to adjust).

We can see that the above list includes, both, factors which in the context of our model would have a favourable, but also those which have an unfavourable impact upon the BOP-constrained growth rate.

As regards the results from simulating various integration scenarios we distinguished – as was mentioned in the introduction – three scenarios of East–West European integration:

Scenario A (the 'Association Scenario'), which is our base scenario, is a rather optimistic extension of current developments of CEEC–EU relationships, but falls short of full EU membership over the forecasting period. Scenario B (the 'Integration Scenario') implies 'near complete membership' of the EU[8] and differs from scenario A in that EU membership leads to more net capital inflows (particularly in the form of FDI and portfolio investment), conditions for new credits and debt repayment get eased, there is stronger integration and specialization in invisible trade and income flows and the remaining (non-tariff) barriers allow full access of EU markets. As a result, also supply-side catching up

Table 7.5 *Summary results from scenarios: Association, Integration and Creeping Disintegration*

Association

	Czech Republic				Hungary				Poland				Slovak Republic				Slovenia			
	1993	1998	2003	2008	1993	1998	2003	2008	1993	1998	2003	2008	1993	1998	2003	2008	1993	1998	2003	2008
Average GDP growth rates: 1993-1998, 1993-2003, 1993-2008		3.5%	4.4%	4.4%		4.0%	4.7%	4.7%		4.8%	4.9%	4.9%		3.2%	4.0%	4.4%		4.7%	4.8%	4.9%
Average GDP growth rates: 1993-1998, 1998-2003, 2003-2008		4.5%	5.5%	4.3%		5.0%	5.4%	4.9%		5.1%	5.0%	4.8%		4.6%	5.0%	5.2%		5.3%	5.0%	5.0%
% of GDP per capita in EU (15)	43%	49%	57%	62%	34%	40%	46%	52%	28%	32%	37%	41%	37%	42%	47%	53%	44%	52%	59%	66%

Integration

	Czech Republic				Hungary				Poland				Slovak Republic				Slovenia			
	1993	1998	2003	2008	1993	1998	2003	2008	1993	1998	2003	2008	1993	1998	2003	2008	1993	1998	2003	2008
Average GDP growth rates: 1993-1998, 1993-2003, 1993-2008		3.5%	5.2%	5.4%		4.5%	5.5%	6.1%		5.3%	5.9%	5.7%		3.5%	5.1%	5.6%		4.8%	5.7%	5.9%
Average GDP growth rates: 1993-1998, 1998-2003, 2003-2008		4.5%	7.2%	6.0%		5.6%	6.7%	7.3%		5.7%	6.6%	5.4%		5.0%	7.0%	6.6%		5.5%	6.7%	6.3%
% of GDP per capita in EU (15)	43%	49%	60%	70%	34%	40%	47%	58%	28%	33%	40%	45%	37%	42%	51%	61%	44%	52%	63%	73%

Creeping Disintegration

	Czech Republic				Hungary				Poland				Slovak Republic				Slovenia			
	1993	1998	2003	2008	1993	1998	2003	2008	1993	1998	2003	2008	1993	1998	2003	2008	1993	1998	2003	2008
Average GDP growth rates: 1993-1998, 1993-2003, 1993-2008		3.3%	3.9%	3.8%		3.8%	4.4%	4.4%		4.5%	4.4%	4.4%		2.9%	3.5%	3.8%		4.5%	4.7%	4.7%
Average GDP growth rates: 1993-1998, 1998-2003, 2003-2008		4.2%	4.7%	3.6%		4.7%	5.1%	4.3%		4.4%	4.2%	4.3%		4.2%	4.1%	4.5%		5.2%	4.8%	4.8%
% of GDP per capita in EU (15)	43%	48%	54%	56%	34%	39%	45%	49%	28%	32%	35%	39%	37%	41%	44%	49%	44%	51%	58%	64%

Figure 7.4   CEEC-5: GDP growth rates for periods starting 1993, weighted averages

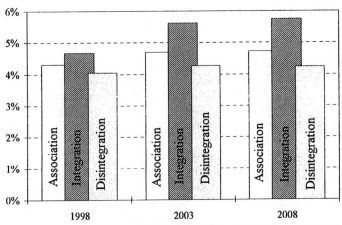

Scenarios for the periods 1993-1998, 1993-2003, 1993-2008

(of the quality and composition of exported commodities and of productivity, but also of wage levels) proceeds more rapidly. Scenario C (the 'Creeping Disintegration Scenario') is one in which CEEC–EU relations deteriorate relative to the path of continuous further liberalization and economic integration as outlined in scenario A. Instead, the FDI and portfolio investments grow more slowly, the conditions for new credit and debt repayment deteriorate, non-tariff barriers (such as the more extensive use of anti-dumping procedures) make access to the EU markets more difficult and less integration also implies slower catching-up on the supply side. Table 7.5 and Figures 7.4 and 7.5 give an overview of the results from the three scenarios.

All scenarios lead to some closure of the GDP (per capita) gap between the CEEC economies and the EU member states, but substantial gaps still remain at the end of the forecasting period (2008). Thus, for example, the Czech Republic moves from a 43 per cent (below average EU) position to a 62 per cent position in scenario A, a 70 per cent position in scenario B and a 56 per cent position in scenario C (all by the year 2008). As mentioned above, the differences between the three scenarios in our model result from differences in net capital inflows (through budgetary transfers, FDI and portfolio investment flows) implying more or less technology transfer and hence faster or slower 'quality' and 'productivity' catching up, a faster or slower reduction in

Figure 7.5 CEEC-5: GDP per capita relative to the EU average in 2008

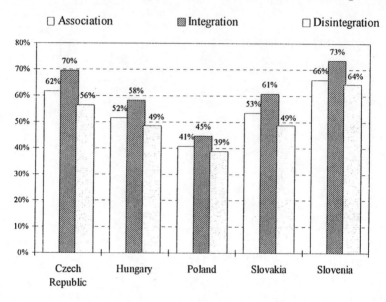

the elasticity asymmetries, but also a faster closure of the real wage gap and more pressure towards a revaluation (reduction of the ERDI[9]) of CEEC economies' currencies (Figure A1 in the Appendix gives an overview of the divergent paths of net capital inflows for selected years in the different scenarios).[10] The net effect from full integration is estimated to be positive although it should be noticed that the model takes account of positive and negative effects of full membership in the EU by the years 2003 for the Czech and Slovak Republics, Hungary, Poland and Slovenia, and 2005 for Bulgaria and Romania.

Detailed information about the simulation results of the three different scenarios can be obtained from Landesmann and Pöschl (1995). We should remind the reader that, like in any model simulation, these projections should not be interpreted as actual forecasts but as analytically coherent scenarios constructed by means of a specific model and specific assumptions about the developments of particular structural parameters and variables. The advantage of such an explicitly stated model structure is that it provides a basis for discussion.

6 Conclusions

The paper has outlined a framework within which scenarios of longer-term growth in CEEC economies can be developed and which are consistent with the balance-of-payments constraints to be faced by these economies when they attempt to catch up with Western Europe.

As we could see, the different economies had different starting positions regarding: (i) the structure of invisible trades which could become important positive or negative items in the balance of payments; (ii) the levels of productivity, real wages and thus of unit labour costs, which allowed us to make conjectures concerning the extent of catching up which might take place in the components determining real competitiveness; (iii) the levels of initial 'undervaluation' as expressed by the ERDI which gives an indication of the longer-term pressures to appreciate the currency in real terms; (iv) the compositional structure of exports including an assessment of initial 'quality' differences across the different CEEC producers which affected our estimates of initial differences in income- and price-elasticities and also provided some scope to develop our conjectures regarding 'quality catching up'.

Given the starting points it was up to us to draw country-specific pictures concerning the extent and speed of a catching-up process over a fifteen year period starting in 1993. The country profiles of these catching-up processes were affected by our views regarding the impact of geographical location and of the speed and directions of economic reforms in the different CEECs.

Finally, we analysed the potential impact which (almost complete) CEEC–EU integration would have (we left out any consideration of the impact on agriculture and any budgetary implications for the CEECs). We pointed out that – within the framework of our model – (near complete) EU membership by the year 2002 had positive as well as negative implications for the BOP-constrained growth paths of the different CEEC economies. On the positive side, there could be faster 'supply-side catching up', partly through higher induced FDI and portfolio investment, partly through more infrastructural support; there could be more favourable terms of debt repayment and in issuing new credits, an easier access of EU markets; while on the negative side we pointed towards a more rapid upward valuation of the domestic currencies (in real terms) given their initial positions of strong undervaluation, as well as, possibly, high rates of import penetration in certain (goods and non-goods) areas of economic activity.

The economic policy conclusions which emerge from this exercise are the following:
(1) Catching up is not an automatic process. It takes place 'against the odds' if one considers the fragile balance-of-payments position of small, open economies with (given the political commitment and obligation

under the Europe Agreements) a commitment to very limited use of protectionist measures, pressures towards the longer-term revaluations of highly undervalued currencies, real wage aspirations and a structure of income- and price-elasticities for exports and imports that are stacked in a way – at least initially – as not to facilitate easily differential growth between CEEC economies and the EU.

(2) Components of the balance of payments that have played less of a role – so far – in the discussion concerning CEEC–EU integration should gain more prominence if the BOP's constraint on economic growth is focused on: the net surplus or deficit positions in the various items of the invisible (service trade) accounts and income transfers, the flows of FDI and of portfolio investments, the conditions under which new loans are given and old debt is repaid. All these items play a prominent role in further CEEC–EU integration and, particularly, the difference that EU (or expected EU) membership might make to the growth prospects of CEEC economies.

(3) 'Supply side upgrading' has a vital role to play in growth and closer EU integration has an impact on such supply-side upgrading. The channels are manifold. More FDI and general corporate integration across the EU–CEEC divide has an impact on the speed of technology transfer, access to international finance has an impact on credit constraints, the takeover of the Acquis Communautaire has an impact on market organization and firm strategies, etc.

(4) Our simulations show that the relationship between the BOP-constrained growth paths and the real exchange rate is very sensisitive. They indicate that any short-term pressures towards exchange rate appreciation which are not anchored in the longer-term improvement of 'quality adjusted' cost competitiveness would be very detrimental to the BOP position of the CEEC economy and hence for economic growth.

All in all, we consider a careful use of the BOP-constrained model of economic growth for CEECs as successful in that it brings together in a coherent framework a large number of factors which already do and will increasingly play important roles in the longer-term growth performances of CEEC economies.

Notes

1. By 'near full membership' we mean membership but exclusion from the Common Agricultural Policy (the CAP) as the implications of CAP membership have not been considered in this paper.
2. In principle we could introduce different rates of 'quality catching up' in competition of domestic producers with importers on domestic markets or with foreign producers on export markets; this, however, requires an overall decomposition of the model and thus to keep the

model simple, we assume that the quality catch-up proceeds in both these two markets at the same rates.

3. We should interpret net debt here in a broad sense as all obligations to the outside world which arise from net capital inflows in all its forms (see equation (7.6)).

4. In the model specification used in table 7.2 we calculated the positive components in equation (7.6) simply as an exogenously specified share of the value of exports in that year.

5. We can observe other examples of this type of process, such as the currently very high export growth rates in India which resulted from the recent process of liberalization.

6. Note that this argument does not rely on the other longer-run reason that Western exporters supply higher income-elastic commodities.

7. For a fuller argument of why the ERDI should decline in the course of a successful reform and growth process of Eastern European economies, see e.g. Dietz (1994).

8. By 'almost complete' we mean membership but with exclusion from the Common Agricultural Policy (the CAP) as the implication of CAP membership has not been considered in this paper.

9. The ERDI – the exchange rate deviation index – measures the ratio between the nominal exchange rate and the PPP (purchasing power parity) rate.

10. One should keep in mind that net capital inflows include net debt servicing which means that net capital imports can become negative, as they do in the cases of Hungary and Poland in the Creeping Disintegration scenario.

References

Abramovitz, M. (1986), 'Catching Up, Forging Ahead and Falling Behind', *Journal of Economic History*, vol. 46, 385–406.

Abramovitz, M. (1994), 'The Origins of the Postwar Catch-Up and Convergence Boom', in J. Fagerberg, B. Verspagen and N. von Tunzelmann (eds), *The Dynamics of Technology, Trade and Growth*, Aldershot: Edward Elgar.

Baldwin. R. (1994), *Towards an Integrated Europe*, Centre for Economic Policy, London.

Baumol, W. (1986), 'Productivity growth, convergence and welfare: what the long-run data show', *American Economic Review*, vol. 76,5, 1072–83.

Ben-David, D. (1994), 'Income Disparity Among Countries and the Effects of Freer Trade', in L.L. Pasinetti and R.M. Solow (eds), *Economic Growth and the Structure of Long-Term Development*, London: Macmillan.

Buigues, P. et al. (1994) 'The Economic Interpenetration between the EU and Eastern Europe', *European Economy*, no. 6.

Collins, S.M. and D. Rodrik (1991), *Eastern Europe and the Soviet Union in the world economy*, Institute for International Economics, Washington, D.C.

Dietz, R. (1994), 'The fall in the level and in the value of economic activities in countries in transition', paper presented at the Third Freiberg Symposium on Economics, 13 September.

Hamilton, D. and L.A. Winters (1991), *Opening up international trade in Eastern Europe*, working paper, Centre for Economic Policy Research, London.

Houthakker, H.S. and S.P. Magee (1969), 'Income and price-elasticities in world trade', *The Review of Economics and Statistics*, vol. LI, 2, May, 111–25.

Landesmann, M. (1995), 'The pattern of East-West European integration: catching up or falling behind?', in R. Dobrinsky and M. Landesmann (eds) (1995), *Transforming Economies and European Integration*, Aldershot: Edward Elgar.

Landesmann, M. and J. Pöschl (1995), 'Balance-of-Payments Constrained Growth in Central and Eastern Europe and Scenarios of East-West Integration', *WIIW*

Research Reports, no. 222, The Vienna Institute for Comparative Economic Studies, September.

McCombie, J. and A. Thirwall (1994), *Economic Growth and the Balance-of-Payments Constraint*, London: St. Martin's Press.

Stern, R.M., J. Francis and B. Schumacher (1976), *Price Elasticities in International Trade. An Annotated Bibliography*, London: Macmillan.

Thirlwall, A. (1979), 'The Balance-of-Payments Constraint as an Explanation of International Growth Rate Differences', *Banca Nazionale del Lavoro Quarterly Review*, March.

Verspagen, B. (1991), 'A New Empirical Approach to Catching Up or Falling Behind', *Structural Change and Economic Dynamics*, vol. 2, no. 2, 359–80.

Appendix:

Figure A1: *Net capital inflows in different integration scenarios
(billion dollars)*

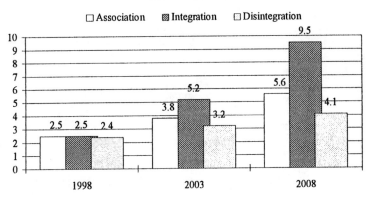

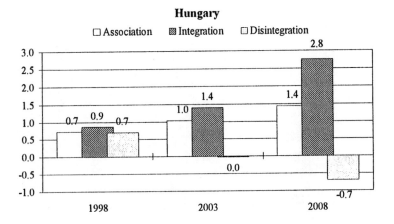

Figure A1 (continued):   *Net capital inflows in different integration scenarios (billion dollars)*

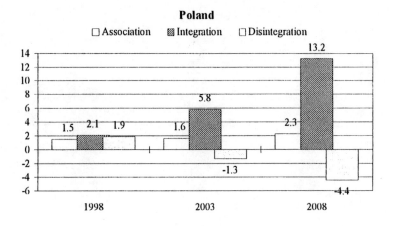

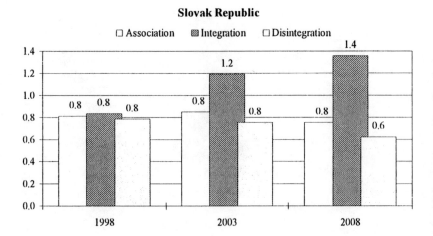

Figure A1 (continued):   *Net capital inflows in different integration scenarios (billion dollars)*

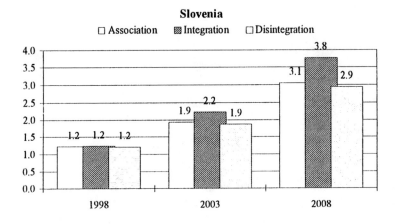

8 Growth Consequences of Systemic Transformation[1]

Vladimir Gligorov and Niclas Sundström

1 Introduction

What are the long-term effects of systemic transformations? We can approach this question with a version of 'new growth theory' that uses Schumpeter's idea of creative destruction. This idea covers the broad area of knowledge creation, transmitting, destruction and evolution. Moreover, it connects the use of knowledge with an appropriate incentive structure. The key idea is that knowledge growth and evolution is a function of profit earning possibilities. This idea introduces dynamic elements that depart significantly from the standard neoclassical assumptions of perfect competition, factor substitutability and price-taking behaviour. Yet, this new approach is not all that clearly defined and charted.

Aghion and Howitt (1992) develop the idea of creative destruction to explain how innovation appears as improvements in the quality of goods. In this approach, creative destruction is modelled as a patent-race game. Assuming there is a new invention with some probability of being adopted, the right to obtain profits from the innovation is expressed as the value of a patent. If the growth rate depends on the knowledge used, and if the rate of innovative activity is dependent on investment in research and development, and if the level of investment is dependent on the expected profits from patented innovations, it follows that economic growth depends on the incentive structure and the consequent evolution of its knowledge stock. Thus, the idea of creative destruction developed by Schumpeter and formalized by Aghion and Howitt takes growth potential of an economy as endogenous. This approach is especially suitable for economies undergoing systemic transformation like those in Central and Eastern Europe.

In this chapter, we first formulate the question of the growth consequences of systemic transformations in broadly Schumpeterian terms. We then introduce some ideas from neo-Schumpeterian growth theory. Finally, we use these ideas to compare a stylized version of

Central and East European transformation with the policy prescriptions and dilemmas that are emerging from research based partly on the theory of creative destruction. The conclusion we reach is that the transformation policies adopted in Central and Eastern Europe can take the respective economies off the desirable or prosperous long-run growth path.

2 The idea of creative destruction

The theory of growth and development is increasingly relying on the idea of creative destruction. Schumpeter (1928) puts his central idea in the context of economic progress and the roles played by innovations and entrepreneurs:

> What we, unscientifically, call economic progress means essentially putting productive resources to uses *hitherto untried in practice*, and withdrawing them from the uses they have served so far. This is what we call 'innovation'...

After defining the process of creative destruction, Schumpeter askes what are supply incentives that encourage entrepreneurs to search for innovations:

> *Why* this is so, is a question which it would lead very far to answer satisfactorily. Successful innovation is ... a task *sui generis*. It is a feat not of intellect, but of will. It is a special case of the social phenomenon of leadership. Its difficulty consisting in the resistances and uncertainties incident to doing what has not been done before, it is accessible for, and appeals to only a distinct type which is rare.

Finally, Schumpeter gives a name to this economic role:

> Whilst differences in aptitude for the routine work of 'static' management only result in doing what every one does, differences in this particular aptitude result in only some being able to do this particular thing at all. To overcome these difficulties incident to change of practice is the function characteristic of the entrepreneur.

Schumpeter used the idea of creative destruction to capture both the entrepreneurial character of capitalism and to predict the rise of socialism. Neo-Schumpeterian growth theory uses the former only. This chapter, however, uses the notion of creative destruction to account for the demise of socialism and the re-emergence of capitalism and to highlight some recurring policy dilemmas.

Creative destruction is an outcome of entrepreneurial activities and describes a process by which inventions create obsolescence. Inventions are discovered and introduced because they increase profits. But these profits are temporary, as innovations are non-rival goods and only partly excludable because it is easy to imitate innovations and new innovations become available (see Aghion and Tirole, 1994 and Murphy, Shleifer and

Vishny, 1989). Thus, the profit motive accounts for both creations and destructions (see Aghion and Howitt, 1992).

Schumpeter (1942) believed the process of creative destruction is self-destructive in the long run by replacing the profit motive with a socialization of investment. Consequently socialism will eventually substitute capitalism.[2] However, the experience of communist countries seems to contradict this view. Yet, the breakdown of communism may have been an outcome of a process of creative destruction working on a large, world-wide scale.[3]

By inverting Schumpeter's metaphor, one can see socialism as an instance of destructive creation. To push this metaphor further, one can see socialism as a political arrangement justified as being designed to enable pure creation, one that does away with the destructiveness of the anarchical functioning of market economy. It certainly ends up with an almost pure destruction. Neo-Schumpeterian growth theory captures this development.[4] The lack of a profit motive in the centrally planned economy diminished the incentive for technical change and technological learning. As a result, they have got considerable adjusting and catching up to do.

Just as socialism engendered a misapplication of resources through a type of destructive growth process, transformation policies may not lead to sustainable long-term growth. The statistics on real GDP, industrial output, investment and employment in the chapter by Havlik (see also Gligorov and Sundström, 1994) illustrate the magnitude of destruction following real socialism and uncovered by the transformation process.[5] One might expect that such ongoing large-scale destruction should foster long-run creativity on an equally or comparably large scale. But, as the Schumpeterian growth theory shows, this process is not automatic. First, the policies may follow an agenda that does not have growth as a priority. Second, they may create new problems that induce these economies to invest resources in political or other disputes over redistribution, instead of activities that promote growth and innovation.[6]

3 Creative destruction and endogenous growth

Unlike the Solow-type models developed in the 1950s and 1960s, 'new growth theory'[7] attempts to make technical progress endogenous (see Hammond and Rodriguez-Clare, 1993). At present, new growth theory has only started to turn up results with possibly far-reaching consequences. Those following Romer (1993a; 1993b) believe that new growth theory is revolutionary, providing an altogether new theory of economics. Others following Lucas (1988; 1993) believe that the new growth theory is a reaffirmation of neo-classical economics. Whatever the result, many of the ideas that new growth theory uses to explain the accumulation of knowledge and learning processes are developed sufficiently to take into account the complexities that are well known in philosophy and sociology of science (e.g. Quine, 1981; Merton, 1975; see also Gligorov, 1994 for a discussion of the possibilities and limits of new growth theory). Following the neo-Schumpeterian version of new growth theory, we simply assume that the supply of knowledge, responds positively to profit incentives (see also Aghion and Howitt, 1992; 1994, Grossman and Helpman, 1991a; Krugman, 1993; Corriveau, 1994; Easterly et al., 1994; and Dosi et al., 1994).

Two types of stylized facts concern new growth theory. First, the apparent lack of sustainable long-term growth rates and of the convergence of per capita income across countries. Second, the apparent correlation of economic policies that countries rely on with a long-run rate of growth of output (or income).

These stylized facts lead to the conclusion that standard neo-classical growth theory (and the aggregate production function) cannot adequately explain growth. If policy could influence long-term growth, then there would be no reason to expect that growth rates would be constant and converging unless the policies pursued over time and across countries are constant and converging (see Solow, 1994). The important question is what kind of policies would promote long-term growth? To answer that question, it is necessary to identify the fundamental determinants of growth.

Growth theory identifies two sources of long-run growth. The first is the growth of knowledge.[8] The second is externalities of all kinds, that is, economies of scale, integration, the extent and openness of the market as well as others. A simple production function parable illustrates the role played by both sources (see Solow, 1988). We can do this without any commitment to the aggregate production function used in conventional growth theory. It is possible to use this parable to show the inadequacy of the analysis. Let Y stand for output (a collection of goods), A for technology (a library of production blueprints), K for capital (a set of intermediate goods), I for inventions (probable additions to the list of blueprints), L for labour (the original factor of production), and H for human capital (a classification of skills associated with labour). We can write this function such that output depends on all the mentioned inputs:

$$Y = Y(K, L; A, I, H) \qquad (8.1)$$

Another way to write the same function could be:

$$Y = Y(AI(K), H(L)) \tag{8.2}$$

Let us assume, in accordance with (8.2), that only K and L get rewarded, that is, Y gets distributed on r, the rate of profit (or the real rate of interest), and w, the wage rate. Then, all the other factors become externalities of various kinds, In other words, the whole income gets distributed to capital and labour, but if the existing capital and labour are doubled, the output and income grow by more than double (superscript dots stand for derivatives):

$$\dot{Y} > \frac{\dot{Y}}{\dot{K}} + \frac{\dot{Y}}{\dot{L}} \tag{8.3}$$

and capital and labour do not get paid their marginal products, that is, social and private benefits diverge. Assuming uniform profit and wage rates, then

$$r < \frac{\dot{Y}}{\dot{K}} \tag{8.4}$$

and

$$w < \frac{\dot{Y}}{\dot{L}} \tag{8.5}$$

Thus, there are rewards distributed to entrepreneurs that come out of externalities.[9] The question is how are they supplied and what determines their rate of growth? Essentially, the new growth theory of any kind attempts to answer this question.

There are two sources of externalities. The first is in the increasing returns associated with the levels or scales of the factors used in production (economies of scale). The old theory of growth argued that growth rates changed while the economy was adjusting to parameter shocks, that is, while it was moving from one level to another. But once the economy had settled down, its level should have no effects on its steady-state rate of growth. The story changes if the capital stock or technology influence the growth rate. This is what new growth theory asserts. Much of the theory has to do with the descriptions of the avenues through which the level of one factor or another influences either its growth or the growth of another factor.[10] For instance, the theory assumes that the level of fixed capital has significant learning-by-doing effects. Also, the level of human capital influences the growth of inventions. And there are many other ways in which the sheer size of a factor influences its growth.

The parameters that control the economy are the second source of externalities. Let s be the rate of saving, d the discount rate that captures the utility of the future output or income, A the technology, i the frequency of inventions, e the labour efficiency, and l the efficiency of learning. It is then possible to associate these parameters with the respective factors and enter them into the production function.

$$dY = f(Ail(sK), lH(eL)) \qquad (8.6)$$

It is possible to specify the parameters such that there are constant returns to scale in the production function, with decreasing returns on separate factors. At the same time one can assume increasing returns to scale. For instance, there may be firm-specific decreasing returns, but industry-wide increasing returns or *vice versa*. Also, an innovation may have industry- or economy-wide external effects, that the innovator cannot entirely capture. Specifically, if we take (8.6) as a firm production function, then one can either change the parameters by the innovations that particular firm introduces (an externality for the industry), or supplied by the industry (a source of the firm's increasing returns). It is possible to describe all types of influences of this kind (see Romer, 1990, Grossman and Helpman, 1991a and Krugman, 1993).

In new growth theory externalities and the growth of knowledge determine economic growth. In neo-Schumpeterian new growth theory, the fundamental assumption is that imperfect competition leads to creative destruction. As a consequence there are different institutional and policy implications. One can argue in the Schumpeterian manner, that the world of perfect competition is irrelevant for theory of growth (see Romer, 1989). When there is a profit motive, creation of new knowledge has a price in the destruction of old knowledge. New processes substitute the old ones; new goods drive out old goods. Instead of looking at the capital–labour substitution, one should look at the substitution of new for old ideas and for the incentive structure that supports this process of the growth of knowledge.

It is for that reason that one can relax the usual assumptions of the production function, and the parameters are free to take values that were impossible to envisage under perfect competition. That has significant implications for both economic theory and policy. Economic policy may determine or influence the production function parameters. Thus, long-term growth depends on the policy agenda and, eventually, on the underlying institutions of public choice. One can also concentrate on the parameters, directly dispensing with the idea of the production function altogether except as a convenient way to tell the macroeconomic story.

4 Policy implications and dilemmas

New growth theory makes growth almost synonymous with externalities (indeed, creative destruction itself is a type of externality). But these externalities are institutions, government or political intervention, or regulation in general. Moreover, new growth theory argues for the fundamental role of public choice and economic policy. The question is what role? That brings in the Schumpeterian policy dilemma not always made explicit in the new growth theory's considerations. This becomes a question of how to influence the values of the variables and parameters identified in (8.6) above.

One possible answer is to assume that an increase in the amount of new capital, or capacity utilized (see DeLong and Summers, 1992), does not bring the growth rate down because of externalities: the larger the stock of capital the larger is the social opportunity set and there are greater learning-by-doing effects. There are, in other words, increasing returns to capital accumulation. That makes capital a kind of a (partially) public good.[11]

From that, one could conclude that public concentration of investment would be the policy that would cause an increase in the actual growth rate. This is, of course, a conclusion of questionable policy validity. An example that might be of interest for the development implications of the new growth theory could be a city deliberately built by a government to put in place a new industrial or administrative centre (see Krugman, 1993 for an opposite evolutionary account of urban concentration). There are quite a number of examples from socialist and other states on the inefficiencies of such developmental strategies.

There are alternative ways to benefit from the larger capital stock. If a firm, a region, or a country opens up to competition, it will acquire access to the larger capital stock. In that sense, deregulation and liberalization put an economic unit in the position to partake in the internalization of externalities. In this case, government actions will still be very important, but the policy the government pursues will be quite different. One can question this policy advice because of the possibilities of liberalization leading to specialization in activities that a country has comparative advantages in, but has low rate of growth.

The dilemma is this: should the government try to influence the investment function directly or through trade policies? The socialization of the investment function or liberalization of trade are the alternatives.

The same dilemma appears when considering policies conducive to the development of human capabilities. Human capabilities augment with learning. Indeed, the more people exposed to education or training, either as students or as labourers, the faster is the increase in the aggregate human capabilities. This suggests the introduction of a comprehensive scheme of public education and instruction. But there is also an alternative or a complement. A country well integrated into the world market will expose its labour force to new technologies and will thus profit from a mass process of learning-by-doing. Thus, there are alternative ways of knowledge propagation (see Arrow, 1994).

One can make a similar case for invention. Assume that a larger stock of knowledge induces an increasing frequency of inventions.[12] That may suggest different policies for a developing economy (especially if it is small). But the most promising one is to try to acquire access to the knowledge as it develops so that the developing country can benefit from the larger stock of knowledge already accumulated in the world. Given the profit motive, this also suggests that competition is important for research and development. Romer (1993a; 1994a) discusses the types of trade and investment policies that provide the incentive for the creation and diffusion of knowledge.

Thus, both institutions and economic policy influence technological accumulation through the invention rate, the rate of increase of human capital, the learning efficiency, and other parameters (such as culture, norms and beliefs). Indeed, for every interventionist policy there is the alternative one that relies on policies of liberalization.

How does one relate interventionism and liberalization? Contrary to Schumpeter's judgement, if long-term growth is sustainable, and if the evidence of the collapse of communism is taken into account, liberalization should second-best Pareto-dominate the former precisely because of the process of creative destruction going on. The argument is essentially as follows. With externalities, public goods and complementarities, it is possible to improve the market outcomes. That suggests government intervention. But, government decisions, being non-market ones, may also be inefficient. Rather than leading to Pareto-improvements, increased government intervention may lead to further Pareto-deterioration (Stiglitz, 1994). In that sense, free trade policies that approximate the efficient market allocation and that endogenize the economic policies second-best Pareto-dominate the neo-classical advice for outright social interventionism. Though at times it does not look that way, one can say that, neo-Schumpeterian growth theory generally supports free-trade policies, investment-friendly fiscal schemes (see King and Levine, 1993) that give incentives to innovate and investments in human and capital goods, equipment, and infrastructure.

5 Transformation and creative destruction

The ongoing transformation in Central and Eastern Europe is an attempt at catching up with the European Union. It is possible to characterize the transformation by a set of stylized policies. By a stylized policy, due to the short-term transformation experience, some hybrid of the policy prescribed and the one actually implemented is meant. Thus, the first two are closer to the actual policies that we observe in Central and Eastern Europe, while the last two are closer to the policies advised:[13]

(a) gradual stabilization;
(b) selective, at places comprehensive, liberalization;
(c) large-scale privatization;
(d) comprehensive restructuring.

One should gear policies toward long-run growth by influencing the parameters of the economic system in a favourable way. However, a closer look at these policies, as recommended and as actually developed, gives a rather different picture.

(a) *Stabilization.* Though it is widely believed that shock-type stabilization is the best for transforming economies and that price liberalization occurred in a shock-like way in at least some of the CEECs,[14] actual stabilization has been essentially gradual. In most cases the inflation rate trend has decreased every year. The reason has been the need to rely on inflation tax for purposes of achieving other transformation policy targets, that is, for easing the transition from the soft-budget to hard-budget constraint.

Though there is some evidence that stabilization is conducive to growth (see Fischer, 1993; Alesina and Summers, 1993), there is very little if any evidence that so-called moderately high inflation is beneficial for long-run growth. There is a broad consensus among Keynesian and neo-classical economists that even moderately high inflation is generally adverse to long-run growth. There are two reasons for the adverse influence of inflation on growth: distributional and allocative. The former affects investment through an increase in the level of uncertainty and policy-induced risks. The latter affects the level of aggregate output and the productivity of labour, because entrepreneurs spend more time on money balances management at the expense of regular activities.

Inflation correlates with the fiscal problems. Not surprisingly, the CEECs face serious fiscal problems, especially given the fall in output, the rise in tax evasion and corruption, the changing tax laws, and the persistent foreign debt and/or balance-of-payments problems (except in Slovenia and the Czech Republic). The problem is that further stabilization, though it could help solve these problems, would lead to a fall in government expenditures and to a further decline in output, as well as to a similar decline in the use and accumulation of human capital.

Given the connection between inflation and growth, the high inflation in the CEECs and their persistent budget deficits, and the foreign-debt burden in some of these countries, the impact of stabilization policy on the prospects for long-run growth is rather ambiguous. It is possible that these countries are trading short-term gains for long-term advantages (for a general discussion on that trade-off see Bruno, 1993).

(b) *Liberalization.* The second shock-like policy introduced in the CEECs was comprehensive liberalization. In theory, the CEECs are open economies and their internal markets were highly deregulated. They have become foreign-investment friendly, they have opened up their financial and other markets, and they have relaxed the stringent socialist regulations on their labour markets.

In reality, however, the CEECs followed a more cautious liberalization policy. There are three reasons why they followed this policy. First, the level of subsidies extended to state firms and to state and private farms (as well as to the emerging private sector through the tolerance of persistent tax evasion) is still significant. What is more important, the CEECs still use subsidies to support lossmaking enterprises or to shield some sectors from competition rather than as an industrial policy instrument.

Second, the process of creative destruction presumes the level of unemployment is high but often not as high as is the fall in output. Its persistence creates obvious problems with the waste of human capital.

Third, though marginal (except in Hungary) and often fluctuating, foreign direct investment has often been selectively welcomed creating significant structural and industry concentration problems that are increasingly being recognized.[15] In addition, liberalization of the labour market has not been as complete as is usually believed.

The neo-Schumpeterian growth theory makes a strong case for liberalization. There are some doubts as to the possible negative effects of free trade on long-run growth rates, but it is possible to alleviate these effects. New growth theory (in all its versions) suggests that liberalization enhances long-term growth. One could argue that new growth theory advises, though not always strongly because of the second-best Pareto-improvement arguments, against countries following some type of comprehensive industrial policy (at worst central planning). The theory recommends, however, policies that increase human capabilities, stimulate research and development and bring down obstacles to competition.

Another way to make the above point is to say that liberalization is a necessary but not a sufficient condition for long-term growth. Seen in that light, the liberalization policy of the transforming economies seem to be only partially growth-conducive. Indeed, one could very well argue that selective liberalization that seems to be the rule in transforming economies can cause quite ambiguous results for economic growth.

(c) *Privatization.* Central and East European transforming economies have targeted privatization as one of their most important tasks, which it certainly is from the point of view of entrepreneurship. However, it has been slow and gradual. In addition, the introduction of comprehensive privatization schemes has not sufficiently changed the incentive structure.

One aspect of privatization that has not received too much attention, but is of fundamental importance for new growth theory, is its entrepreneurial character, or rather the lack of one. Neo-Schumpeterian growth theory emphasizes the contribution of the innovative entrepreneurs through the process of creative destruction. Unfortunately, privatization schemes in the CEECs have not taken that into account and have more of a redistributional and political character than the entrepreneurial one (see the revealing testimony given in Boycko et al., 1994). From a Schumpeterian point of view, privatization is growth enhancing because it introduces the right principal–agent relationship and the income distribution that supports the incentive structure necessary for such a relationship. The privatization process in the CEECs is favouring insiders, introducing unnecessary rent-seeking and targets redistribution rather than entrepreneurship and inventiveness. This is exasperated by the slow privatization of the banking sector that should play a crucial role in the Schumpeterian type of transformation and growth. Privatization in the CEECs has yet to show its growth potential because of its indecisiveness, its politicization, the unclear incentive structure and the mainly redistributionary character.

(d) *Restructuring.* The process of restructuring is perhaps the one that is the most connected to the creative destruction idea of the neo-Schumpeterian growth theory. In the CEECs, the mass destruction that has occurred because of the lack of creativeness has been huge and it is far from over. One could very well argue that the most important part of it is yet to come. Indeed, one could encourage it for the following reason.

A developing country may find it profitable to specialize in the low-growth industries to gain a comparative advantage. Thus, if Central and Eastern Europe decides to restructure in such a way as to preserve as much of its existing industry as possible, it might end up with a low-growth economy in the long run. Moreover, if one accompanies restructuring with a fall in R&D and by an increase of a specific kind of inequality, the emerging private sector may move onto a long-term low-growth path.

New growth theory has discussed the possibility of this type of development. This relates to the theoretical possibility of multiple equilibria that are Pareto-ranked. That means that there will be growth equilibria that are Pareto-dominated. This is another way to say that there will exist growth equilibria that will not be efficient. Indeed, this could prove to be the most serious problem that the restructuring process in the post-socialist CEECs faces.

The path that these transforming countries have taken may not lead to sustainable long-run growth. There are two indications of that. First, there is still very little creative destruction (the number of bankruptcies is still significantly low and the overall level of subsidies, tax shields, as well as other types of rent-seeking related activities are all relatively high). Second, there is still very little inventiveness. Indeed, one would expect a surge of inventiveness, if not in new ideas, then in the implementation of the existing ones. But that phase is yet to come. Indeed, there is increasing awareness that the quite dramatic fall in research and development activities will have long-term consequences. The overall index of these developments is the slowly progressing restructuring. Also, one can argue that what restructuring there is, is moving into the direction of specialization that may lead to the reliance on the low-growth activities in which these countries have comparative advantages.

Having in mind the discussed stylized facts, and especially the process of restructuring, we would like to allude to an important theoretical possibility. Intuitively, transformations are shocks that require policy adjustments. In a sense, they are a process of growth and development that starts with radical changes in the fundamentals of the transforming economy. There is a sense in which the early policy responses may have quite far-reaching consequences: they may lock up an economy on to a long-term growth and development path (see Arthur, 1989 and David, 1994). The lock-in effects have been studied with the idea that small events can have long-run consequences, but the same sorts of effects should be expected to exist in the case of historical discontinuities and breakdowns. This is indeed what seems to us to be important in the case of transformations. They are such momentous shocks that one should expect the policy responses to have consequences for much of future history.

The Schumpeterian idea of creative destruction captures this type of lock-in effect. This involves the start of an evolutionary process that has some significant dynamic properties for growth and development. The detection of the initial process of creative destruction can lead to the judgement that an economy has been locking in to a fast long-run growth. The lack of such a process should alert to the opposite possibility. Therefore, it is interesting to study the early policy responses in the CEECs in relation to the process of creative destruction.

6 Conclusion

Though we have argued that neo-Schumpeterian growth theory does not yet give an unambiguous policy agenda for development, much of the transformation policy agenda goes against the policy proposals this theory suggests. After the long period of socialist destructive creation, the CEECs find it difficult to turn to creative destruction. On the one hand, the destruction caused by the demise of socialism has robbed these countries of many of the externalities connected with the advanced level of capital endowment. On the other hand, most of the policies adopted do not work on the fundamental parameters in a way that is conducive to long-run growth. It will take a further change in policy to reverse the current growth trend.

Notes

1. An earlier version of this chapter was discussed at a seminar at the Department for East European Studies of Uppsala University. The authors appreciate the criticism and the suggestions of the participants.
2. 'Capitalism, whilst economically stable, and even gaining in stability, creates, by rationalizing the human mind, a mentality and a style of life incompatible with its fundamental conditions, motives, and social institutions, and will change, although not by economic necessity and probably even at some sacrifice of economic welfare, into an order of things which it will be merely a matter of terminology to call Socialism or not.' (Schumpeter, 1928).
3. Schumpeter can be said to have anticipated that possibility too. See Schumpeter's 'The Crisis of the Tax State' in Schumpeter (1991), published originally in 1918.
4. Kondratiev and Oparin (1926) develop a theory of world-wide creative destruction that Schumpeter endorsed in his work on business cycles.
5. In addition there is a well-recognized fall in the level of investment and especially in the investment in research and development.
6. All these results rely on the existence of the multiple-equilibria problem. See Shleifer (1986) and Krugman (1991b) and (1993).

7. It is debatable and it is indeed debated how new the 'new growth theory' is (on that see Solow, 1994 and Pasinetti, 1994). We think that both Solow and Pasinetti are right in arguing that the new growth theory is essentially an extension of the old growth theory. What is new is the more concentrated treatment of the process of the growth of knowledge as well as of the growth effects of different policies. These aspects are the most important for our paper (we acknowledge the help of the editor of this volume who pressed this point on us repeatedly).

8. This is the corner-stone of the conventional neoclassical growth theory (see Solow, 1988 for a review).

9. It is not necessary to assume increasing returns to have the same distributional problems. On that see Caballé and Manresa (1994).

10. Assuming, of course, that the factors, K and L, can be consistently defined. As is known from the so-called Cambridge controversy, this is impossible. Indeed, one way to see that it is so is to look at function (8.6) and see how complicated the properties of these factors can become. It may very well be that all the excitement with the new growth theory may be due to the fact that by introducing externalities, increasing returns, creative destruction and similar ideas it is both acknowledging this conceptual impossibility and drawing the desired conclusions from them.

11. It is to be understood here when we are discussing the aggregation of human capabilities (or human capital) that we are aware of the difficulties that the aggregation of the factors of productions brings. Indeed, we both want to use the new growth theory's language and to point to its limitations advocating the Schumpeterian approach instead.

12. That is, the probability of an invention coming in per unit of time increases. To repeat, this is an assumption. It is not a proposition in philosophy, sociology, or history of science.

13. For an early and detailed treatment see Blanchard et al. (1991); it is interesting to note that this book was written by a group of economists some of whom are among the leading contributors to the new growth theory literature, but that has very little reflection on their analysis of transformation processes.

14. For a general dilemma that stabilization highlights in developing countries see Bruno (1993).

15. For a discussion see ECE (1995).

References

Aghion, P. and P.H. Howitt (1992), 'A Model of Growth through Creative Destruction', *Econometrica*, 60, 323–51.

Aghion, P. and P.H. Howitt (1994), 'Endogenous Technical Change: The Schumpeterian Perspective', in L.L. Pasinetti and R.M. Solow (eds) (1994).

Aghion, P. and J. Tirole (1994), 'Opening the Black Box of Innovation', *European Economic Review*, 38, 701–10.

Alesina, A. and L.H. Summers (1993), 'Central Bank Independence and Macroeconomic Performance: Some Comparative Evidence', *Journal of Money, Credit, and Banking*, 25, 151–62.

Arrow, K.J. (1962), 'Economic Implications of Learning by Doing', *Econometrica*, 29, 155–73.

Arrow, K.J. (1994), 'The Production and Distribution of Knowledge', in G. Silverberg and L. Soete (eds) (1994).

Arthur, W.B. (1989), 'Competing Technologies, Increasing Returns, and Lock-In by Historical Events', *The Economic Journal*, 99, 116–31.

Barro, R.J. (1990), 'Government Spending in a Simple Model of Endogenous Growth', *Journal of Political Economy*, 98, S103–S125.

Barro, R.J. and X. Sala-I-Martin (1992), 'Public Finance in Models of Economic Growth', *Review of Economic Studies*, 59, 645–61.

Blanchard, O., R. Dornbusch, P. Krugman, R. Layard and L. Summers (1991), *Reform in Eastern Europe*, Cambridge, Mass.: The MIT Press.

Boycko, M., A. Shleifer and R.W Vishny (1994), *Privatizing Russia*, Cambridge, Mass.: The MIT Press.

Bruno, M. (1993), *Crisis, Stabilization, and Economic Reform*, Cambridge: Cambridge University Press.

Caballé, J. and A. Manresa (1994), 'Social Rents, Interest Rates, and Growth', *Economics Letters*, 45, 413–19.

Corriveau, L. (1994), 'Entrepreneurs, Growth and Cycles', *Economica*, 61, 1–15.

David, P.A. (1994), 'Why are Institutions the "Carriers of History?": Path Dependence and the Evolution of Conventions, Organizations and Institutions', *Structural Change and Economic Dynamics*, 5, 205–20.

DeLong, J.B. and L.H. Summers (1992), 'Equipment Investment and Economic Growth: How Strong is the Nexus', *Brookings Papers on Economic Activity*, 2.

Dinopoulos, E. (1994), 'Schumpeterian Growth Theory: An Overview', *Osaka City University Review*, 29, 1–21.

Dosi, G. et al. (1994), 'The Diversity of Development Patterns: Catching Up, Forging Ahead and Falling Behind', in L.L. Pasinetti and R.M. Solow (eds) (1994).

Easterly, W., R. King, R. Levine and S. Rebelo (1994), 'Policy, Technology Adoption and Growth', in L.L. Pasinetti and R.M. Solow (eds) (1994).

ECE (1995), *Economic Survey of Europe in 1994–1995*, United Nations, New York and Geneva.

Fischer, S. (1993), 'The Role of Macroeconomic Factors in Growth', *Journal of Monetary Economics*, 32, 485–512.

Gligorov, V. (1994), 'Science as a Vocation Revisited', unpublished.

Gligorov, V. and N. Sundström (1994), 'Growth Consequences of Transformations', Working paper 20, Department of East European Studies, Uppsala University.

Grossman, G.M. and E. Helpman (1991a), *Innovation and Growth in the Global Economy*, Cambridge, Mass.: The MIT Press.

Grossman, G.M. and E. Helpman (1991b), 'Quality Ladders in the Theory of Growth', *Review of Economic Studies*, 58, 43–61.

Grossman, G.M. and E. Helpman (1994), 'Endogenous Innovation in the Theory of Growth', *The Journal of Economic Perspectives*, 8, 23–44.

Hahn, F.H. and R.C.O. Matthews (1964), 'The Theory of Economic Growth: A Survey', *Economic Journal*, 74, 779–902.

Hammond, P.J. and A. Rodriguez-Clare (1993), 'On Endogenizing Long-Run Growth', *Scandinavian Journal of Economics*, 95, 391–425.

King, M. (1992), 'Growth and Distribution', *European Economic Review*, 36, 585–92.

King, M.A. and M.H. Robson (1993), 'A Dynamic Model of Investment and Endogenous Growth', *Scandinavian Journal of Economics*, 95, 445–66.

King, M.A. and R. Levine (1993), 'Finance and Growth: Schumpeter Might be Right', *The Quarterly Journal of Economics*, 108, 717–37.

Kondratiev, N.D. and P. Oparin (1926), *Bolshoy cikli konyukturii*, Moscow.

Krugman, P. (1991a), *Geography and Trade*, Leuven, Belgium: Leuven University Press and Cambridge, Mass.: The MIT Press.

Krugman, P. (1991b), 'History versus Expectations', *Quarterly Journal of Economics*, 106, 651–67.

Krugman, P. (1993), 'Toward a Counter-Counterrevolution in Development Theory', Proceedings of the World Bank Annual Conference, The World Bank.

Krugman, P. (1994), 'Competitiveness: A Dangerous Obsession', *Foreign Affairs*, March/April.

Lombardini, S. and F. Donati (1994), 'Economic Development: A Quasi-Schumpeterian Model', in L.L. Pasinetti and R.M. Solow (eds) (1994).

Lucas, R.E., Jr. (1988), 'On the Mechanics of Economic Development', *Journal of Monetary Economics*, 22, 3–42.

Lucas, R.E., Jr. (1990), 'Supply-Side Economics: An Analytical Review', *Oxford Economic Papers*, 42, 293–316.

Lucas, R.E., Jr. (1993), 'Making a Miracle', *Econometrica*, 61, 251–72.

Merton, R.K. (1975), *Sociology of Science*, New York: The Free Press.

Murphy, K.M., A. Shleifer and R.W. Vishny (1989), 'Industrialization and the Big Push', *Journal of Political Economy*, 97, 1003–26.

Pasinetti, L.L. (1994), 'The Structure of Long-Term Development: Concluding Comments', in L.L. Pasinetti and R.M. Solow (eds) (1994).

Pasinetti, L.L. and R.M. Solow (eds) (1994), *Economic Growth and the Structure of Long-Term Development*, London: Macmillan.

Persson, T. and G. Tabellini (1992), 'Growth, Distribution and Politics', *European Economic Review*, 36, 593–602.

Przeworski, A. (1993), 'Economic Reforms, Public Opinion, and Political Institutions: Poland in the Eastern European Perspective', in L.C. Bresser Pereira, J.M. Maravall and A. Przeworski (1993), *Economic Reforms in New Democracies*, Cambridge: Cambridge University Press.

Quine, W.V. (1981), *Theories and Things*, Harvard University Press.

Rivera-Batiz, L.A. and P.M. Romer (1991), 'Economic Integration and Endogenous Growth', *Quarterly Journal of Economics*, 106, 531–55.

Romer, P.M. (1989), 'Capital Accumulation in the Theory of Long-Run Growth', in R.J. Barro (ed.) (1989), *Modern Business Cycle Theory*, Harvard University Press.

Romer, P.M. (1990), 'Endogenous Technological Change', *Journal of Political Economy*, 98, 71–102.

Romer, P.M. (1993a), 'Two Strategies for Economic Development: Using Ideas and Producing Ideas', Proceedings of the World Bank Annual Conference, The World Bank.

Romer, P.M. (1993b), 'Idea Gaps and Object Gaps in Economic Development', *Journal of Monetary Economics*, 32, 543–73.

Romer, P.M. (1994a), 'New Good, Old Theory, and the Welfare Costs of Trade Restrictions', *Journal of Development Economics*, 43, 5–38.

Romer, P.M. (1994b), 'The Origins of Endogenous Growth', *The Journal of Economic Perspectives*, 8, 3–22.

Rosenstein-Roden, P.N. (1943), 'Problems of Industrialization of Eastern and South-Eastern Europe', *Economic Journal*, 53, 202–11.

Schumpeter, J.A. (1928), 'The Instability of Socialism', *Economic Journal*, 38, 361–86.

Schumpeter, J.A. (1942), *Capitalism, Socialism and Democracy*, New York: McGraw-Hill.

Schumpeter, J.A. (1991), *The Economics and Sociology of Capitalism*, Princeton University Press.

Siebert, H. (ed.) (1993), *Overcoming the Transformation Crisis*, Tübingen: J.C.B. Mohr (Paul Siebeck).

Silverberg, G. and L. Soete (eds) (1994), *The Economics of Growth and Technical Change*, Aldershot: Edward Elgar.

Solow, R. (1988), *Growth Theory*, Oxford: Basil Blackwell.

Solow, R. (1994), 'Perspectives on Growth Theory', *Journal of Economic Perspectives*, 8, 45–54.

Stiglitz, J. (1994), *Whither Socialism?*, Cambridge, Mass.: The MIT Press.

Young, A. (1993a), 'Invention and Bounded Learning by Doing', *Journal of Political Economy*, 101.

Young, A. (1993b), 'Substitution and Complementarity in Endogenous Innovation', *Quarterly Journal of Economics*, 108.

9 Prospects of Building Science and Technology Capabilities in Central and Eastern Europe

Slavo Radošević

1 Introduction

Research and development (R&D) and production capabilities are two of the most important inherited comparative advantages of the Central and East European countries (CEECs). It is a common assumption that the austere macroeconomic stabilization programmes advocated for the CEECs should give rise to 'natural' comparative advantages. If so, one could expect the acquired comparative advantages in R&D and production knowledge to materialize quickly in market outcomes. This Ricardian assumption lies behind much of the economics of transition.[1]

An alternative view would be that the acquired capabilities in R&D and production could be easily lost if micro and sectoral aspects of restructuring are not taken into account. Whether the Ricardian assumption or the alternative view is taken, radically changed economic incentives have led to a significant re-configuration and re-evaluation of acquired capabilities in the CEECs. As capabilities are a 'specific commodity', it is important to analyse what has happened to them during the transition process. This applies equally to 'in-house' R&D and production capabilities as well as to non-business based science and technology capabilities. Changing economic incentives has important long-term effects on science and technology in the CEECs.[2]

This chapter looks at the importance of capability building in Central and Eastern Europe. Section 2 assesses the inherited absorptive and innovation capacities in the CEECs. Section 3 describes reform changes and their macroeconomic effects. Section 4 estimates the effects of changed macroeconomic incentives on science and technology and sectoral capabilities. And the final section suggests three possible scenarios for improving the prospects of building science and technology capabilities in the CEECs.

2   Inherited absorptive and innovation capacities[3]

Apart from inherited socialist institutional specificities, the CEECs have had exceptionally high levels of R&D investment. In relative terms, these activities significantly surpassed those of comparable countries at the medium income level. However, the absorptive capacity of these economies did not quite match the high levels of R&D investments. This applies equally to domestically developed technologies as well as to imported ones.

A comparison of the gross enrolment ratios for selected countries and regions provides a rough approximation of absorptive capacity.[4] Table 9.1 shows that secondary enrolment in the CEECs appears between Latin American and second-tier East Asian countries on the one side, and the European periphery on the other. However, fifteen to twenty years ago these countries ranked much higher, being much closer to the European periphery and significantly ahead of Latin America. This 'loss of tempo' is the essential characteristic of the CEECs that also appears in other indicators.[5]

At the tertiary level, the CEECs do not have an advantage in relation to other regions. At this level the enrolment ratios are behind Latin America and the European periphery. 'Loss of tempo' is somewhat stronger at this level than at the secondary level. The average increase in enrolment ratios during the last twenty years is the slowest in the CEECs. The most puzzling observation is that Hungary, Poland, Slovakia and the Czech Republic appear in the lowest percentile. Also, differences within the CEECs are much bigger than in the European periphery. The slowdown in increase of the relative number of students in the CEECs is much more pronounced.

The comparative enrolment ratios show a more favourable position for the CEECs at the beginning of the 1970s than at the end of the 1980s. The CEECs still rank higher on average than Latin America in secondary education. At the tertiary level they are similar to Latin America. In relation to the less developed EC countries, the gap has somewhat widened at both educational levels. Educational indicators put the CEECs at a rank in keeping with the income level of those countries. However, where R&D activities are concerned the situation is very different.

To compare R&D levels in financial and manpower terms would give an unrealistically favourable picture of the CEECs.[6] From the dynamic perspective, however, simple average annual growth rates of research scientists and engineers during the 1970s and 1980s are more than two times slower compared to other regions. Table 9.2 contains comparable figures on R&D gross expenditures (GERD) based on purchasing power

Table 9.1   Education indicators in selected countries and regions, 1980 and 1990

| | Enrolment ratios | | | | | | Number of students per 10,000 inhabitants | | |
| | Secondary | | | Tertiary | | | | | |
	1980	1990	change	1980	1990	change	1980	1990	change
Eastern Europe									
Bulgaria	84	74	88%	16	31	193%	1144	2092	183%
Czechoslovakia	89	84	94%	17	18	104%	1287	1215	94%
GDR	80	79	99%	30	34	111%	2395	2683	112%
Hungary	69	79	114%	13	15	112%	944	970	103%
Poland	77	82	106%	18	22	124%	1656	1418	86%
Romania	71	110	155%	11	9	78%	868	712	82%
Average	78	85	108%	18	21	121%	1382	1515	110%
USSR	93	94	101%	21	26	120%	1971	1820	92%
Developed Europe									
Austria	73	83	114%	23	33	143%	1811	2174	120%
Denmark	105	109	104%	29	32	110%	2074	2466	119%
Finland	98	93	95%	32	47	145%	2577	3331	129%
Average	92	95	103%	28	37	133%	2154	2657	123%
European periphery									
Greece	81	99	122%	17	29	166%	1256	2200	175%
Ireland	90	98	109%	20	26	130%	1610	2308	143%
Spain	87	107	123%	24	32	134%	1859	2730	147%
Portugal	37	59	159%	11	18	164%	944	1525	162%
Average	74	91	123%	18	27	145%	1417	2191	157%
Latin America									
Argentina	56	74	132%	22	41	188%	1741	3079	177%
Brazil	34	39	115%	12	12	97%	1162	1064	92%
Peru	59	70	119%	19	36	184%	1771	3450	195%
Urugay	62	77	124%	18	50	286%	1338	3751	280%
Chile	53	74	140%	...	...	...	1305	1698	130%
Average	53	67	127%	18	35	196%	1463	2608	175%
East Asia									
Korea	76	88	116%	18	28	175%	1698	3953	233%
Malaysia	48	56	117%	4	7	163%	419	671	160%
Average	62	72	116%	10	17	173%	1059	2312	196%

Note: Gross enrolment ratios equals total enrolment, regardless of age, divided by the population of the age group in a specific level of education. Simple averages are calculated for each country group.

Source: UNESCO, *Statistical Yearbook 1992.*

parities.[7] GERD per capita figures show that R&D expenditures in the CEECs were two times higher than expenditures of Spain and Ireland and four times higher than those of Greece and Portugal.[8] The levels of GERD/GDP for Hungary show similar differences.[9]

Table 9.2 GERD/GDP in CEECs and the European periphery

	1985	1986	1987	1988	1989	1990
Bulgaria	2.49	2.48	2.53	2.77	3.63	2.38
Hungary	2.36	2.55	2.65	2.33	1.98	1.6
Yugoslavia	0.79	0.88	0.94	0.98	0.91	0.92
Greece	0.34	0.33	0.35	0.37	0.47	...
Ireland	0.82	0.89	0.87	0.85	0.85	0.92
Portugal	...	0.45	...	0.5	...	0.61
Spain	0.55	0.61	0.64	0.72	0.75	0.81

Source: OECD, *Main Science and Technology Indicators 1992*, Simeonova (1993).

The trend for Hungary is typical of the CEECs; almost no growth of relative expenditures in the 1980s and a sharp decrease at the end of the 1980s, resulting in CEECs going into a lower spending group. Despite overestimated figures on manpower and expenditures, much higher relative spending for R&D indicates that its position is still significantly above that of the European periphery.

This comparatively hyper development of R&D is in stark contrast with educational indicators. It implies that more developed innovative activity was faced with a much less developed assimilation capability. On the other hand, a hyper developed R&D sector may indicate its lower productivity, too. The comparison with respect to that is equally limited and partial.

The number of citations per publication indicates the scientific impact of this 'production'. Comparisons with Portugal show similar 'scientific productivity' if measured by published papers. Table 9.3 shows a similarity between the CEECs and the European periphery (*Science Watch*, 1991). The East Asian countries are far above the CEECs in 'science production' (*Science Watch*, 1993). Taking into account R&D investment in the CEECs, one might expect the impact of these expenditures to be much higher. Reasons for this discrepancy might include a lower 'science productivity' or too much inward and applied orientation of their R&D systems.[10]

Finally, in terms of US patents the CEECs have activities equal to or higher than the European periphery. In terms of the absolute level this indicator underestimates their innovative activities as these economies were closed.[11] The lack of dynamics in US patenting is fully compatible with other indicators confirming a 'loss of tempo' in science and technology activities during the 1980s.

Table 9.3 Selected educational indicators, 1970 and 1989

	scientists and engineers			citations per paper[a]		
				number of papers	number of citations	mean citation per paper
	1970[a]	1989[b]	1989[b]/70[b]			
Bulgaria	22452	50585	13%	...	...	...
Czechoslovakia	36927	65475	9%	26764	63779	2.38
GDR	90836	127449	10%	32791	84683	2.58
Hungary	16282	20431	7%	21072	69951	3.32
Poland	59000	32500	3%	35886	105307	2.93
Romania	20764	59670	15%	...	...	...
Yugoslavia	...	...	...	11965	31265	2.61
Belarus	21863	44100	11%	...	...	...
Ukraine	129781	348600	14%	...	...	...
Greece	2634	5340	29%	11165	32558	2.92
Ireland	1857	6351	20%	12874	50780	3.94
Spain	5842	31170	30%	42907	135825	3.17
Portugal	2187	5004	13%	...	...	...
Argentina	6500	11088	9%	15490	36624	2.36
Brazil	21756	52863	61%	20037	50200	2.51
Peru	1925	4858	23%	...	...	...
Chile	3469	4630	19%	10141	22168	2.19
Korea	5628	56545	56%	...	...	...

Notes: [a]Countries publishing more than 10,000 papers. [b]Or the closest available year.
Sources: UNESCO, *Statistical Yearbook 1992*; *Science Watch* (1991).

In short, the absorptive capacity in the CEECs is similar to that of Latin America and behind the European periphery, while innovative capacities are much more developed and are, despite statistical problems, significantly above the two other regions. The basis for the growth of absorptive and innovative capacities was enormous physical investment. The problem of socialism was not of mobilizing finance to increase aggregate savings. For a long time the CEECs and the former Soviet Union invested relatively very high shares of GDP. These relative shares were much higher than US levels and surpassing Japanese levels (McKinnon, 1991). However, it is difficult to estimate the intangible investments. The studies of firms in the CEECs show that these intangible investments were far too insufficient for the level of physical investments, and also unbalanced, with a dominance of R&D investments over vocational training.

The CEECs imbalance between investment and outcome leads to a conclusion similar to Dahlman and Nelson (1993). Despite high R&D investments and relatively high, though for that level of R&D insufficiently developed, social absorptive capability, these economies mainly lacked an adequate incentive environment. This implies two things. First, as Dahlman and Nelson (1993) conclude, 'social absorption capability is not sufficient to explain why some economies have performed much better than others. High technical human capital may be a necessary but not sufficient condition for rapid economic growth.' Second, an adequate incentive environment to direct investments and people into the most economically productive activity is as important as social absorption capability.[12] That is why the next section provides a brief overview of the current changes in macroeconomics in the CEECs. This enables us to see how the changed incentives might influence the development of science and technology capabilities.

3 Radical changes in economic incentives and their effects
The result of bad allocative efficiency in the CEECs, either static or dynamic, was the inherited industrial structure characterized by the lack of small firms,[13] significant budget transfers,[14] macroeconomically significant distortions in relative prices and closed economies.[15] The latter was an indispensable condition to maintain such a structure of relative prices. As a result of decreasing growth during the 1980s some of these economies have inherited significant debt problems.[16]

The results of marketization of previously centrally planned economies have surprised economic experts. Contrary to expectations, stabilization has been relatively fast and successful, and prices were rapidly freed from administrative control. Markets replaced administrative allocation for goods and services, and microeconomic imbalances have been mainly eliminated in producer goods as well as in consumer goods markets. Inflation has come down markedly but after some time the fiscal position tended to deteriorate (Portes, 1993).

An unexpected result is the significant and protracted fall in industrial output and the reappearance of the 'soft-budget' constraint in the non-payment of inter-enterprise credit.[17] Although subsidies have been removed in the CEECs the 'soft-budget' constraint has shifted into inter-enterprise debts located in banks. Firms have explored how far they could go with arrears, non-payment of interest and non-payment of taxes. Firms have survived but restructuring has barely started (Blanchard, 1993).

Although exports to the West have grown rapidly (see Table 9.4), their durability and sustainability are questionable due to relatively income-inelastic demand for Central and Eastern European exports. It is not yet clear whether it is a stock-adjustment type of growth, i.e., growth based on the redirection of the existing products from Eastern to Western markets. CEECs export low-growth commodities, where export is usually increased through reduced market share of competitors, and not through the market growth.

Table 9.4 Exports from the CEEC-7 (percentage change in dollars)

	1988	1989	1990	1991	1992	1993	1994
Bulgaria	8	−13.8	−1.7	7.8	27.9	−28.6	0
Czech Republic	10.3	8.5	10.1	39.2	35.2	20.3	20.4
Hungary	8.9	17.1	−1.6	45.9	8.3	−19.3	−5
Poland	17.6	4.5	43.4	17.5	9.7	−2.9	15.8
Romania	8.6	−7.9	−44	−1.7	22.9	13.6	28
Slovak Republic	...	8.5	10.1	39.2	35.2	−16.9	25
Slovenia	...	3.2	20.8	−6	8.1	−9	11.9

Notes: Figures are based on balance-of-payments statistics. Figures for the Czech Republic exclude trade with Slovakia. 1994 figures are estimates.
Source: EBRD (1994) and EBRD (1995).

Institutional transformation has been slower than initially expected, especially because of political and technical delays to privatization. However, in all countries the development of small-scale private enterprises, mainly in services, is vigorous.

The fall in output has caused problems since mainly state companies and the tax base in the CEECs shrink rapidly. The private sector is not yet developed enough to compensate for the deterioration of the state sector while the institutional capability needed to build an efficient fiscal system is still underdeveloped. A fall in public consumption is accompanied by a fall in private consumption leaving only export demand as a source of increasing demand. Nevertheless, it seems that domestic, not export, demand is the main source of recovery in Poland.

What are the explanations for the protracted fall of output? Nuti and Portes (1993) classify explanations in four groups. The first group is 'J-curve' hypothesis: sharp contraction is unavoidable during the transition, it is the inevitable cost of restructuring and cutting back of the public sector. Second, there is statistical under-reporting of the private sector and services. Third, a strong negative demand shock is the result of wrong macroeconomic stabilization policies whose implicit assumptions were: excess demand, monetary overhang and the virtue of free market exchange rates (see Laski, chapter 5 in this volume). The excessive devaluation led to an unnecessarily large inflationary shock, which required restrictive policies to stop inflation. This led to credit squeeze. As a result big firms forced their banks to lend, while small firms and the private sector were left without credits. McKinnon (1991) sees the problem in a premature pressure to decontrol prices, float the exchange rate, privatize and decentralize decision-making before securing proper fiscal and monetary control over the economy. The fourth group is demand- and terms-of-trade shock coming from the former Soviet Union, which, although self-inflicted, halted trade within the former CMEA (Council for Mutual Economic Assistance) area. Even when experts take into account all these factors they, naturally, differ in the weighting of each factor.

From our perspective, it is interesting to ask: has allocative efficiency been achieved and has restructuring begun? Nuti and Portes (1993), as well as most experts, hold that a significant amount of capital still flows to defunct state-owned enterprises, thus starving the nascent private sector. Deficits created in this way through the banking system hide the danger of excessive inflation. In such circumstances the price mechanism does not properly guide the allocation of resources. The market will not work well if the credit market does not function. Also, because of slow privatization, state enterprises still do not behave as proper market agents. Estrin et al. (1993b) find that Polish state-owned enterprises (SOEs) failed to increase supply to activities whose relative price and therefore profitability increased; exports were not significantly reduced in activities whose relative profitability fell. This brings into question the relevance of the policy formulated on the assumption that firms will respond rationally to price signals after liberalization.

With respect to restructuring, the views are not in such conformity. In the case of some countries (Bulgaria, Romania, the Czech and Slovak Republics) it seems that sectoral restructuring has not yet taken place (Borensztein et al., 1993). In the case of Poland and Hungary, there are weak signs that structural change has started (Commander and Coricelli, 1993 and Landesmann and Pöschl, chapter 7 in this volume). Experts are not yet in agreement on the relative role in the output decline of aggregate demand (cuts in consumption), shifts in the composition of demand and negative supply shocks (changed relative prices of inputs).

The linkages between structural (institutional) and macroeconomic adjustment has provided an important lesson for the economics of transition as Bruno (1993) points out:

> Eastern Europe has confirmed the conventional lesson that economy in a fundamental macro-economic disequilibrium cannot successfully transform its micro structure as long as the fundamental imbalance prevails. (...) The new lesson from eastern Europe is that macro-economic adjustment can often not be achieved without at least some simultaneous structural reform.

Contracting effective demand may not necessarily increase unemployment and eliminate negative value-added activities unless there is structural change. Inadequate micro-foundations and lack of structural reforms have had substantial macroeconomic effects (property rights, lending discipline, managerial motivation, etc.). These are key factors behind the lack of supply response ('supply inertia') that were neglected in macroeconomic policy programmes.

Perhaps the most important issue is the perverse link between incentives and capabilities, as is explained in McKinnon (1991). Its importance stems from the evidence that much of the lost output was not in negative value-added activities as was expected (Nuti and Portes, 1993). Estrin et al. (1993b) recognize that the processes of financial decline in Polish firms appear to operate independently of factors associated with the underlying potential profitability or international competitiveness of the sectors in which the enterprises operate. 'Firms, which one might expect to be highly competitive on international markets, such as furniture or footwear manufacture, find themselves in a financially worse state than firms in many of the less obvious candidates for sunrise industries, such as steel, plastics and pharmaceuticals.' (Estrin et al., 1993b)

'Getting prices right' does not always lead to the improvement of capabilities with comparative advantages. McKinnon (1991) explains this refutation of the law of comparative advantage in the following way. Textbook wisdom says that, despite low average productivity, the comparative efficiency of at least some major domestic industries would soon assert itself. Such Ricardian-type reasoning lay behind the wish to liberalize foreign trade. If the 'real' exchange rate was sufficiently devalued, this model suggests that a substantial proportion of domestic industry would be viable in the short term and could quickly begin to expand in export markets. However, McKinnon starts from a different assumption, which he defines as the substitution model. It is based on the circular flow of production where goods and services can be combined in variable proportions. Producers of finished manufactures use labour and capital to add value to industrial raw materials and energy in combinations reflecting the previously highly protected domestic market.

The key point is that once the socialist economy is open to unrestricted foreign trade, McKinnon's approach admits the possibility of absolute inefficiency in existing domestic manufacturing. At the beginning of the transition, industries producing finished goods might well exhibit negative added value at world market prices, whether or not they turn out to be viable in the long run once free trade is attained. Most domestic industry need not be viable in the short term and massive real devaluation would not be all that useful in easing the burden of adjustment to world prices. This is possible because of the starting assumption: a combination of output and input with negative (or very low) value added at world market prices.

The long-term viability of industry depends not only on its production efficiency, but also on the prevailing costs of domestic factors of production, after a new trade equilibrium is established. To solve the problem McKinnon suggests setting the exchange rate in such a way as to equate (average) domestic prices of material inputs with those prevailing in world markets. This potentially stable 'real' exchange rate now provides a benchmark for converting the old implicit tariff protection associated with quota restrictions and with the existing system of exchange controls into explicit tariff equivalents. He recognizes the need for temporary protection in order to save viable production.

McKinnon's solution to the problem implies that the link between incentives and capabilities is not straightforward. Situations approaching 'perfect markets' are not necessarily the most conducive for the realization of comparative advantages. Dynamic adjustment requires a certain, though probably minimal, degree of deviation from the 'free trade' solution.[18]

This leads us back to Dahlman's and Nelson's (1993) proposition that the main problem in the CEECs is (was) not the investments in technical human capital but the incentive environment. The next section analyses the effects of new macroeconomic incentives on the acquired science and technology capabilities in the CEECs and the new types of capabilities that are likely to be developed within the new environment.

4 The effects of changed economic incentives on science and technology capabilities

Capabilities are mainly firm- and/or sector- (network-)specific. For this reason it is important for new market economies to ensure that firm and sector competencies are reflected in market outcomes.

Studies cited in the previous section had somewhat opposite conclusions regarding the extent of restructuring the CEECs. From the science and technology perspective, we can formulate this problem in the following way: have macro shocks prevented the structural adjustment of national R&D or have they enabled R&D competencies, embodied and disembodied, to be realized on the market? If the financial position of a sector is independent of its competitiveness, due to high macroeconomic shocks, then such a prolonged situation will have deteriorating effects on the acquired science and technology capabilities. Instead of being put to best use, human resources and knowledge can (through drastic demand cuts or through prolonged supply inertia caused by adaptations to new relative prices of inputs) in fact be wasted. If sector or industry is not a significant determinant of the pattern of adjustment, a situation in which macro stability is implemented for its own sake, and not as an enabling factor of firm and sector adjustments, is created. The net benefit of such an operation can in the end be negative. If, on the other hand, restructuring has started, the main problem is to understand which capabilities will be highly priced and which will be valued as irrelevant in a new incentive environment. We will try to sketch the problem on all three levels: aggregate R&D trends, sectoral adaptations and firm-level competencies.

A fall in R&D. Table 9.2 shows a decrease in GERD/GDP expenditures in the period 1985–90. Generalizing on the basis of these countries, it is possible to conclude that there is a decrease of 0.5 per cent of GDP. Since the biggest reductions actually took place in the last two years for which data are available (1991 and 1992–93), the total reduction since 1989 is around 1 per cent of GDP. This means that the R&D expenditures in these countries are now close to or below 1 per cent, which puts them into a category that seems 'natural' for medium-income economies. However, this does not say much about the current and future role of R&D.

The number of research scientists and engineers (RSE) is also decreasing at a rapid pace. Table 9.5 gives an idea of the extent of the decrease in the number of research scientists and engineers in the CEECs. The data for the Czech Republic (Muller, 1993), Romania (Sisesti and Sandu, 1992) and Estonia (Koorna, 1993) show that the decrease is about 30 per cent. The decrease in the number of the Eastern German RSE, which will be used as a reference point, was 53 per cent in three years.

The figures in Table 9.5 show that the reduction of a hyper-developed R&D system is underway. The interim result of the marketization of the

Table 9.5 Decrease of RSE employment in Eastern Europe, 1989–92

	1989	1992/93	1992(3)/89
Romania	60000	43000	0.72
Eastern Germany[a]	140000	66000	0.47
Bulgaria[b]	31616	26184	0.83
Czechoslovakia[c]	13400	9600	0.72
Russia[b]	1389000	778800	0.56
Hungary[b]	20431	11818	0.58
Czech Republic	7854	5639	0.72

Notes: [a]Data for 1992 estimated, based on Meske (1993). [b]Data for 1993. [c]Data for 1991.

Sources: Meske (1993), Simeonova (1993), Muller (1993), Gokhberg and Sokolov (1995), Inzelt (1995).

former socialist economies is a reduction of GERD/GDP of 1 per cent and a reduction of RSE of 30 per cent. Is this fall in expenditures and RSE a fall to a 'natural' level appropriate for middle-income economies which thus only reflects their 'natural' comparative advantages? Or is it the result of a fall in output, which is not based on the 'real' competitiveness of these economies but is primarily the result of macroeconomic mismanagement?

Table 9.6 Estimation of the East European RSE and the effects of the 'Eastern German scenario'

	nominal figures	norm. by Eastern German ratio	after Eastern German scenario
Bulgaria	50585	34398	23775
Czechoslovakia	65475	44523	30773
GDR	127449	86665	59901
Hungary	20431	13893	9603
Poland	32500	22100	15275
Romania	59670	40576	28045

Source: UNESCO, *Statistical Yearbook 1992.*

In the first instance, assume that Eastern German 1992 GERD/RSE levels are a reference point for comparing with the CEECs. In order to make the Eastern German scenario realistic, we must first try to get the estimations of OECD-compatible CEEC figures. Meske (1993) gives us GDR figures on OECD basis. In a rather crude manner, we normalize the figures on the number of research scientists and engineers in the CEECs by 0.68, that is, the proportion by which GDR figures had to be reduced to obtain OECD comparable data. On these figures we apply the Eastern German scenario, that is, a decrease in RSE figures by 0.47. This gives us the effects of the Eastern German scenario on the CEECs (Table 9.6). Tables 9.7 and 9.8 give us RSE figures per 10,000 inhabitants, before and after this procedure, compared to other countries.

Table 9.7 Number of RSE per 10,000 inhabitants before and after 'Eastern German scenario'

	nominal figures	norm. by Eastern German ratio	after Eastern German scenario
Bulgaria	56	38	18
Czechoslovakia	42	28	13
Hungary	19	13	12
Romania	26	18	8

Source: UNESCO, *Statistical Yearbook 1992.*

In the second instance we will take a more evolutionary stance and presume that the process of restructuring R&D is highly conditioned by the institutional heritage of R&D systems. The most important institutional characteristic of the CEEC R&D systems is the relatively high degree of externalization of R&D and/or small 'in-house' R&D capacities.[19] Again, an important contribution by Meske (1993) confirms this. The share of non-university based R&D in GDR was almost two times higher than in West Germany. In Table 9.9, estimates for the Czech Republic and the former USSR are included, based on Muller (1993), Glaziev and Schneider (1993) and Koorna (1993). If the share of West German non-university-based R&D (independent institutes) is taken as

Table 9.8 Number of RSE per 10,000 inhabitants during the 1980s

Austria	10	Greece	5
Denmark	21	Ireland	18
Finland	23	Spain	8
		Portugal	5
Argentina	4		
Brazil	4	Korea	13
Peru	3	Malaysia	3
Uruguay	7		
Chile	4	Turkey	4

Source: UNESCO, *Statistical Yearbook 1992.*

100, the estimates of shares of research scientists and engineers working in independent institutes are between two to four times higher than for West Germany.[20] This institutional heritage, based on weak incentives to appropriate R&D in centrally planned economies, creates a starting point for the restructuring of domestic R&D. As the relationships in R&D in Eastern Europe are now indeed mainly market-based, the development of this market seems crucial for the survival of Eastern European R&D capacities. It is especially so as shares of independent institutes in research scientists and engineers employment are around 30 per cent and under the biggest threat in the current situation.

Table 9.9 Institutional structure of RSE employment in FR Germany and in Eastern Europe (in percentages)

	FRG	GDR	Czech Rep.[a]	SSSR[b]
	1989[c]	1989[c]	1992	1989
University R&D	12.94%	10.00%	8.59%	9.10%
Non-university-based R&D	12.00%	22.86%	54.38%	51.50%
Industrial R&D	69.88%	61.43%	37.03%	39.50%
R&D in human-social sciences	5.18%	5.71%	...	...
Total	*100.00%*	*100.00%*	*100.00%*	*100.00%*

Notes: [a]Based on R&D manpower data. [b]Estimation based on the assumption that half of 'industrial sector' RSE are employed in independent branch institutes. [c]Full-time employment.
Sources: Meske (1993), Muller (1993), Glaziev and Schneider (1993).

Our knowledge of the direction of R&D restructuring is still anecdotal. One of the most interesting directions of R&D restructuring is change towards 'in-house' production or transformation of independent institutes into small manufacturing companies. Many of the previously semi-academic supplier organizations have fragmented into joint ventures, distributing and adding value to imported Western products. Almost all of the great Russian success stories in software development come from 'spin-offs' from big Soviet-era research institutes (Dyker and Stein, 1993).

However, even before a systematic empirical survey can be undertaken, the scarce evidence shows that in most of the CEECs there are several trends: first, a polarization of R&D, second, shifts in R&D towards the low end of the R&D spectrum and third, shrinking domestic R&D markets. Polarization means that the share of applied R&D is shrinking, the scientific community is further marginalized and public policy is unable to bridge the increasing gap between science and technology communities. The biggest victims of such situations are areas called 'transfer sciences', fields dependent on the interaction with basic sciences and production engineering (chemical and software engineering, for example). A shift towards the low end of the R&D spectrum denotes the increasing dominance of non-R&D activities like measuring, testing and quality control. These are areas for which there is a growing demand from domestic exporters.

Sectoral capabilities in a new context. We emphasized that, in the harsh economic conditions prevailing in the CEECs, specific sectoral advantages are not yet reflected in market outcomes. Demand and supply shocks prevent the search processes and the realization of network synergies within sectors. Very strong uncertainties in the environment still make irrational market outcomes possible. As there is not yet enough evidence on restructuring processes within different sectors, the following taxonomy of sectoral or/and capabilities restructuring summarizes several typical situations found in the CEECs.

First, the opening of economies based on an excessive import substitution, of which the CEECs are the best example, means that the 'production' of many irrelevant capabilities will be stopped. This will have effects similar to the stoppage of negative value-added productions. This will not only be the case in production that was the result of intended self-sufficiency but even more in production that was developed as a result of externally imposed restriction on technology access by the Co-ordinating Committee for Multilateral Security Controls (COCOM). A good example of these types of capabilities are information technology (IT) hardware producers. In the face of foreign competition, the IT hardware sector almost collapsed in the CEECs.[21] The capabilities developed within this sector would have never developed had there not been external restrictions. In current conditions the only response is closure of these capacities and, where possible, their transformation into component suppliers for a foreign partner.

Second, although a lot of acquired technological capabilities in the CEECs can be grouped into the import substitution type, it does not mean that all this effort is useless in the new conditions. The closed economy and specific restrictions and constraints to which the CEECs were exposed have in some areas created new trajectories and capabilities that have a promising future in an open economy. In fact, these are now competitive advantages of which some are already commercial high-tech products. Examples of these capabilities are specific skills of Soviet software engineers and several software packages already on the market.

For example, because Soviet computing was isolated from the world markets it followed a different path of evolution – one firmly rooted in mathematics – from that of the West. The result were highly developed skills in programming and algorithms (*Financial Times*, 1993).[22] The best documented story of commercial success is the Hungarian 'Graphisfot', which managed to capture 25 per cent of the world market for architectural design packages on the Apple Macintosh (Bojár, 1993). The second case is ScKi Recognita Corp of Hungary, a spin-off of the old state-owned software monopoly SzKi, which has sold 16,000 copies of its optical character recognition package Recognita Plus, of which over 95 per cent go for export (*Business Central Europe*, 1993). Dyker and Stein (1993) describe a similar success story of ParaGraph, also a venture with Apple.

However, some of the new capabilities developed within a closed economy can be irrelevant in new circumstances due to their bias towards complexity, as with the Hungarian laser industry (Havas, 1993a).[23]

Third, the liberalization and opening of the CEECs will probably do the most harm to capabilities and productions in the process of acquiring competencies that might be promising in an open markets context. These are capabilities whose development is still under the learning curve or that should be significantly reorganized to be profitable. A good example is the Hungarian precision engineering industry. The accumulated knowledge of R&D and manufacturing engineers as well as the experience of the elite of the industrial labour force might become completely worthless and disappear unless new market opportunities can be found quickly (Havas, 1993b). For the current level of demand the sector is too big and needs to be reorganized through vertical disintegration, subcontracting and division into smaller companies.

Finally, there are sectors with accumulated technological experience and significant production know-how whose opening has created incentive pressure. These are mainly traditional industries that are now the main exporters from the CEECs (textiles in Poland, wood and furniture in other countries, etc.). Their main problem is not production capability but complementary capabilities like marketing and design. The second area from which such firms might come is the military/industrial complex.[24]

Firm-level capabilities during the transition. The strength of macroeconomic changes, caused either by demand reductions or by new sets of relative prices, has prevented a clear sectoral adjustment. In that context, it seems that the firm level is currently the most important for restructuring Eastern Europe. The only real adjustment and re-configuration of capabilities are under transformation within the viable firms. Factors that determine motivation for managers, privatization and related conflicts and uncertainties have decisive influence on the pace of firm adjustment (Estrin et al, 1993a).

Irrespective of the pace of these changes, it is possible to get an idea on the processes of re-configuration of capabilities within firms. Török (1991), Hughes (1993) and Radošević (1994a) show that complementary capabilities (finance, marketing and organization) are weakest in the spectrum of firms' capabilities. Production know-how is comparatively better developed.[25] The information technology sector is a good example of a lack of firms that possess marketing skills.[26]

The current firm adjustments are minor structural shifts within the existing product mix. These adjustments are appearing as changes in the organizational structure (thinning of numerous hierarchical layers), increased marketing and sales effort and the elimination of the most unprofitable lines. Depending on the institutional context of a country, 'lay-offs' and privatization also belong to this group of mainly passive responses to new circumstances. More active adjustments would require additional capital and long-term stability. It is important to recognize that often the most active responses come from firms that are privatized through foreign partners (Estrin et al., 1993a).

Most of the enterprises do not have a consistent strategy but contain only a few elements of a consistent market reorientation strategy package, which includes organization, capital resources/financial markets and marketing (Török, 1991, Radošević, 1994a). This reorientation has been financed from the assets of enterprises through assets subtraction. This does not so much harm traditional as capital-intensive industries (Hughes, 1993).

From an R&D perspective, this situation implies that product development, innovation and human resource issues were relegated to the background. Priorities are crisis management and a survival strategy. The reorientation of the demand for R&D has been reduced on quality, measuring and other non-analytical tasks. The shortening of the planning horizon and shallowing of technological effort, accompanied by the increasing cost and price sensitivity of firms, redirected the demand towards non-R&D services.

5 Prospects for survival and growth of CEEC science and technology

Prospects for survival and growth of science and technology (S&T) in the CEECs depend on the dominant type of economic adjustment mechanism in individual countries. Three types of adjustment mechanisms are distinguished: Ricardian, Keynesian and Schumpeterian.[27]

Ricardian Adjustment. This is a continuation of the current macroeconomic orthodoxy that exhausts itself in the principle of 'getting prices right'. It will ensure stable macro-economy and full liberalization but the net price might be negative. The main problem with this type of adjustment is that growth might not follow from stabilization (Dornbusch, 1991). Its implication is the continuation of a fall in output, and, despite its objectives, very irrational effects of price decontrol owing to a combination of outputs and inputs with negative value added at world prices.

The growth element of this adjustment is the so-called 'stock adjustment'. This is the provision of those trade and services activities that were not supplied under the previous regime. This is the main growth area of small businesses, financed by internal funds with high rates of closure, based on low wages and high rates of turnover. On the export side, it is the re-direction of goods, mainly commodity types, that were previously exported to the East and are now sold below the normal price on Western markets. This adjustment process will soon reach its limits (Blanchard, 1993).

In the S&T area, this type of adjustment will lead to a further closure of R&D institutions and a full realization of the Eastern German scenario. The only prospective areas of the R&D system will be those able to offer non-R&D services.

Keynesian Adjustment. This adjustment is based on the revival of domestic and export demand. This will enable the survival of products for which domestic markets are too small and that do not have immediate chances on Western markets.

The conditions for this type of adjustment are domestic demand stimulation, which carries the danger of high inflation, and a regional payment (settlement) system needed to keep trade going. Probably, a payments union is unrealistic and unworkable.

It is difficult to estimate in which areas inter-regional trade could be developed. It is likely to develop along new patterns where the technological component will not be very strong. However, it will stimulate and keep alive a broader spectrum of R&D capabilities outside and inside industry.

The technological push might come only through close contacts with Western exporters through various original equipment manufacturer arrangements. A developed strategy towards direct foreign investment seems crucial in this type of adjustment. However, there will be no automatism between market access, through multinational corporations or export, and technological upgrading. The result of this type of adjustment can be rather fragile growth, based on wage and inputs cost-difference in relation to other competing regions. Without a policy of linking multinational corporations into the domestic economy, this growth can be based on export enclaves, with rather limited technological spillovers into the rest of the economy. The main policy issue here is how to maximize technological effects of foreign direct investment.

Schumpeterian Adjustment. This type of adjustment is based on the understanding that the essential differences between capitalist and socialist economies lie in the factors emphasized in the Schumpeterian perspective and not in those stressed by the neo-classical model.[28] (Murrell, 1990) This implies that the success of the CEECs will not be based on their static allocative efficiency but on their ability to generate new institutions and to choose between new alternatives.

The possibility for this type of adjustment is to be tested through industrial restructuring. Short-term profitability may be a bad indicator of the capacity of a firm to restructure, so to be effective, restructuring needs guidance. As Portes (1993) put it:

> the growth of the small-scale new private firms cannot substitute for restructuring the large state owned enterprises in industry, and it is now evident that the market cannot do that job without guidance. There is a need to work out and implement conscious industrial policies; to 'commercialise' immediately all state enterprises that do not yet have proper legal frameworks; to give appropriate incentives to managers to stop the decapitalisation of the state firms and induce them to reorganise and seek new markets; and to accelerate privatisation with a wide menu of methods.

The difference between this and the Keynesian type of adjustment will be the most visible in the case of foreign direct investment policy. Through coupling of multinational corporations' and local companies' activities, Keynesian growth can be transformed into Schumpeterian growth. This coupling between technology efforts and market access will be determined by the domestic strategies.[29]

6 Conclusions

In conclusion, we should try to envisage what factors are decisive in the choice of possible adjustment of the CEECs. It would be nad've to perceive these choices as politically rational. Growth is a highly political process and is based on political consensus and institutional capability. I define *institutional capability* as an ability to organize the development of firm, sector or economy by coupling appropriate market and non-market incentives with the need to upgrade technological and complementary capabilities. It is obvious that the institutional capability requirements are growing proportionally as we move from the Ricardian to the Schumpeterian type of adjustment. Eastern European countries are realizing that the introduction of a stock exchange is not the only institutional requirement for a mixed economy. Institutional requirements for industrial restructuring might resemble some of the old policy mechanisms and re-examine newly adopted 'free market' orthodoxies.

Unfortunately, the acquired institutional capabilities in most of the Eastern European countries do not seem to match current needs. However, we should not reject the possibility of fast institutional learning in small countries like Estonia, Slovenia, Hungary or the Czech Republic, where political consensus for modernization could be reached in the near future. Even in countries with the less likely prospects for fast catching-up, policy makers could develop mechanisms of co-ordination and change that have minimal administrative costs.[30]

Notes

1. The conventional economic view is that, once macroeconomic incentives are right, this should lead to economic growth: 'Once stabilisation is achieved, structural change will accelerate as credits wither, enterprises will face up to the need for change.' (Layard, 1993) The implicit assumption of a mainstream approach is that capabilities *per se* are not the problem. Once incentives are right capabilities will take care of themselves, i.e., market pressure and allocative efficiency will induce their development. On the other side the neo-Schumpeterian view presumes that the link between incentives and capabilities is not straightforward. Market incentives have limited impact on the development of capabilities, which are equally impacted by non-market factors. The neo-Schumpeterian extremist view is equally misleading as capabilities are not seen in a market context. In that context it is of interest to examine the effects of changed economic incentives on capabilities as these are closely related.

2. The current Eastern European situation contains an important theoretical problem: what happens to capabilities in the conditions of radically changed macroeconomic incentives? The problem of lacking capabilities is tackled by Elliason (1991). However, the problem of acquired, but in a new market context irrelevant, capabilities has to my knowledge, not yet been systematically discussed.

3. An assessment of science and technology capabilities is inevitably partial and biased owing to methodological problems. Technological capability always contains elements of idiosyncrasies, i.e., most capabilities are not fully formalized and are local-specific thus requiring expert opinion in assessing their level. Strong sector specificity poses an insurmountable problem of analysing very disparate industrial situations. The problems are multiplied when one tries to analyse capabilities across different countries. Therefore, I shall have to restrict myself on available indicators that cover only explicit R&D effort and human potential. The evidence of sectoral restructuring processes is still vague and I rely on several papers that give an idea of sectoral restructuring. The CEEC situation can in some elements be compared with the less developed EU, Latin American and East Asian countries.

4. To approximate absorption capabilities I use some of the available education indicators. A disclaimer, regarding the difficulties in measuring technological capability, applies here equally.

5. This indicator says nothing about the quality of second-level education. Also, high gross ratios, which are used in tables, may give a wrong picture as pupils who are also above an appropriate group are measured in relation to the respective age group. Finally, the saturation of ratios at higher levels make it difficult to recognize the differences between countries by using simple algebra.
6. This favourable picture stems from two main problems. First, R&D manpower data for the CEECs contain a significant number of non-R&D employees. Second, in economies where financial categories were used primarily for accountancy purposes absolute expenditure levels should be considered with suspicion. Also, relative indicators like R&D gross expenditures (GERD)/GDP are unreliable because of lack of data on GDP for all years. Instead of that, GERD are measured in relation to Net Material Product, which does not contain most of the services and thus overstates relative shares of GERD.
7. However, these are still figures on GERD which is not based on Frascati manual standards. This gives higher figures for Eastern Europe.
8. According to OECD (*Main Science and Technology Indicators*), the GERD per capita in $PPP are as follows: Hungary 198, Czech Republic 169; Russia 161; Slovak Republic 156; Spain 99.8; Ireland 96.7; Portugal 51.2; Greece 33.5.
9. In comparable GDP. For Bulgaria the source is GDP.
10. This characteristic is especially valid for the 1970s and 1980s, although the widespread perception is that these systems were dominated by R&D irrelevant to industry. For example, the GDR Academy of Sciences had to raise 33 per cent of funds through contracts research already in 1967 (Dore, 1993).
11. In order to correct the data for this bias it would be worth trying to normalize US patenting figures by export openness for Eastern Europe.
12. These conditions for growth – high social absorption capability plus allocative efficiency (good macroeconomic conditions and an appropriate incentives regime) – resembles similar lines of thinking as a recent World Bank (1993) study *The East Asian Miracle.* This approach, which I would call the new World Bank formula for growth, focuses mainly on static allocative efficiency and neglects issues of dynamic adjustments, i.e., directions of changes for which static allocative efficiency does not give justification. Murrell shows (1990) that in Eastern European foreign trade the main problem was not static allocative efficiency but Schumpeterian efficiency. We come back to that in the last section.
13. Hungary and Poland have been at a significant advantage in this respect as their share of small firms was 5–6 times higher than that of other Eastern European countries.
14. Hungary was the least distorted economy if measured by subsidies financed from a central budget.
15. The degree of openness towards CMEA seems today to be a sign of disadvantage. The degree of the export openness toward the OECD varied significantly. It was the smallest in the case of Bulgaria (7.4 per cent of export) and the highest in the case of Poland (45 per cent of export in 1987).
16. Net debt is the biggest in Poland and Hungary, followed by Bulgaria. In these three countries net debt per capita is above $1000 and per $US of export it is above $300. In Romania and the Czech and Slovak Republics it does not represent a macroeconomic problem.
17. This fall has been accompanied by a significant increase in unemployment, although it is not as strong as the fall of output. Unemployment has reached levels above 10 per cent in all CEECs.
18. For the confirmation of this proposition on a large sample of developing countries, see Dornbusch (1991).
19. Estimates of the externalization of R&D in Eastern Europe are as follows (FRG = 100): GDR: 192, Czech Republic: 453, SSSR: 429, Estonia: 298 (based on Meske, 1993, Muller, 1993, Glaziev and Schneider, 1993, Koorna, 1993).

20. The low degree of externalization of R&D for the GDR compared to the other Eastern European countries is caused by the normalization of GDR figures on full-time (FT) equivalents and on OECD standards.

21. As a result of restricted access to foreign IT, a considerable IT sector appeared in Eastern Europe. The biggest was DZU, a Bulgarian hard disk-drive manufacturer, employing some 20,000 workers and turning over $1.5 billion in 1988. Its technology stopped at the level of 40Mb 5.25in disk drives. The company's employment dropped dramatically to under 5,000 and revenues were down to $30 million last year. DEC VAX and IBM clone manufacturers of the Czech Republic have stopped computer-related production completely (*Business Central Europe*, 1993).

22. 'Their work is mathematically based, and despite very low levels of technology, their programming skills are formidable. They have been able to get far more out of low power systems than we would have believed possible. ...their programming doesn't waste a bit or byte' – Bill O'Riordan, *Financial Times* (1993).

23. Hungarian laser manufacturers 'tend to provide expensive, complex systems requiring new skills, supplementary investments and major procedural changes from the would-be customers while somewhat ignoring the cheap, similar type of lasers used in "compact" applications. Not surprisingly there is hardly any demand for the former systems whereas the latter ones are imported in order to meet the Hungarian needs.' (Havas, 1993a)

24. A study on Russian entrepreneurship found that almost 30 per cent of sample entrepreneurs came from the military/industrial complex, which possesses an abundance of technical knowledge and skills (Charap and Webster, 1993).

25. Quality control is also one of the under-developed capabilities in Eastern European firms. However, it can be considered as a mainly organizational weakness and a result of poor management, not a problem caused by the lack of know-how.

26. The following description from *Business Central Europe* (1993) illustrates this point: 'Despite the emphasis on manufacturing, the brightest prospects in the domestic sector are those firms which are able to take imported Western hardware from a range of suppliers, network them together, perhaps add their own software applications and install them at a customer site with consultancy and support services – preferably developing their expertise to serve specific vertical market sectors. Such firms are highly sought after by Western suppliers, but they are relatively few and far between. There are no shortcuts to gaining the necessary skills and perfecting the right supplier relationships.'

27. For a theoretical discussion on these three types of adjustments, see Dosi, Pavitt and Soete (1990).

28. When examining how closely the trade data of different countries fit a neo-classical model of efficient static resource allocation (Heckscher–Ohlin model of trade), Murrell (1990) found that the socialist economies appear to be as efficient as the capitalist economies. Moreover, the socialist economies have a comparative advantage in sectors whose behaviour leads to static inefficiencies in Western economies – the sectors with high concentration levels. Hence it is difficult to argue that static inefficiency and intersectoral resource allocation were the basic problem of socialist economies.

29. A good example of neglect of technological aspects of FDI is the Hungarian decision on the selection of the suppliers to the Hungarian telecommunication network modernization programme. Although it was impossible to preserve the former domestic telecom suppliers capacities and although their survival in its previous form was unfeasible, the policy-makers did not succeed in linking domestic suppliers' restructuring through opening the domestic market (Tóth, 1994).

30. Along these lines in Radošević (1994a), I try to develop theoretical aspects of policies appropriate for Eastern Europe that avoid the dichotomy between market and state failure. See also Kuznetsov (1993).

References

Blanchard, Olivier J. (1993), 'On the dynamics of transition and restructuring', Round Table on Restructuring, *The Economics of Transition*, vol. 1(2), 273–274.

Blejer, M.I., G.A. Calvo, F. Coricelli and A.H. Gelb (1993), 'Eastern Europe in Transition: From Recession to Growth?', *World Bank Discussion Papers*, no. 196.

Bojár, Gábor (1993), *The Graphisfot Story*, Paper presented at the International Conference 'Information Technology and Business Opportunities in Eastern Europe and the Former Soviet Union', Adam Smith Institute, London, 13–14 October.

Borensztein, E. R., D.G. Demekas and J.D. Ostry (1993), 'Output decline in the aftermath of reform: the cases of Bulgaria, Czechoslovakia, and Romania', in M.I. Blejer et al. (1993).

Bruno, Michael (1993), 'Stabilization and the macroeconomics of transition – How different is Eastern Europe?', *The Economics of Transition*, vol. 1(1), 5–19.

Business Central Europe (1993), *Clash Of Titans: Computers & Office Technology: Survey*, October.

Charap, Joshua and Leila Webster (1993), 'Constraints on the development of private manufacturing in St Petersburg', *The Economics of Transition*, vol. 1(3), 299–316.

Commander, Simon and Fabrizio Coricelli (1993), 'Output decline in Hungary and Poland in 1990/1991: structural change and aggregate shocks', in M.I. Blejer et al. (1993).

Dahlman, Carl and Richard Nelson (1993), *Social Absorption Capability, National Innovation Systems and Economic Development*, Paper prepared for the UNU/INTECH, Maastricht.

Dore, Julia (1993), *The Unification of German Science: Transforming the East German Academy of Sciences*, MSc Thesis, SPRU, August.

Dornbusch, Rudiger (1991), 'Policies to Move from Stabilization to Growth', *Proceedings of the World Bank Annual Conference on Development Economics 1990*, The World Bank.

Dosi, G., K. Pavitt and L. Soete (1990), *The Economics of Technical Change and International Trade*, Harvester Wheatsheaf.

Dyker, David and George Stein (1993), *Russian Software: Technology Transfer and Technological Capability*, mimeo, Radio Free Europe.

EBRD (1994), *Transition report. October 1994*, London.

EBRD (1995), *Transition report update. April 1995*, London.

Elliason, Gunnar (1991), *The Micro Frustrations of Privatising Eastern Europe*, Working Paper no. 306, The Industrial Institute for Economic and Social Research, Stockholm.

Estrin, Saul, Alan Gelb and Inderijt Singh (1993a), *Restructuring, viability and privatization: a comparative study of enterprise adjustment in transition*, The World Bank, mimeo.

Estrin, Saul, Mark E. Schaffer and Inderijt Singh (1993b), 'Enterprise adjustment in transition economies: Czechoslovakia, Hungary, and Poland', in M.I. Blejer et al. (1993).

Financial Times (1993), 'Russians show their mathematical might', 18 November.

Glaziev, Sergei and Christian M. Schneider (eds) (1993), *Research and Development Management in the Transition to a Market Economy*, IIASA, CP-93-001, Laxenburg.

Gokhberg, L. and L. Mindely (1993), 'Soviet R&D Resources: Basic Characteristics', in S. Glaziev and C.M. Schneider (eds), 1993.

Gokhberg, L and A. Sokolov (1995), *Overview of S&T Trends and Policy in Russia,* Centre for Science Reseach and Statistics (CSRS), Moscow, mimeo.

Havas, Attila (1993a), *The Hungarian Laser Industry in Transition,* IKU, Innovation Research Centre, Budapest, mimeo.

Havas, Attila (1993b), *COCOM and CMEA abolished: Re-structuring Precision Engineering Industry in Hungary,* IKU, Innovation Research Centre, Budapest, mimeo.

Hughes, Kirsty (1993), *Sectoral Restructurization in Czechoslovakia and Hungary – A Comparison,* Draft Report of the EC ACE Project, mimeo.

Inzelt, Annamaria (1995), *Review of recent developments in S&T in Hungary: Developments in Hungary's S&T since 1991: A Summary,* CCET/DSTI(95)10, OECD, Paris.

Koorna, Estonian A. (1993), *Science in Transition,* Estonian Academy of Sciences, mimeo.

Kuznetsov, Evgenii (1993), 'How Can Economy Adjust to Simultaneous Market and Government Failure? Lessons from the Soviet Union, Contemporary Russia and Countries of Late-late Industrialization', *Communist Economies & Economic Transformation,* vol. 5, no. 4.

Layard, Richard (1993), 'The Future of the Russian Reform', *The Economics of Transition,* vol. 1, no. 3.

McKinnon, Ronald I. (1991), *The Order of Economic Liberalization: Financial Control in the Transition to a Market Economy,* Baltimore and London: The Johns Hopkins University Press.

Meske, Werner (1993), 'The restructuring of the East German research system – a provisional appraisal', *Science and Public Policy,* vol. 20, no. 5, October.

Muller, Karel (1993), *The Transformation of Research Systems in Czech Republic,* Paper presented at Annual Convention, HSA, Miškolc, 7–10 July, mimeo.

Murrell, Peter (1990), *The Nature of Socialist Economies: Lessons from Eastern European Foreign Trade,* Princeton: Princeton University Press.

Nuti, Domenico Mario and Richard Portes (1993), 'Central Europe: the way forward', in Richard Portes (ed.), 1993.

Portes, Richard (ed.) (1993), *Economic Transformation in central Europe: A Progress Report,* CEPR-EC.

Radošević, Slavo (1994a), 'Strategic Technology Policy for Eastern Europe', *Economic Systems,* vol. 18, no. 2, 87–116.

Radošević, Slavo (1994b), 'The Generic Problems of Competitiveness at Company Level in the Former Socialist Economies: The Case of Croatia', *Europe-Asia Studies,* vol. 46, no. 3, 489–503.

Science Watch (1991), 'No Slippage Yet Seen in Strength of US Science', Institute for Scientific Information, January/February, 1–2.

Science Watch (1993), 'Asia's Little Dragons May One Day Breathe Scientific Fire', Institute for Scientific Information, March, 7.

Simeonova, Kostadinka (1993), *Reforms at the Bulgarian Academy of Sciences and their Impact on Academy-Industry Relations,* Paper prepared for the Workshop 'Innovation Potential Embodied in Academy-Industry Links in Eastern Europe', Balaton Lake (Tihany), October.

Simeonova, Kostadinka (1994), *Innovation Capacities Embodied in Academy-Industry Relations: Bulgarian Case,* Bulgarian Academy of Sciences, Sophia, mimeo.

Sisesti, Ileana I. and Steliana Sandu (eds) (1992), *Science and Technology Policy in Romania during the Transition Period to Market Economy*, Proceedings of the Romanian-American Workshop, Commission for Science Policy of the Romanian Academy of Sciences, Bucharest.

Török, Adam (1991), *Market Orientation of Hungarian Enterprises – EC Integration*, Paper prepared in the framework of the ACE Programme of the EC, Research Institute of Industrial Economics, Budapest.

Tóth, Lászlo G. (1994), 'Technological Change, Multinational Entry and Re-Structuring: The Hungarian Telecommunications Equipment Industry', *Economic Systems*, vol. 18, no. 2, 179–95.

van Zon, Hans (1992), *Towards Regional Innovation Systems in Central Europe*, FAST Dossier, vol. 2, FOP 308, EC FAST.

10 Closing the Institutional Hiatus in Economies in Transition: Beyond the 'State versus Market' Debate

Richard Kožul-Wright and Paul Rayment[1]

1 Introduction

As the experience of the last five years has testified, the transition from a centrally planned socialist economy to a decentralized capitalist economy is a difficult process. The initial outburst of euphoria accompanying the removal of entrenched political regimes across the East,[2] has given way to a more sombre and dispirited mood in the face of a deep transition slump (Kornai, 1993; ECE, 1993 and 1994). The drop in output in the East over this period has been unprecedented.[3] The average decline in GDP between 1989 and 1994 was close to 40 per cent and was most severe in the former Soviet Union (ECE, 1995). Although a decline in output after 1989 was generally regarded as unavoidable, most East European governments (as well as those providing them with advice from abroad) expected the recession to be short and not very deep (ECE 1992, p. 46; ECE 1995, ch. 1).[4] With the possible exception of the ex-German Democratic Republic, no recovery has been investment led,[5] although investment in machinery and equipment is beginning to rise quite strongly in Poland, Slovenia, and the Czech Republic (ECE, 1995). Severe domestic and external imbalances have dominated economic management since 1989; accumulating fiscal deficits have proved difficult to reverse and although trade deficits in Eastern Europe were generally much reduced in 1994 (except in Hungary), due to strong export growth, it appears unlikely, given the relatively weak inflows of foreign capital, that significant current account deficits can be sustained even if desirable from a development point of view. Although the initial acceleration of price rises – following liberalization and currency devaluations – had by 1993 been contained in most Eastern countries (with the exception of most of the countries of the former Soviet Union), inflation rates remain relatively high and persistent. Unemployment has risen rapidly in most of the transition economies, although it is below what might be expected given the fall in output; high rates of structural unemployment look set to persist for a number of years to come.

The depth of this crisis, in part, reflects unanticipated external developments including slower growth across much of the world economy, particular economic difficulties in Western Europe and volatile international financial markets. Together these have dashed hopes of a Western aid package comparable to the Marshall Plan, foreclosed any fast-track membership of the European Union and generated difficult negotiations with the international lending institutions. But just as important has been the approach to policy-making adopted by many governments in the East that ignored or underestimated obstacles that needed to be at the centre of any transition agenda from the outset.[6] To date, the transition debate has divided those advocating the therapeutic value of shocks from those wishing to see a more measured process of reform. But for a number of reasons, this distinction is not a particularly helpful one. First, given the common objectives of eliminating central control over the production and pricing of goods and services, establishing a private sector and integrating with the international economy, shocks were unavoidable. Still, in many cases monetary and fiscal shocks have been extreme, and to the extent these have given rise to persistent macroeconomic disequilibria, control over money and credit and budget discipline have become prevailing concerns in the minds of most policy-makers. Second, the distinction tends to reduce the problem of transition to correcting the misallocation of resources due to the suppression of market forces under central planning. The only real grounds for disagreement then lies with the speed at which markets can be expected to fill the co-ordination gap left by the collapse of the planning system.

Narrowing the transition agenda in this way has crowded out alternative strategies, particularly those that see the economic challenges facing transition economies as inseparable from the 'institutional hiatus' that has opened up with advanced industrial economies.[7] Approaching the design of transition agendas from this perspective certainly implies expanding the operation of markets. But liberalization – whether rapid or gradual – can be no substitute for a comprehensive agenda of institutional catching-up in the East (UNCTAD, 1993; ECE, 1994; North, 1994). This paper applies this reasoning to reforms at the enterprise and industry levels and suggests that entrepreneurship not efficiency is the more suitable concept for constructing an agenda to close the institutional hiatus in these parts of transition economies. Moreover, and counter to much conventional wisdom, emphasizing the role of entrepreneurship in the transition leads us to conclude that reforming the state in the East, rather than seeking its removal, is central to the process of institutional catch-up in the East.

The chapter begins with a short survey of theories of entrepreneurship. The dynamic qualities of the Austrian, neo-institutional and Schumpeterian approaches distinguish them from the kind of economic analysis which has helped design transition strategies. However, these approaches still fall short of analysing the full range of institutional conditions necessary to ensure productive entrepreneurship becomes an integral part of a comprehensive transition process. In particular, we suggest that accepting rent-seeking as inherent in any development process provides a connecting thread between entrepreneurship, industrial strategy and the reform of the state in the East. The next section argues that an important part of the institutional hiatus left by central planning is the absence of a development state in the East. The final section considers how a development state might evolve in the East once the need to manage the creation and destruction of economic rents becomes a central feature of any transition agenda.

2 Entrepreneurship and economic development

According to Vacláv Klaus, one of the architects of reform in the Czech Republic, the transition in the East poses a stark choice between the state and the market (Klaus, 1991). Making the choice for markets has certainly been simplified by trends in Western economic thought and policy-making since the mid-1970s. According to a revitalized neo-liberal agenda, economic stagnation, particularly in Western Europe, has been the cumulative product of various obstructions to market flexibility; loss-making state enterprises, bureaucratic inertia and rent-seeking behaviour, and distorted economic incentives through ill-conceived social programmes have, on this account, all contributed to the ossification of economies increasingly ill-equipped to make the structural adjustments needed to meet the challenges of international competition.[8] The broad thrust of policy advice to remove state-created rigidities and enlarge the sphere of market relations was eagerly accepted in the East since it accorded well with the prevailing distrust of the state bureaucracy and institutions, a legacy of decades of communist rule.

But a possibly more direct influence on the architects of reform, given the urgency of financial and technical assistance in all the transition economies, has been the international financial agencies. Structural adjustment programmes, established as an integral part of a new economic agenda in developing countries during the 1980s, appeared to lend themselves to the tasks of correcting imbalances in the East (Rybczynski, 1991) and these agencies quickly became the conduit for an 'economists' consensus' on the transition (Summers, 1992, p. 112). The World Bank has confidently summarized this consensus in terms of a linear sequencing of reforms to correct price distortions and establish more competitive markets as the essential means to the efficient organization of production and distribution of goods and services, renewed entrepreneurship and technological progress (World Bank, 1991, p. 1). Accordingly, a combination of rapid price and trade liberalization, and monetary and fiscal austerity was expected to rapidly create competitive markets in the East and, thereby, establish the right environment to discipline existing firms and, in conjunction with wholesale privatization programmes, encourage the formation of small and medium-sized enterprises and attract needed foreign investment, new technologies and managerial skills.[9] Although the economists' consensus implies a small, but perceptible, shift from a neo-liberal to a market-friendly agenda, both shared the objective of containing any active economic role for the state; the provision of traditional public goods, the formation of human capital, and the creation of an effective social safety net establish the economic boundaries for state activity (Biersteker, 1990).

Although the details of 'shock therapy' varied among advisers in the early 1990s, the consensus was consistent with, and helped reinforce, the desire for quick results, which was certainly a strong motivation for both the designers and users of policy advice at the beginning of the transition process (Caselli and Pastrello, 1991; Portes, 1994, p. 1182).[10] The description of economies in the East as a collection of distortions and imbalances went hand in hand with a belief that, with the removal of central co-ordination of economic activity, markets would spontaneously generate the desired economic improvements. Such a description also implied a marginal role for the state in managing the transition. This was clearly the case with Poland's Economic Programme of October 1989 – the Balcerowicz plan – which had no place for an industrial policy alongside the privatization programme.[11]

Critics have subsequently faulted the 'consensus' for idealizing an Anglo-Saxon model of capitalist development (Amsden et al., 1995) and disregarding the region's historical and institutional legacies in the design of transition strategies (Köves, 1992; van Brabant, 1993). Much of this criticism is valid. But perhaps a more crippling consequence of the consensus was its drastic narrowing of the debate on policy options at exactly the moment – given the fundamental economic and social adjustments that were facing the East – when the emphasis needed to be on as wide a choice of policies as possible to encourage the development of market and non-market institutions.[12]

The attractiveness of the economists' consensus was certainly reinforced by the denial of any credible alternative. Whilst this was, in large part, true in the case of extreme macroeconomic imbalances, such a claim was always lacking in intellectual honesty when the issue was how to address structural imbalances inherited from the planning system and was no less credible when the issue was restoring economic growth. Not only has a vast historical literature on industrialization patterns in the 19th and 20th centuries revealed the different paths taken by successful, newly industrializing economies, but in all cases – albeit to different degrees and with different policy measures – the process of catching up has involved guidance from the state.[13] A full account of the dynamics of comparative capitalist development is beyond the scope of this paper, but one conclusion that deserves more careful attention given the existing consensus on transition, is that an emphasis on the role of entrepreneurship fails to confirm the simple choice between the state and market in the management of economic development (Murrell, 1992; Chang and Kožul-Wright, 1994; Chang and Rowthorn, eds, 1995).

Even a passing familiarity with the history of economic thought confirms that the 'disappearance of the entrepreneur' from economic analysis (Casson, 1987, p. 121) coincides with the rise of ideas of market perfection (and, indeed, market friendliness) of the kind that currently underpin much of the debate on transition. Entrepreneurship, far from emerging from an economics of competitive equilibrium, has always been part of the heretical tradition of growth dynamics and economic progress. The nature of the heresy is clear; in one form or another, entrepreneurship highlights the central role of rents in the process of economic development.

The Austrians, beginning with Carl Menger, have, perhaps, been most consistent in integrating the creative role of the entrepreneur with the dynamics of market economies. In this tradition a radical individualism is married to a world where uncertainty and unpredictability create rent opportunities from information asymmetries that an agile entrepreneur will be able to exploit (Reekie, 1984, pp. 48–51; Binks and Vale, 1990). Thus the Austrians do not take market dynamics as given but see them as depending upon the attributes of risk-taking, leadership and alertness possessed by the entrepreneur. Moreover, as Hayek recognized, forming these attributes is a social and historical process (Hayek, 1960).[14] Although pointing to this cultural dimension is of obvious relevance in the East where the economic value system has evolved through very different principles, the Austrian approach is of less value in the actual design of an alternative transition agenda. Not only does it assume that prices convey all information and fails to consider how economic agents can change prices or whether all actions of entrepreneurs are welfare enhancing; but their radical individualism leads them to a world in which the larger institutional dynamics of the capitalist firms are absent and where rent-seeking activity is unconnected to processes of wealth creation.

A second – neo-institutionalist – approach to entrepreneurship associates it with a larger managerial response to various market frictions and resistances – 'failures' – and in particular, those arising when prices convey insufficient or inappropriate information to ensure an efficient use of resources. The origins of this approach can probably be traced to Marshall's fourth factor of production, but its modern lineage lies in the Coasian theory of the firm (Coase, 1937; Putterman, 1989). In this tradition, Harvey Leibenstein's description of entrepreneurship as gap-filling and input-completing, in a world where shirking creates a state of persistent slack or X-inefficiency, has been particularly influential (Leibenstein, 1968). More recently, the transaction costs literature (Williamson, 1975) and the economics of information (Casson, 1987) has extended this approach in important ways. In transition economies where markets are missing, information distorted and economies operate under conditions of extreme slack, these approaches deserve considerably more attention than most policy-makers have given them. However, it is doubtful that an economics of market failure can provide a comprehensive framework for policy-makers where a basic issue remains creating markets. Moreover, non-market institutions largely appear in this literature as imperfections rather than as integral parts of the economic environment. Consequently, the allure of equilibrating forces retains a powerful hold over the analysis of economic problems: successful performance continues to be defined as the effective allocation of resources – with technology and institutions as exogenous – while production – as much as in the Austrian tradition – remains something of a black box (Hodgson, 1988).

Both the Austrian and neo-institutional approaches see entrepreneurship as an activity aimed at capturing economic rents created by factors outside their control. A final notion of entrepreneurship, deriving from the work of Joseph Schumpeter, emphasizes the rent-creating role of entrepreneurship. Schumpeter began, like the Austrians, with a rejection of equilibrium analysis, insisting that plausible capitalism 'is by nature a form or method of economic change and not only never is but never can be stationary' (Schumpeter, 1987, p. 82). But unlike the Austrians, Schumpeter located the forces of change in the strategic actions of firms. In particular, Schumpeterian entrepreneurship describes a process of rent-seeking through the introduction of new products or production processes. As such, entrepreneurship implies the temporary establishment of a monopoly position through which innovative activity could be encouraged and existing industrial activity challenged and ultimately replaced – a process Schumpeter called 'creative destruction'.

The nature of transition in the East, involving the destruction of existing structures and the creation of new economic relations, readily lends itself to a Schumpeterian interpretation (Murrell, 1992; Gomułka, 1992). However, too strict an adherence to Schumpeterian prescriptions unduly limits the scope of transition strategies. For Schumpeter, economic progress was very much the result of isolated and discontinuous events and the institutional conditions for innovative activity were very thinly defined as the provision of appropriate incentives to stimulate the ingenuity of the independent entrepreneur or firm. Neo-Schumpeterians have broadened this analysis by recognizing that incremental changes, tacit knowledge and cooperation play an important part in the innovative activities of the capitalist firm (Nelson and Winter, 1983; Dosi et al., 1993). The importance of this revision to our understanding of entrepreneurship lies in its connection to the long-standing notion of economic development as a cumulative and continuous process of calling forth and organizing for development purposes, resources that are often hidden, scattered or badly utilized (Hirschman, 1987, p. 210; Kaldor, 1985, pp. 61–2). Combining these two strands, it is possible to describe entrepreneurship as the bundle of 'social capabilities' (Abramovitz, 1989) required to organize development at the firm, industry and national levels; not only the willingness to take risks and the ability to visualize new opportunities but also the searching out of available information and the creation of new knowledge through constant learning and experimenting. Moreover, because the activities resulting from such capabilities cannot be exclusively identified with one individual or firm, entrepreneurial capabilities will only be fully developed and made effective within a network of institutional relations, at the local, national and international levels. As such, entrepreneurship is as much a collective process as it is individual, located in the interaction of various functions inside the firms, between the users and producers of a product, between firms and other economic institutions (such as banks and labour unions) and in their interaction with non-economic institutions such as universities and government agencies. In all these respects, the collective values of voice and loyalty must coexist with more individualistic values associated with entry and exit in defining entrepreneurship.[15]

Equating entrepreneurship with the process of building capabilities is particularly suited to the design of more evolutionary transition agendas (ECE, 1992). However, if entrepreneurship is to become a useful thread in designing transition agendas, it must also be linked to the process of capital accumulation. This is a large and still inadequately explored area of analysis.[16] Even under the best of conditions, investing in new firms and industries (or expanding existing ones) involves committing resources to an uncertain future. But where the investments are large and the risks are high, sizeable profits are a necessary condition of rapid accumulation. Innovation, by creating rents, provides one possible link between accumulation and entrepreneurship. But this link can be a tenuous one. Indeed, once entrepreneurship is understood to involve rent-seeking, it is necessary to distinguish between productive, unproductive, and destructive entrepreneurial activities (Baumol, 1990). Individuals or enterprises can engage in profit-seeking activities by using asymmetric information, establishing illegal barriers to entry or reinforcing a monopoly position through political, financial or other organizational constraints to the entry of potential competitors. Such activities will require the unproductive use of resources in securing these rents and if these redistributive strategies become entrenched, they can begin, in a very destructive manner, to erode existing assets by encouraging predatory types of behaviour.

Consequently, the success of any institutional environment will be the extent it helps direct resources towards more productive entrepreneurship.[17] This environment will certainly include an appropriate incentive system to encourage risk-taking – what Kaldor called 'the creative role of markets' (Kaldor, 1989) – as well as a variety of formal and informal firm-level linkages which support more lasting relations than those established through purely market transactions (Richardson, 1972). But, if the market can not provide adequate profits, the state becomes instrumental in creating and managing rents (Akyuz and Gore, 1994). Successful development states have used a variety of mechanisms to this end, including selective protection, controls over credit allocation and access to foreign exchange, controlled expansion of capacity and technological acquisition, and cartelization and other restrictions on firm-level entry.[18] But the introduction of all these measures poses a subtle dilemma for policy-makers. On the one hand, the use of rents can stimulate development by redistributing resources to areas of rapid growth and fuelling the process of capital accumulation (Chang and Kožul-Wright, 1994; UNCTAD, 1994). On the other hand, to the extent that unproductive entrepreneurship becomes established in the routines of enterprises, the tendency to seek redistributive rather than creative activities could eventually undermine the economy's growth potential (Olson, 1982). Consequently, an industrial strategy must find ways to keep the costs incurred in managing rents low and non-productive forms of wealth accumulation, such as real estate speculation, must be closed off. Moreover, the measures used to create rents must be selective, with a definite life span and attached to well-defined performance criteria. All of this assumes that a good economic bureaucracy exists to manage the process of rent creating and destruction in a way that enhances, rather than retards the growth process.

3   Investment without profits: legacies of the command economy

In the absence of reliable measures of inputs and outputs, growth accounting has always proved a difficult exercise in the East. Still, there is probably little disagreement that any success in meeting the twin goals of rapid structural transformation and narrowing the technological and income gaps with Western economies was the result of mobilizing and organizing resources on a large scale to augment the physical and human capital stock. In this respect, the resulting growth path resembled other late developing countries, particularly to the extent that priority was given to the industrial sector (Hirschman, 1992; Feinstein et al., 1990). However, the degree of formal central allocation of resources was a distinguishing feature.[19] In addition, the state owned almost all natural resources and capital assets (with the exception of agricultural land and housing in some countries and at different times) and retained a strict monopoly over foreign trade. The allocation of labour and management was bureaucratically prescribed and mobility of factors was significantly constrained. Although private activity was allowed, primarily in agriculture and some service activities, it was subject to stringent central controls and was vulnerable to changing political sentiment. The near absence of market relations reduced the search options available to decision-makers over supplies of inputs as well as distribution of the final product. Price setting was the responsibility of the central authority and scarcity pricing was abandoned for a variety of social-welfare and administrative reasons. Money acted primarily as a means of payment, controlled through a monobank system which acted as an accounting mechanism for overseeing planned credits to the enterprise system. There was no need for commercial banks and there was little role for monetary policy to influence economic activity. Prices remained unchanged for long periods and quantity rationing under shortage conditions resulted in perverse imbalances.[20] In addition, and of critical importance to the actual functioning of Eastern economies, the intrusion of political oversight added a further layer of organization to the co-ordination of economic activity. The 'leading role' of the Party, inscribed in Soviet and Eastern European constitutions, extended to formally independent institutions and economic agents.

Whilst the architects of this type of *ex-ante* co-ordination saw extensive advantages over its more anarchic Western market rival, there is little doubt that the superior design of a planned economy as an economic mechanism was expected to reside in its organization and control of saving and investment decisions. Rather than leaving economic development to the uncertain profitability calculations of a myriad of independent firms, the central state could, it was believed, by reducing uncertainty and mastering the complementarities which emerge between expanding firms and industries, produce a smoother, speedier and more balanced growth path under social ownership.[21] The paradoxical economic history of the East has been a slow, and ultimately futile, search for a scientific basis for capital accumulation that could underpin this alternative investment regime (Nove, 1983, pp. 90–7). Behind this paradox lies the failure to create the kind of state which could combine the rapid pace of capital accumulation with the kinds of social and economic capabilities needed for sustained technological progress and economic development.

Despite the semblance of a tightly controlled hierarchical system of central co-ordination and management, in practice planning embodied a mixture of both formal and informal routines of co-ordinating economic decision-making between the state authorities and enterprises. In the absence of a profit motive, scale provided the basis for centrally planned investment decisions. However, under the particular conditions of economic backwardness and political competition with the West, the ambitious growth targets set by the central bureaucracy and reinforced by one-party rule, led to a dysfunctional system of over-investment and plan fulfilment. This 'curse of scale' (Nove, 1983, p. 75) is a major factor behind the institutional hiatus currently found in the East.

The concentration of responsibility for overall design at the central level quickly encountered information constraints as the bounded competence of the planning authorities faced the increasingly complex needs and problems of an expanding economy. Moreover, bureaucrats persistently refused to share information across ministerial jurisdictions, protecting their vertical links as a means to secure established positions and reinforce political authority (Goldman, 1991, p. 278). Although the chain of command was simplified by the formation of large enterprises, the evolution of large firms with privileged access to resources, operating under monopoly conditions and with no real threat of bankruptcy, did little to improve the quality of information required to co-ordinate the decision-making process or reduce the uncertainty which grew from an excessive intertwining of political and economic factors.[22] Enterprise managers could expect to sell all their output domestically and there was little incentive to seek markets outside the Council for Mutual Economic Assistance (CMEA); consumer and user needs were of marginal concern.

As the economies in the East became more industrialized, diversified their product structures, moved into more sophisticated technological areas and created a more complex division of labour, the limits and inconsistencies in the formal planning system added to the discretionary power of local bureaucrats and enterprise managers, generating *ad hoc* measures and informal relations – including barter arrangements, secondary markets, bribes and theft – to create a coherent economic outcome. Contrary to the impression given by much analysis of the transition, entrepreneurship was not absent from enterprise behaviour under central planning. Under shortage conditions, simply maintaining enterprise performance often required remarkable initiative and foresight. These efforts, however, were increasingly channelled into procurement rather than production, marshalling scarce resources to meet predetermined targets rather than directing resources into new endeavours. Most enterprises employed individuals to expedite the procurement process through long-term relations with suppliers and considerable managerial effort was directed into establishing a network of political ties with higher authorities in the bureaucracy and Party, to secure subsidies and privileged access to resources.[23] Under these conditions the opportunities for rent-seeking activity expanded; political connections had to be reinforced with the appropriate 'gifts' and opportunistic behaviour at the enterprise level – such as hiding the true capabilities of the firm, hoarding manpower, overusing resources, manipulating production schedules and outright theft – shifted private costs on to the state.[24] Similarly, because particular skills and knowledge were required of the labour force under shortage conditions to ensure the continuity of production, certain groups of workers were in a position to establish firm-specific skills which were highly valued by management and enabled them to acquire rents at the expense of other groups.[25] Many of these activities quickly became destructive through the degradation of product quality, manipulation of the product mix and the general resistance to new products and technologies which could threaten existing routines.[26]

Rent-seeking activity was not confined to the large state firms but was equally characteristic of smaller firms in the second economy. Many small entrepreneurs were subsidized through the state sector in numerous ways, such as the use of plant and equipment, the theft of materials and the transfer of labour to private activities (Comisso, 1989; Stark, 1990, p. 389). Not surprisingly, the relaxing of central control under various reform efforts in the East often opened up new opportunities in this direction; the proliferation of such activities accompanied the extension of business partnerships between state enterprises and workers in Hungary from the late 1970s (Galasi and Sziráczki, 1985) and the formation of cooperatives in the Soviet Union from the mid-1980s (United Nations, 1992). Moreover, the shortage economy produced a sellers' market and the administered restrictions on the second economy meant that surviving firms were able to establish their own monopoly position which often yielded quick and sizeable returns; retaining such a position often required agreement from the appropriate authorities through payments of one kind or another (Mokrzycki, 1991, p. 211). Although the environment of protection and shortage did stimulate some truly innovative activity and despite the recent attention paid to the second economy as a potential source of entrepreneurship in the transition, the absence of trust and the requisite degree of organization between firms in this sector did not, in most cases, foster the required capabilities to enhance productive entrepreneurship (Gabor, 1990).

Despite a considerable acceleration in rates of fixed investment in the 1970s, the slowdown in rates of output growth continued, and both capital and labour productivity fell steadily (ECE, 1986, pp. 209–23). Difficulties in adapting Western technology meant that imports of Western goods had little impact on productive efficiency. These and other factors, such as inadequate transport and communication networks, all point to a strong secular decline in systemic efficiency. The consequences of this decline were, in part, delayed by rising imports paid for by foreign borrowing. But the second oil shock changed the situation radically. Both domestic consumption and fixed investment fell sharply in 1982 throughout the East, and, although consumption recovered somewhat thereafter, most of the adjustment continued to fall on fixed investment for the rest of the 1980s. Indeed, the characterization of the 1980s as a 'lost decade', although usually referring to developing country experiences, applies with particular force to the East;[27] during the 1980s, economic growth in the East fell behind not only the new industrializing Asian economies but also the developed market economies (Table 10.1).

Table 10.1   Relative growth rates: Catching up and falling behind[a] in the East, 1965–89

	1980–89	1965–80
Eastern Europe	−0.4	2.6
ex-Soviet Union	0.6	1.2
ex-GDR	1.0	2.1
East Asia	4.9	3.5
Sub-Saharan Africa	−0.9	0.4
Latin America & Carribean	−1.4	2.2

Note: [a]The figures are obtained by subtracting the average annual regional growth rate from the annual growth rate of high income economies
Sources: Marer et al. (1993); World Bank (1991); UNCTAD (1981).

The missing routines and habits, as well as more formal institutional linkages required to support interactive learning, experimentation and imitation became more noticeable with the slowdown of investment. Efforts were made at decentralizing responsibility through market-oriented reform, earlier in Hungary and the former Yugoslavia and later in Poland. However, these efforts were often introduced in an *ad hoc* manner, limited to certain types of transaction (mainly on the goods market including in some cases foreign markets) and subject to reversal.[28] Indeed, as the experience of Poland in the 1970s and 1980s already suggested, any efforts to revive rapid accumulation as a substitute for more widespread institutional reforms appeared doomed to failure.

The legacies of central planning are as familiar as they are deep-seated and pervasive. This section has not attempted to detail the full extent of the institutional hiatus left by the rise and collapse of central planning. Rather, it has suggested that a regime of investment without profits produced a rapid rate of accumulation, alongside the steady drain of creative capabilities required for dynamism in a modern economy, by rigid vertical linkages, oversized firms, the fragmentation of horizontal ties and a destructive rent-seeking behaviour. In this respect, the kind of state that evolved in the East combined an unhealthy mixture of paternal and hierarchical structures and routines. This proved inconsistent with a more development state that could oversee the transition from extensive industrial development to transformative growth through innovative activity.[29]

4 Entrepreneurship and industrial strategy in the transition

In a recent assessment of transition experiences, Richard Portes (1994) has challenged the narrow foundations on which most policy reforms have been built and argued that a better sequencing of reform must encompass a comprehensive range of policies, particularly at the enterprise level.[30] A somewhat similar sentiment has been expressed from a different angle by András Köves (Köves, 1994, pp. 156–60), who argues that any sequencing of reforms should aim to revive economic growth and maintain social consensus. These calls to widen the transition agenda reflect a growing recognition that neo-liberal strategies make little sense in an environment dominated by missing markets and that the recovery of economic growth will depend on the performance of industrial enterprises. However, advocates of a wider reform agenda must, themselves, face up to the institutional hiatus in the East and particularly the problem of missing, weak or inappropriate state institutions. In this respect, whilst the concept of sequencing is a healthy antidote to neo-liberal ideology, it is almost certainly too technocratic an idea to initiate a process of institutional catch-up in the East.

The task, rather, is to find credible policies which simultaneously address the fundamental problems in the East and begin to establish a more effective set of state institutions. In the light of earlier arguments, the introduction of credible industrial policies to encourage productive forms of entrepreneurship in both state-owned and private enterprises, provides one such starting point for reform. Once the building of new institutional capabilities is placed at the centre of reforming the state in the East, industrial strategies can be seen as a potentially powerful channel both for creating an economic bureaucracy and for familiarizing the administrative apparatuses of the state with domestic management objectives that are very different from those associated with either central planning or unregulated markets. Accordingly, the design of industrial policies should be approached less as an exercise in 'picking winners' and more as one of encouraging and co-ordinating investment and innovation through the *strategic* management of economic rents.[31]

Whilst there is considerable scope for formal training to learn new policy objectives and the use of new policy instruments, there will be a very important process of learning-by-doing and interacting with newly independent firms, to establish effective channels of communication with the emerging enterprise sector and to ensure that rents are used productively to support investment and innovation.[32] The obstacles facing such reform efforts – and not least the lack of political will and vision to convince a sceptical public that *creating* and managing market-type economies needs a strong and active state which is very different from the one established under central planning (Panic, 1993) – cannot be underestimated. But to deny a more encompassing dialogue between the government, firms and the wider public – as has been the case with most transition agendas – will simply delay the start of an unfamiliar and difficult learning process. It is in this learning process that policy-makers, private and state managers and representatives of labour begin to interact in a way that establishes a sustainable transition path that leads from economic recovery to longer-term growth and technological catching up.

The immediate context for designing and implementing industrial policies in transition economies will almost certainly be a state of systemic disequilibrium, where economic uncertainty and institutional instability dramatically shorten the time horizons of decision-makers recently released from the strict hierarchical tutelage and dependence on the central state. The profit-making activities of this *incipient* form of entrepreneurship are as likely to be unproductive as they are productive, and leaving the market to pick winners alone is as or more likely to reflect leverage and connections inherited from the past rather than long-run productive potential. Any fledgling development state will have to confront enterprises seeking to protect already established rents and with little or no interest in committing resources to a long and uncertain process of restructuring. Moreover, this institutional mix of old and new is continuously expanding the opportunities for arbitraging and rent-seeking behaviour and the loopholes, inconsistencies and inadequate sanctions in the emerging regulatory framework and legal codes, can quickly turn any activity into more destructive types of entrepreneurship. The criminalization of economic activity presents the most invidious form of destructive entrepreneurship (Handelman, 1994). But the problem is of a more deep-rooted nature. Many of the largest corporations have already used liberalization to increase prices and incomes rather than carry out necessary investment and restructuring, and foreign investors attracted by undervalued assets have responded to the wider institutional hiatus by seeking various forms of subsidy and protection. Most experiences with the privatization process, including in the former German Democratic Republic, have been marred by speculative and fraudulent activities; 'spontaneous privatization' in Hungary and 'political capitalism' in Poland, have revealed the potential damage from such activity,[33] and the privatization programme in Russia –

which began later than in other transition economies – has, if anything, provided even greater opportunities for destructive entrepreneurship (Ash and Hare, 1994).

In these circumstances, the financial, managerial and technological restructuring of enterprises should be accepted as a responsibility of the state and exercised through an independent public agency. But it is important from the outset that such an agency not only takes responsibility for the restructuring of state enterprises but also links structural measures to the promotion of new private enterprises and to policies aimed at encouraging capital accumulation.

In this respect, there is no single model from experience that can be transplanted to the conditions in the East. However, there are lessons which can be drawn upon in the formation of such an agency. The parallels drawn by some Japanese policy-makers between their own experience of organising successful catching up and socialist planning provides one obvious starting point.[34] The lessons from Japan can be expanded by looking at the experience of other newly industrializing countries in Asia. Whilst there are significant differences between these countries, in all cases a strong economic bureaucracy has assumed some responsibility for the pace and direction of investment and structural change and developed policy measures to this end (Singh, 1994; Chang, 1994). These experiences are of interest to economies in transition for a number of reasons other than the rapid pace of economic growth. First, these countries were not naturally endowed with the institutional capacity for rapid growth but were, rather, highly successful institutional imitators. Moreover, when countries such as South Korea and Taiwan began their imitation of the Japanese model in the late 1950s and early 1960s, accusations of incompetence and corruption were commonplace among critics of their economic bureaucracies, much as they are in the East today. Second, the fact that a number of the rapidly growing economies in Asia have evolved through a close association between the state and large corporate structures, is likely to be of particular relevance in the East, where concentrated industrial structures will remain in place for some considerable time. But East Asia is not the only model. The reconstruction and transformation of post-war Western Europe also offers lessons for policy-makers in the East. Although planning wartime economies was a very different exercise from central planning, the task of dismantling controls at the end of hostilities did not give way to a simple or unique model of a market economy. Rather attempts to improve the efficiency of the market system and accelerate the pace of technological and structural change was understood to require policies to correct for market failures, especially in non-competitive markets, and to promote collaboration among enterprises and government in such areas as long-term investment, research and development, and training. Again the opportunity to accelerate institutional learning through imitation merits a more careful assessment of these experiences than has so far been given them by most Eastern policy-makers (Panic, 1991; Landesmann, 1994). Finally, there are also some models from the transition process itself, such as the German Treuhand, which might be successfully replicated or adapted in other Eastern countries (ECE, 1994). The important lesson that the fledgling bureaucracies of the East need to take from these experiences is that creating state institutions involves a difficult learning process,[35] but one where openness to a wide range of experiences is almost certain to increase the chances of success.

Whatever the precise institutional form assumed by such an agency, at this stage of the transition, the introduction of effective governance mechanisms at the firm level is critical to industrial recovery (van Brabant, 1993). Changing the formal rules of ownership through privatization represents only one element – though probably not the most important (UNCTAD, 1995) – in a broader strategy. Although the privatization of small businesses has been popular across the East and moved ahead rapidly, the problems involved in transferring the large state-owned enterprises to the private sector has been an altogether different matter. This, in part, reflects problems endemic to the legacy of socialist enterprise formation – including their size, social responsibilities and indebtedness – which has left them unattractive to private investors. But it also reflects the limits of privatization measures themselves. On the one hand, and regardless of the form privatization takes, the behaviour of enterprises will not change dramatically until the wider institutional hiatus begins to close in the East.[36] Whether the state is a good or a bad seller of assets, in a situation of endemic rent-seeking behaviour considerable effort will be required to prevent unproductive entrepreneurship turning destructive. On the other hand, a one-sided emphasis on ownership, because it focuses on the reorganization of state-owned assets, is less likely to address the broader task of equipping all firms – whether state-owned or private – with the right capabilities to manage their assets under conditions of restructuring and recovery. This problem is clearly apparent in the case of small and medium-sized enterprises which are not only the easiest to privatize but also the most likely to be neglected in the subsequent design of policies.

Most observers would now probably agree that widening the scope for market incentives will require consistent contract and bankruptcy laws backed by effective enforcement mechanisms, a transparent fiscal system and new accounting procedures. The state must also find measures to regulate competition in ways that foreclose both the destructive aspects of monopolistic tendencies and too easy exit. These measures will only take effect over the medium and longer term. Indeed, it quickly became clear, in Hungary and to the Treuhand in Germany, for example, that bankruptcy laws which are intended to penalize imprudent management and economic failure in individual enterprises operating in a market economy, were likely to generate systemic failure in the East destroying potentially viable enterprises along with those that anyway would have been closed down. This prospect, together with the concomitant threat of a rapid rise in mass unemployment, led to the suspension of bankruptcy laws or, at least, to delays in implementing them.

Of possibly more immediate impact on corporate restructuring will be the use made of state subsidies. Stopping open-ended subsidies to state-owned enterprises will be the most effective way of hardening budget constraints. However, there is unlikely to be an abrupt halt to subsidies and with strict market criteria unable to guide restructuring and determine which industries should be expanded, profit and loss calculations must be supplemented by other performance criteria. Although assessing the extremes of potential success and failure might be relatively easy, the broad mass of enterprises will exhibit uncertain potential, and devising alternative criteria which could help allocate the limited resources available for restructuring has been obstructed by the problems of pricing existing assets and gauging the relative efficiency of firms and industries (Hughes and Hare, 1992 and 1994; Glyn, 1994). Pragmatism will be inevitable and the likelihood of mistakes needs to be recognized and accepted. Whatever criteria are selected, the process of restructuring will take a long time to complete and policy-makers must use this opportunity to learn the discretionary use of such intervention by attaching performance criteria to the provision of any subsidies and gaining credibility by making sure the time frame adopted is realistic and enforced.[37] Moreover, the state should not forgo the option of changing property rights in both the private and public sectors, whenever the use of subsidies and the management of assets clashes with the longer-term objectives of the chosen industrial strategy.

But the state cannot, and should not, take sole responsibility for economic restructuring. Measures aimed at strengthening corporate governance must be combined with access to appropriate financing to ensure restructuring and growth over the longer term. Despite the enthusiasm of some Western advisers, stock markets will not, for a considerable time to come, provide the institutional basis for successful financial intermediation or corporate discipline in the East (Singh, 1992). Similarly, foreign direct investment (FDI), which in addition to capital can bring organizational and other skills (Junz, 1991), is unlikely to be a decisive factor in restructuring economic activity in the first stages of the transition (ECE, 1994). This is partly because FDI tends to lag behind economic development even under more favourable economic conditions than are now common in the East. But also any understanding of transnational corporation (TNC) activity must include their efforts to dominate markets and engage in predatory behaviour, particularly where economic and social institutions are relatively weak. Indeed, emphasizing the role of FDI in the early stages of transition is almost certainly a diversion from the wider task of closing the institutional hiatus in the East.

Rather, reform of the banking system will be key. The creation of a genuine two-tier banking system has been recognized as an immediate task of the transition. However, the imperfect nature of financial markets is a prevailing feature of the East. One major obstacle to a more effective system of financial intermediation is undoubtedly the legacy of enterprise debts which includes the inherited stock of bad loans from the monobank system but also bad loans accumulated since 1989. Consequently, restructuring state-owned enterprises is intimately linked to the development of a sound financial sector. Despite the possible dangers of excessive economic power, the adoption of 'insider' financial models of enterprise control, where banks acquire considerable control over management, seems more likely to enforce a hard budget constraint, by reducing inter-firm credit and assessing profitable loans, than reliance, for example, on stock markets. However, in light of the financial relations inherited from the command economy, the banks themselves must undergo restructuring and refinancing and be given time to learn necessary skills (Székely, 1992; Begg and Portes, 1993), and there must also be time to build complementary institutions of financial intermediation. Under the current circumstances of excessive reliance on inter-firm credit, considerable cooperation between the State, emerging financial intermediaries and enterprises will be required to impose a harder budget constraint on firms whilst simultaneously strengthening the banking system. Experiences in the East to date suggest that this is a particularly difficult process. However, there are enough lessons from 19th and 20th century development experience to suggest that, if properly organized, closer ties between finance and industry, along with selective state supervision and intervention, can be a particularly powerful tool of rapid accumulation and economic restructuring.

Many of the challenges associated with incipient entrepreneurship are peculiar to the transition. However, even as economies progress towards greater macroeconomic stability, a more complete financial system and a strong and dynamic private sector, many of the activities that emerge will hold little potential of evolving into the kind of productive entrepreneurship necessary for long-term development. Thus, from an early stage, state institutions must begin managing the process of rent creation and destruction in a way that fosters longer-term and dynamic relations with particular firms and industries. Restoring profits and investment is certainly a prerequisite of this process. But of perhaps greater importance in light of the failures of central planning, many potentially viable projects may founder because they lack some of the individual and institutional capabilities required to upgrade and improve product structure, enhance the quality and availability of goods and services, adopt and adapt frontier technologies, and reach new markets. Although the absence of specific knowledge and skills required to pursue productive activities is largely a legacy of central planning, the experience-based nature of these capabilities implies a lengthy period of learning-by-doing and training. Infant entrepreneurship describes the process of institution building for productive entrepreneurship. Policies aimed at maintaining high rates of investment will have to be complemented by measures to support the formation of human capital and skills, and advancing this agenda in the East will require a further transformation of the state, divesting it of some responsibilities associated with incipient entrepreneurship and adding new ones.

Arguably, as Eastern economies enter this stage of transition, the lessons from experience become all the more instructive. A common ingredient in the catching-up experience of most European and East Asian countries has been successful integration in the international division of labour, particularly through export promotion. However, the broad lesson from history is that international integration cannot outpace domestic economic development: openness is a gradual and strategic process whose success requires a continuous transformation in economic and technological processes. The policy mix best suited to linking structural reforms to a process of export promotion is still disputed. However, there is considerable agreement that as economies in the East enter this pattern of development, measures aimed at maintaining a rapid pace of capital accumulation will become intertwined with the process of technological catching-up (Radošević, 1994). What also seems certain is that unless an economic bureaucracy has been firmly established with a clear vision of domestic development needs, and with the experience and skills to devise and implement effective measures to support the private entrepreneurial activities, these economies are as likely to be shipwrecked by the gales of international creative destruction as they are to turn these winds to their own advantage.

A number of more specific observations concerning infant entrepreneurship are worth making. First, in many smaller countries, technology policies will probably become more closely linked to the activities of transnational corporations (Lall, 1994). But building these linkages cannot be a substitute for stronger domestic industrial policies (Kožul-Wright, 1995; Cantwell and Basu, 1994). Indeed, FDI is not the only transmission belt for obtaining new technology and governments in the transition economies should not be inhibited from making a careful assessment of the costs of premature inflows of FDI. Second, one area of increasing importance will be policies aimed at strengthening research and development linkages. Managing resources in such crucial areas as R&D will involve a more refined set of instruments which whilst familiar in the West – such as general R&D tax credits, financial subsidies and the creation of a pre-competitive R&D infrastructure – have not been used in the East. But just as important will be the need to ensure that private firms and remaining state-owned enterprises have the necessary capabilities which enable the identification, expansion and exploitation of potential technology sets in engineering-based and design-based activities, as well as those in more traditional research and development areas. Moreover, in a period of rapid economic change in the global economy many of these measures will involve organizational changes at the enterprise and industry levels. The extension of flexible manufacturing systems and strategic alliances have already widened the institutional hiatus in the East since the fall of communism. Responding to these institutional changes will require considerable social investments and co-ordination; consequently the need to monitor these changes and to find effective responses is perhaps one of the greatest challenges facing the fledgling economic bureaucracies in the East.

Because of its close links with building new skills for industry, reform of the education system will be a third priority area in strengthening infant entrepreneurship.[38] Education was previously a truly public goods in the East, freely available to virtually everyone. Relative to their income levels, most transition economies begin with a large stock of human capital. However, the bias against linking formal training in both the tertiary and secondary sectors, to commercial and workplace demands has left important gaps which will have to be filled. Moreover, the change to a market economy creates a demand for new skills that the previous regimes decided they did not need, such as marketing, accounting and exporting skills, as well as more formal legal, economic and statistical skills. A new concept of the supply of education will undoubtedly take a long time to evolve and should provide not only diversified channels to acquire professional skills but also curriculum changes that can serve to remodel old mentalities, habits and attitudes. There will, of course, be new opportunities to train abroad, including in cooperation with private sector firms, but these must be matched against the possible drain of human capital. Moreover, the effectiveness of the reforms to the formal education system will depend on the strength of domestic linkages between training and research institutions and the newly independent enterprises. Vocational training schemes, both for shop floor workers and management, will need to be strengthened and the establishment of business schools, regional educational centres and technology colleges, in many cases geared to the needs of the local economy, will be required. Such changes to the education system, which should not be *ad hoc* or distorted by short-term considerations, will certainly involve considerable investments. However, there is a concern across the East that the educational base of the population instead of being strengthened, might be eroded by cuts in funding because of current macroeconomic stringencies.

5 Conclusion

There is an understandable desire in the East to normalize the process of policy-making. However, this desire should not be used to divorce policy-making from actual economic circumstances. In many respects, it is precisely such a response that has been one of the most damaging aspects of the first five years of reform. East European economies currently contain a mosaic of separate and largely unco-ordinated decision-making arenas, new departures and continuing features of the previous system. This situation is best described as an institutional hiatus and whilst the growing share of output produced by the private sector can be taken as a sign of the gap being closed, there are other signs that suggest this hiatus is growing, not only with respect to developed market economies but also the more rapidly growing developing countries.

To date the institutional hiatus has been interpreted as a problem of missing markets in the East. The shock therapy versus gradualism debate has largely revolved around this problem, and the description of economies in the East as a collection of distortions and imbalances has directed the policy debate towards a search for a more stable and efficient equilibrium. Against this, the slow pace of structural reforms poses a constant challenge to the conventional approach. Political obstacles to the restructuring of state enterprises, the lack of funds for new investment and the rehabilitation of existing capacities, and the problems involved in the large-scale reallocation of resources, all conspire to slow down the reform process. Consequently, policy measures need to be constructed both with the objective of recovery and growth as well as building up a different set of state institutions from those associated with either central planning or unregulated markets.

As much as markets, the institutional hiatus in the East concerns the organization of the firm and industries. In this respect, entrepreneurship needs to be an integral part of any larger conceptual framework for discussing transition agendas. However, and counter to much conventional wisdom, policies to encourage entrepreneurship do not imply removing the state from the economy. Indeed, entrepreneurship highlights the central importance to any transition agenda of missing state institutions in the East. This means that the question of industrial policy needs to be placed on the transition agenda despite the ideological hostility towards it in both the East and the West, an hostility which, it should be said, is often more apparent in the rhetoric of governments than in their practice. In this paper, we have suggested one possible approach to the question of industrial policy, and whilst fully aware of the problems and pitfalls that it poses, the peculiar problems of transition, as well as the lessons from experience, present opportunities for institution- and capability-building around industrial policies which deserve the full attention of policy-makers in the East.

Notes

1. The views expressed in this paper are the authors' own, and in no way reflect those that may be held by the United Nations Secretariat. Comments by Ha-Joon Chang, Željka Kožul, Mark Knell, István Székely and Jozef van Brabant on earlier drafts were valuable. Final responsibility rests with the authors.
2. The appropriate geographical designation for these economies is somewhat arbitrary. In this paper, East is used to refer to Eastern Europe (Bulgaria, the former Czechoslovakia, Hungary, Poland and Romania), the former Yugoslavia and Albania, the former German Democratic Republic and the former Soviet Republics.
3. Only in Poland was the slump in the 1930s of a comparable magnitude to the transition slump, see ECE (1992), p. 42.
4. Thus, for example, the Polish government expected GDP to fall by 3 per cent in 1990 and to rise by 3.5 per cent in 1991; in fact, it fell by 12 and 7 per cent respectively. In Hungary, the government forecast output growth of 2 to 3 per cent a year for 1991–93, but instead output fell each year and in 1993 GDP was 20 per cent below its level in 1989.
5. In 1993, four countries registered positive growth rates: Albania, Poland, Romania and Slovenia. In 1994 output rose in all the East European countries except the former

Yugoslav republic of Macedonia. The former GDR, which began to recover in 1992, has posted the most impressive growth rates, reaching nearly 9 per cent in 1994. In Russia and the other CIS countries, however, output was continuing to fall in 1994.

6. Unlike the recent assessment by Portes (1994) we do not accept that many of the 'transformation traps' which he describes were unavoidable. Rather, many were the consequence of deliberate policy choices.

7. See ECE (1993). It should be noted that all transition economies have experienced unexpectedly large output declines regardless of whether explicit shock therapy programmes have been adopted, and along with the positive correlation between output declines and the acceleration of inflation, the slump in the East points to the predominance of structural problems in the transition.

8. For general discussions of the neo-liberal agenda see Chang and Rowthorn (1995); Przeorwski (1992); Grahl and Teague (1989).

9. For recent assessments of the stabilization debate see ECE (1992, 1993); Bruno (1992); Fischer (1992) and the comments on Fischer by Summers (1992) and Nordhaus (1992); Sachs (1995); Balcerowicz and Gelb (1995).

10. More generally, post-communist politics was marked by a strong populist strain which was often not only anti-intellectual and anti-democratic, but also generally impatient of debate and complex solutions, see Schöpflin (1993).

11. This general spirit was expressed by the then Polish Minister of Industry and Commerce who declared that 'the best industrial policy was no industrial policy' (quoted in ECE, 1994, p. 199).

12. The irrelevance of neo-classical reasoning in guiding the transition because of its failure to distinguish between the operation and development of markets has been emphasized by Douglas North (North, 1994, p. 359). The preoccupation of economists with a narrow set of remedies also ignored the fact that the governments of the East are also embarked on a programme of building democratic institutions and nurturing democratic practices. Open, democratic government requires, among other things, that the pace and scope of policy-making be such that there is genuine discussion of different options and consideration of the electorate's fears and interests, see Rayment (1995).

13. A wealth of historical studies on the evolution of capitalist institutions confirm the value of distinguishing between the operation and development of market and non-market institutions. Karl Polanyi was among the first to explore these issues in detail. Subsequently the literature has built on the work of economic historians such as Alexander Gershenkron, Alfred Chandler, Moses Abramovitz and others, as well as development theorists such as Gunnar Myrdal, Albert Hirschman and Raul Prebisch; see Taylor (1994) for an overview.

14. See Binks and Vale (1990) pp. 12–13. Keynes's description of entrepreneurship as akin to 'animal spirits' shares something in common with this tradition.

15. See Hirschman (1970). On the collective nature of entrepreneurship see Reich (1991); Lall (1991); Johnson and Lundvall (1989); and Jorde and Teece (1990). A more comprehensive critique of Schumpeterian analysis would add its failure to recognize the role of aggregate demand in creating a favourable climate for investment and innovation.

16. It is a fault of endogenous growth theory that it has ignored or downplayed this link. Allyn Young's seminal 1928 article (Young, 1928) remains as good a point of departure as any for further exploring this link.

17. The following relies heavily on Chang and Kožul-Wright (1994).

18. The term 'development state' is due to Chalmers Johnson and is used to identify the kinds of government–business relations which characterize late industrializing economies and, in particular, a state apparatus directly involved in the organization and direction of domestic industry and concerned with promoting an economic structure that enhances the nation's industrial competitiveness, Johnson (1992), p. 19. See also Singh (1994).

19. See Brus and Laski (1989); Goldman (1991); Erikson (1991); Gershenkron (1962). It is also the case that the bias towards the industrial sector, particularly heavy industry, was excessive under central planning.
20. Whether these imbalances are best described as macroeconomic or structural has been debated by economists proposing a 'disequilibrium' or 'shortage' approach to the analysis of command economies. The closer attention paid to institutional detail in the shortage approach is in line with the arguments in this paper. However, this approach has paid inadequate attention to the more dynamic issues discussed here.
21. Maurice Dobb's account of the expected dynamic advantages of Soviet-type planning remains one of the clearest (Dobb, 1978, particularly pp. 1–11). It is of some interest to note, in this respect, that Dobb's earliest work on entrepreneurship and the theory of the firm enabled his analysis to avoid the essentially static perspective that marred the socialist calculation debate.
22. Formally, state preferences concerning the wants (both current and future) to be satisfied gave rise to a series of plan targets and corresponding material balances, whereby resources were consistently allocated at the enterprise level. Following a period of interactive bargaining in each branch of the economy, these targets became legally binding. Over time, however, the evolution of planned economies gave rise to an increasingly dispersed authority structure and chain of command to match the task of managing a modern and increasingly complex economy. However, the generality of many Party instructions, competing economic and social demands at the enterprise level, and ambiguities over responsibility for decision-making induced considerable political uncertainty and planning targets had to be carefully interpreted by enterprise managers. The adverse economic effects of this politically induced uncertainty are discussed extensively by Berliner, 1989. See also Jowitt (1992), ch. 8.
23. See Litwack (1991), pp. 80–81; Hare (1990), p. 598; and Galasi and Szirácki (1985).
24. See Staniszkis (1991); Mokrzycki (1991); and Erikson (1991).
25. See Galasi and Sziráczki (1985), pp. 206–7.
26. Even much so-called innovative activity was little more than falsely ascribed novelty as a means of meeting plan requirements. This practice was particularly common in engineering but was also found in the consumer goods sector. Brus and Laski, suggest that such practices may explain the inflated growth rates attributed to centrally planned economies, Brus and Laski (1989), p. 46; see also Balcerowicz (1990). A related institutional failure under these conditions was the inability of centrally planned economies to capitalize on their large investment in research and development and the poor performance of imported technology (Hanson and Pavitt, 1987; Rosenberg, 1988).
27. Between 1980–88, the growth rate in the Soviet Union fell to 3 per cent per annum from over 5 per cent over the previous decade and in Eastern Europe from over 6 per cent to under 2 per cent; the two epicentres of change in the late 1980s, Poland and Hungary, exhibited even more precipitous declines.
28. Because such reforms undermined the performance of state enterprises but did not offer a sustainable transformation through the creation of an independent sector, they were subject to reversal by the political authorities. The reintroduction of restrictions over enterprise responsibility was required to ensure the continuation of government-set priorities, both economic and political, and to ensure that planning was itself functional rather than subject to the uncertainties and vagaries of price fluctuation. In reaction to the initial openness, these reversals often expanded hierarchical control over the allocation decisions and the macroeconomic control of the economy. This in turn implied a further extension of responsibility over judicial matters of contractual dispute, location decision and the entry and exit of firms. See Nove (1983); Comisso (1989); and Galasi and Szirácki (1985).
29. Gomułka was one of the first to advance this thesis; see Gomułka (1986); also Goldman (1991) and Panic (1991). Institutional conditions must include the creation of an ideological framework. The expectation of catching up and surpassing Western levels of

technology and standards of living was continuously reinforced by Communist Party ideologues and bureaucrats. The growing gap between expectations and reality was undoubtedly a major factor in the demise of central planing.

30. The problem is well demonstrated by the comments of some of the champions of market-led transition. Lipton and Sachs, for example, whilst insisting that the 'seamless web' of the transition process necessitates a comprehensive set of macroeconomic and structural adjustments under the pressures of tight demand (Lipton and Sachs, 1990, p. 99) appear to assume that functioning markets will automatically accompany the introduction of proper incentives. János Kornai, who describes the goal of transition as 'a system that encourages individual initiative and entrepreneurship, liberates this initiative from excessive state intervention, and protects it by the rule of law' (Kornai, 1990, p. 23), whilst confident in prescribing a managerial role for the state in the transition appears less sure whether individual initiative and entrepreneurship could, by themselves, bring about this desired goal. Similarly, Václav Klaus (1990, pp. 13–14), whilst calling on 'mainstream economics' to help guide the economies of the East to 'an economic system based on scarcity prices, on sound incentives, on transparent general rules', provides a comprehensive account of why such guidance is likely to fail.

31. This is not to deny that individual policies will discriminate between particular firms and industries under the particular circumstances of transition.

32. The network of public and private institutional linkages that encourage risk-taking, learning, imitating and experimenting, the co-ordination of investment and the adoption of a longer-term vision by those with responsibility over economic resources has been described elsewhere as systems of entrepreneurship (Chang and Kožul-Wright, 1994). We do not wish to give the impression that the possibility of government failure is irrelevant to this discussion, on the contrary. However, the fact that governments sometimes fail is no more ground for seeking their removal than the fact that private firms also fail is grounds for large-scale nationalization. On government failures and their implications, see Datta-Chaudhuri (1990); Stiglitz (1992); Chang (1994); van Brabant (1993).

33. See Stark (1990), and Stanizskis (1991), respectively.

34. Thus Shinyasu Hoshimo, former vice minister of the Economic Planning Agency, has suggested that 'The postwar Japanese approach was something close to a planned economy, not true capitalism, but capitalism under strict control ...' and professor Hauro Shimada describes MITI's industrial policy as 'In a sense, ...similar to what takes place in a planned economy of a socialist economy', both quoted in Johnson (1993).

35. It is worth recalling in this context that, outside the centrally planned economies, the countries with the highest concentration of large firms were precisely the rapidly growing Asian economies of South Korea and Taiwan.

36. Deciding which enterprises should and which should not be privatized, will be complicated by the need to recognize the already implicit property rights established through pension funds, banks and other intermediaries (Köves 1994, p. 162).

37. It is also true that in the East enterprises were often responsible for delivering a broad range of social services to their workforce, and that restructuring consequently carries far broader implications than is given to the term by Western economists. The resulting burden of adjustment will carry significant social ramifications which must be addressed by any transition policy (Komárek 1992). At the very least, this suggests that, in this early stage of the transition, the design of adequate social safety nets to facilitate enterprise restructuring, if not directly under the auspices of this agency needs to be designed in close co-ordination with those responsible for industrial restructuring. The effectiveness of these policy measures will also depend on the kinds of trade union structures and industrial relations practices that emerge during the transition. The pressure of unemployment, still not fully felt in many transition economies, will almost certainly put any fledgling labour movement on the defensive. This could be a particularly destructive outcome in these early stages of

transition. So far, reform of trade unions has been almost entirely absent from the discussion of transition.
38. This is the conclusion of endogenous growth theory.

References

Abramovitz, M. (1989), 'Catching up, forging ahead and falling behind', in *Thinking About Growth*, Cambridge: Cambridge University Press.

Akyuz, Y. and C. Gore (1994), 'The investment–profits nexus in East Asian industrialization', *UNCTAD Discussion Papers*, no. 91.

Amsden, A., J. Kochanowicz and L. Taylor (1995), *The Market Meets its Match: Restructuring the Economies of Eastern Europe*, Cambridge: Harvard University Press.

Ash, T. and P. Hare (1994), 'Privatisation in the Russian Federation: changing enterprise behaviour in the transition period', *Cambridge Journal of Economics*, 18.

Balcerowicz, L. (1990), 'The Soviet type economic system, reformed systems and innovativeness', *Communist Economies*, 1.

Balcerowicz, L. and Gelb, A. (1995), 'Macropolicies in Transition to a Market Economy: A Three-Year Perspective', in Proceedings of the World Bank Annual Conference on Development Economics 1994, World Bank, Washington, DC.

Baumol, W. (1990), 'Entrepreneurship: productive, unproductive and destructive?', *Journal of Political Economy*, no. 5.

Begg, D. and R. Portes (1993), 'Enterprise debt and financial restructuring in Central and Eastern Europe', *European Economic Review*, 37.

Berliner, J. (1989), *Soviet Industry from Stalin to Gorbachev*, Ithaca: Cornell University Press.

Biersteker, T. (1990), 'Reducing the role of the state in the economy: a conceptual exploration of IMF and World Bank prescriptions', *International Studies Quarterly*, no. 4.

Binks, M. and P. Vale (1990), *Entrepreneurship and Economic Change*, New York: McGraw-Hill Book Company.

Bruno, M. (1992), 'Stabilization and reform in Eastern Europe – a preliminary evaluation', *IMF Staff Papers*, no. 4.

Brus, W. and K. Laski (1989), *From Marx to the Market*, Oxford: Clarendon Press.

Cantwell, J. and A. Basu (1994), 'The internationalisation of business and the economic development of Central and Eastern Europe', mimeo, University of Reading, United Kingdom.

Caselli, G. and G. Pastrello (1991), 'Poland: from plan to market through crash', in P. Havlik (ed.), *Dismantling the Command Economy in Eastern Europe*, Boulder: Westview Press.

Casson, M. (1987), 'Entrepreneurs', *The New Palgrave*, London: Macmillan.

Chang, H.-J. (1994), *The Political Economy of Industrial Policy*, London: Macmillan.

Chang, H.-J. and R. Kožul-Wright (1994), 'Comparing national systems of entrepreneurship', *Journal of Development Studies*, July.

Chang, H.-J. and B. Rowthorn (eds) (1995), *The Role of the State in Economic Change*, Oxford: Clarendon Press.

Coase, R. (1937), 'The nature of the firm', *Economica*, 4.

Comisso, E. (1989), 'Market failures and market socialism: economic problems of the transition', *Eastern European Politics and Society*, no. 3.

Datta-Chaudhuri, M. (1990), 'Market failure and Government failure', *Journal of Economic Perspectives*, no. 3.

Dobb, M. (1978), *Soviet Economic Development Since 1917*, London: Routledge and Keegan Paul.

Dobrowski, J. et al. (1991), 'Polish state enterprises and the properties of performance: stabilisation, marketisation and privatisation', mimeo, Center for International Affairs, Harvard University.

Dosi, G., C. Freeman, S. Fabiani and R. Aversi (1993), 'On the Process of Economic Development', *CCC Working Paper*, no. 93–2, Center for Research and Management, University of California at Berkeley, Berkeley, CA.

ECE (1986), *Economic Survey of Europe in 1985–1986*, United Nations, New York.

ECE (1990), *Economic Survey of Europe in 1989–1990*, United Nations, New York.

ECE (1992), *Economic Survey of Europe in 1991–1992*, United Nations, New York.

ECE (1993), *Economic Survey of Europe in 1992–1993*, United Nations, New York.

ECE (1994), *Economic Survey of Europe in 1993–1994*, United Nations, New York and Geneva.

ECE (1995), *Economic Survey of Europe in 1994–1995*, United Nations, New York and Geneva.

Erikson, R. (1991), 'The classical Soviet-type economy: nature of the system and implications for reform', *Journal of Economic Perspectives*, no. 4.

Feinstein, C. et al. (1990), *Historical Precedents for Economic Change in Central Europe and the USSR*, Oxford: Oxford Analytica.

Fischer, S. (1992), 'Stabilization and economic reform in Russia', *Brookings Papers on Economic Activity*, 1.

Gabor, I. (1990), 'On the immediate prospects for private entrepreneurship and re-embourgeoisement in Hungary: a pessimistic meditation in the wake of Istvan Szeleney's prognosis of continuity and János Kornai's program of discontinuity', *Working Papers on Transition from State Socialism*, Cornell University.

Galasi, P. and G. Szirácki (1985), 'State regulation, enterprise behaviour and the labour market in Hungary, 1968–83', *Cambridge Journal of Economics*, no. 9.

Gershenkron, A. (1962), *Economic Backwardness in Historical Perspective*, Cambridge, Mass.: The Belknap Press.

Glyn, A. (1994), 'A comment on Hughes and Hare', *Oxford Economic Papers*, 46.

Goldman, M. (1991), 'Diffusion of development: the Soviet Union', *American Economic Review, Papers and Proceedings*.

Gomułka, S. (1986), *Growth, Innovation and Reform in Eastern Europe*, Brighton: Harvester Press.

Gomułka, S. (1992), 'Polish economic reform, 1990–91: principles, policies and outcomes', *Cambridge Journal of Economics*, vol. 16, no. 3, September.

Grahl, J. and P. Teague (1989), 'The costs of neo-liberal Europe', *New Left Review*, 174.

Handelman, S. (1994), *Comrade Criminals: The Theft of the Second Russian Revolution*, London: Michael Joseph.

Hanson, P. and K. Pavitt (1987), *The Comparative Economics of Research and Development and Innovation in East and West: A Survey*, London: Harwood Academic Publishers.

Hare, P. (1990), 'From central planning to market economy: some microeconomic issues', *The Economic Journal*, June.

Hayek, F. (1960), *The Constitution of Liberty*, Chicago: University of Chicago Press.

Hirschman, A. (1970), *Exit, Voice and Loyalty: Response to Decline in Firms, Organisations and States*, Cambridge, Mass.: Harvard University Press.

Hirschman, A. (1987), 'Linkages', *The New Palgrave*, London:Macmillan.

Hirschman, A. (1992), 'Industrialization and its manifold discontents: West, East and South', *World Development*, no. 9.

Hodgson, G. (1988), *The Economics of Institutions*, Cambridge: Polity Press.

Hughes, G. and P. Hare (1992), 'Industrial policy and restructuring in Eastern Europe', *Oxford Review of Economic Policy*, 8.

Hughes, G. and P. Hare (1994), 'Reply to Glyn', *Oxford Economic Papers*, 46.

Johnson, C. (1992), *MITI and the Japanese Miracle: The Growth of Industrial Policy, 1925–1975*, Stanford: Stanford University Press.

Johnson, C. (1993), 'Comparative capitalism: The Japanese difference', *California Management Review*, Summer.

Johnson, B. and B. Lundvall (1989), 'Limits of the Pure Market', in *Samhällsventenskap, Economioch Historia – Festskrift till Lars Harlitz*, Goteborg: Daidalos.

Jorde, T. and D. Teece (1990), 'Innovation and cooperation: implications for cooperation and antitrust', *Journal of Economic Perspectives*, no. 3.

Jowitt, K. (1992), *New World Disorder – the Leninist Extinction*, Berkeley: University of California Press.

Junz, H. (1991), 'Integration of Eastern Europe into the world trading system', *American Economic Review*, 2.

Kaldor, N. (1985), *Economics Without Equilibrium*, Cardiff: Cardiff University Press.

Kaldor, N. (1989), 'The irrelevance of equilibrium economics', reprinted in F. Targetti and A.P. Thirlwall, *The Essential Kaldor*, London: Duckworth.

Klaus, V. (1990), 'A perspective on economic transition in Czechoslovakia and Eastern Europe', *Proceedings of the World Bank Annual Conference on Development Economics*, World Bank, Washington DC.

Klaus, V. (1991), 'Quotation of the month: we need an untainted market economy and we need it now', *The World Bank/CECSE*, 2.

Komárek, V. (1992), 'Shock therapy and its victims', *New York Times*, 5 January.

Kornai, J. (1990), *The Road to a Free Economy*, New York: W.Norton and Co.

Kornai, J. (1993), 'Transformational Recession: A General Phenomenon Examined Through the Example of Hungary's Development', *Economie Appliquée*, no. 2.

Köves, A. (1992), 'Shock therapy versus gradual change: economic problems and policies in Central and Eastern Europe (1989–1991), *Acta Oeconomica*, 44.

Köves, A. (1994), 'From 'great leap forwards' to normalcy: some issues in transitional policies in Eastern Europe', *UNCTAD Review*.

Kožul-Wright, R. (1995), 'Transnational corporations and the nations state', in J. Michie and John Greaves Smith, *Managing the Global Economy*, Oxford: Oxford University Press.

Lall, S. (1991), 'Explaining success in the industrial world', in V.N. Balasubramanyan and S. Lall (eds), *Issues in Development Economics*, London: Macmillan.

Lall, S. (1994), 'Industrial policy: the role of government in promoting industrial and technological development', *UNCTAD Review*.

Landesmann, M. (1994), 'Industrial Policy and the Transition in East-Central Europe', in G. Hunya (ed.), *Economic Transformation in East-Central Europe and in the Newly Independent States*, Boulder, CO: Westview Press.

Leibenstein, H. (1968), 'Entrepreneurship and development', *American Economic Review*, 58, papers and proceedings.

Lipton, D. and J. Sachs (1990), 'Creating a market economy in Eastern Europe: the case of Poland', *Brookings Papers on Economic Activity*, 1.

Litwack, J. (1991), 'Legality and market reform in Soviet-type economies', *Journal of Economic Perspectives*, fall.

Marer, P., J. Arvay, J. O'Conner, M. Schrenk and D. Swanson (1993), *Historically Planned Economies: A Guide to the Data*, World Bank, Washington DC.

Mokrzycki, E. (1991), 'The legacy of real socialism and western democracy', *Studies in Comparative Communism*, no. 2.

Murrell, P. (1992), 'An antidote to shock therapy: an evolutionary approach to the East European transition', The Woodrow Wilson Centre, Occasional Paper no. 37, Washington DC.

Nelson, R. and S. Winter (1983), *The Evolutionary Theory of Economic Change*, Cambridge, Mass.

Nordhaus, W. (1992), 'Comment on Fischer', *Brookings Papers on Economic Activity*, 1.

North, D. (1994), 'Economic performance through time', *The American Economic Review*, June.

Nove, A. (1983), *The Economics of Feasible Socialism*, London: George, Allen and Unwin.

Nuti, M. and R. Portes (1993), 'Central Europe: The way forward', in R. Portes (ed.), *Economic Transformation in Central Europe: A Progress Report*, London: Centre for Economic Policy Research.

Olson, M. (1982), *The Rise and Decline of Nations*, New Haven: Yale University Press.

Panic, M. (1991), 'The future role of the state in Eastern Europe', paper presented at the 10th Keynes Seminar, University of Kent.

Panic, M. (1993), 'International economic integration and the changing role of National governments', in H.-J. Chang and B. Rowthorn (eds) (1995).

Portes, R. (1994), 'Transformation Traps', *The Economic Journal*, 104.

Przeorwski, A. (1992), 'The neo-liberal fallacy', *Journal of Democracy*, no. 3.

Putterman, L. (1989), *The Economic Nature of the Firm: A Reader*, Cambridge: Cambridge University Press.

Radošević, S. (1994), 'Strategic Technology Policy for Eastern Europe', *Economic Systems*, vol. 18, no. 2.

Rayment, P.B.W. (1995), 'The hard road to the market economy: realities and illusions', *MOCT-MOST*, no. 2.

Reekie, W. (1984), *Markets, Entrepreneurs and Liberty: An Austrian View of Capitalism*, Brighton: Harvester Press.

Reich, R. (1991), 'Entrepreneurship reconsidered: the team as hero', in *Participative Management*, Harvard Business School.

Richardson, G.B. (1972), 'The organisation of industry', *The Economic Journal*, no. 327.

Rosenberg, N. (1988), 'Technical Change under Capitalism and Socialism', mimeo, Department of Economics, Stanford University.

Rybczynski, T. (1991), 'The sequencing of reform', *Oxford Review of Economic Policy*, no. 4.

Sachs, J.D. (1995), 'Russia's Struggle with Stabilization: Conceptual Issues and Evidence', Proceedings of the World Bank Annual Conference on Development Economics 1994, World Bank, Washington, DC.

Schöpflin, G. (1993), *Politics in Eastern Europe*, Oxford: Oxford University Press.

Schumpeter, J. (1987), *Capitalism, Socialism and Democracy*, London: Unwin.

Singh, A. (1992), 'The stock market and economic development: should developing countries encourage stock markets?', *UNCTAD Review*.

Singh, A. (1994), 'Openness and the market friendly approach to development: learning the right lessons from development experience', *World Development*, December.

Stanizskis, J. (1991), 'Political capitalism in Poland', *East European Politics and Societies*, no. 1.

Stark, D. (1990), 'Privatization in Hungary: From plan to market or from plan to clan?', *East European Politics and Societies*, 4.

Stiglitz, J. (1992), 'Comment on "Toward a counter-counterrevolution in development theory" by Paul Krugman', in Proceedings of the World Bank Annual Conference on Development Economics, World Bank, Washington DC.

Summers, L. (1992), 'Comment on Fischer', *Brookings Papers on Economic Activity*, 1.

Székely, I. (1992), 'Economic transformation and the reform of the financial system in Central and Eastern Europe', mimeo, United Nations, Department of Economic and Social Development, New York.

Taylor, L. (1994), 'Growth, the state and development theory', paper presented to Economic Research Workshop on 'Endogenous Growth and Development', University of Siena, July.

UNCTAD (1981), *Trade and Development Report 1981*, United Nations, Geneva.

UNCTAD (1993), *Trade and Development Report 1993*, United Nations, Geneva.

UNCTAD (1994), *Trade and Development Report 1994*, United Nations, Geneva.

UNCTAD (1995), *Privatization in the Transition Process: Recent Experiences in Eastern Europe*, United Nations, Geneva.

United Nations (1992), *World Economic Survey*, United Nations, New York.

van Brabant, J. (1993), *Industrial Policy in Eastern Europe*, Dordrecht: Kluwer Academic Publishers.

Williamson, O. (1975), *Markets and Hierarchies: Analysis and Antitrust Implications*, New York: Free Press.

World Bank (1991), *World Development Report*, World Bank, Washington DC.

Young, A. (1928), 'Increasing returns and economic progress', *The Economic Journal*, 38, December.

Index